GLOBAL CRIME CONNECTIONS
Dynamics and Control

Simplistic assumptions about crime are widespread: that crime is caused by bad individuals, acting alone or conspiring, and that crime can be adequately dealt with by increasing conventional police activity. Such assumptions fail to recognize a number of key global developments since the Second World War. Changes in social, economic and political environments have made systematic crime more profitable and more destructive.

The authors of these essays examine the dynamics and control of organized crime in their national and international contexts. Among the subjects they discuss are American organized crime, US foreign policy and drug control, the influence of the US on British drug control, the international linkages between organized crime and legitimate business in toxic waste disposal, the *Camorra* in Naples, the extent and control of fraud in the European Community, the destructive capacity of corporate crime, and the attempts to control it.

Frank Pearce is Professor of Sociology at Queen's University, Ontario.

Michael Woodiwiss is a member of the Department of American Studies, University College of Swansea.

Global Crime Connections

Dynamics and Control

Edited by

FRANK PEARCE

and

MICHAEL WOODIWISS

University of Toronto Press
Toronto and Buffalo

© Lumière (Co-operative) Press Limited 1993

All rights reserved. No reproduction, copy or transmission
of this publication may be made without written permission.

First published in Great Britain by
THE MACMILLAN PRESS LTD

First published in Canada and the United States in 1993 by
UNIVERSITY OF TORONTO PRESS
Toronto and Buffalo

ISBN 0–8020–2838–1 (hardcover)
ISBN 0–8020–7716–1 (paperback)

Canadian Cataloguing in Publication Data

Main entry under title:

Global crime connections

Includes index.
ISBN 0–8020–2838–1 (bound)   ISBN 0–8020–7716–1 (pbk)

1. Organized crime.   2. Commercial crimes.
3. Organized crime – Prevention.   4. Commercial
crimes – Prevention.   5. Narcotics, Control of.
6. Organized crime – United States.   7. Commercial
crimes – United States.   8. Organized crime –
United States – Prevention.   9. Commercial crimes –
United States – Prevention.   10. Narcotics,
Control of – United States.   I. Pearce, Frank.
II. Woodiwiss, Michael.

IIV6441.G56   1993   364.1'06   C91–095728–2

Printed in Hong Kong

To George and Cecelia Pearce, John and Audrey Lawrence,
Jo, Mary, Simon, Min and Anthony Woodiwiss,
and Rachel and Helen Cooper

Contents

Preface

This volume examines the dynamics and control of organised and corporate crime in their national and international contexts. There are essays on American organised crime, US foreign policy and drug control, the influence of the United States on British drug control, the international linkages between organised crime and legitimate businesses in toxic waste disposal, the *Camorra* in Naples, the extent and control of EEC fraud, the destructive capacity of corporate crime, and the attempts to control corporate crime.

Global developments since the Second World War have combined to produce social, economic and political environments which have increased both the profitability and destructive impact of systematic illegal activity. The contributions to this volume challenge the simplistic assumptions that crime is caused by bad individuals, acting alone or conspiring together, and that crime can be adequately dealt with by increasing conventional police activity. This assumption does not square with the available empirical evidence. The essays are all new, and have been specially written for this volume by leading academics.

Acknowledgements

Frank Pearce would like to thank Anthony Woodiwiss, Laureen Snider, Steven Tombs, Elaine Stavro and, for their continuous challenges, Rory and Blake. Michael Woodiwiss would like to thank Philip Vinall, and Damien and Teresa Hoyles. We would both like to thank Queen's and Swansea Universities for financial support during the writing and editing of this book. Thanks are also due to June Pilfold, Sharon Hansard, Audrey Bamber, Valery Rose, Frances Arnold, Margaret Cannon, Rose Gann and Clive Bloom.

Introduction

International developments since the Second World War have combined to produce a social, economic and political environment which has increased both the profitability and the destructive impact of systematic illegal activity. Governments are not equipped to deal with a rapidly changing situation, and show little or no interest in attempting to remedy their inadequacies. Their current efforts at control are often counter-productive, producing as many problems as they are designed to solve. Some, or parts of some, governments, are even actively involved or knowingly complicit in the types of crime we are concerned with in this volume. The chapters that follow are about the dynamics and control of organised and corporate crime; both national and international aspects are covered.

Most government officials and media commentators tend to analyse crime in a framework which assumes that the world is made up of 'good guys' and 'bad guys'; a framework that admits only one solution: give conventional policing agencies the resources and legal powers to lock up more wrongdoers. Investigate, arrest and incarcerate; then, theoretically, the problem is solved. Periodically a prominent mobster or a particularly unsubtle white-collar criminal is led off to jail, and the authorities take the credit for effective enforcement. The police and the courts are kept busy, the media has a constant supply of stories. According to this framework, most of us, at least in the West, are reasonable, law-abiding individuals. At the same time our Western pluralist democracies are seen as the culmination of social development, the goal to which history has been moving. But this leaves the problem of explaining why, at the same time, many of our societies suffer such high crime rates. Why, in other words, are there so many 'bad guys'?

The United States is the Western country with the highest crime rate, and the US has long been able to externalise the blame for many of its problems, not just the proliferation of crime. White, Anglo-Saxon Protestant Americans, or those with economic or political power, are rarely considered to be responsible for serious crime. For the US the sources of evil usually originate outside the US, in backward areas and backward peoples. Both the ethnicity and motives of these 'backward' peoples vary at different times, but the assumption that they hold 'un-American' values and are not to be tolerated never does. Asians, Southern and Central Europeans, Latin Americans and Afro-Americans have all at one time or another been singled out to explain the extent or incidence of crime. All these groups, at some time, have been represented as aliens, often conspiring to corrupt the body politic. Law-enforcement agencies have placed great emphasis on the outsider status of those assumed to be the cause of social problems and have helped develop demologies based on highly tendentious conclusions from dubious and even fabricated evidence. McCarthy's ever-changing lists of Red state employees, fragments of taped conversations between Italian-American gangsters, for example, or accusations of involvement in drug trafficking by Central American governments have helped to justify extraordinary measures by the American state both at home and abroad. At home, more and more people have been locked away in American gaols as policing activities have expanded. Abroad, the US has felt free to invade sovereign states, give military support to those attacking elected governments, support repressive regimes and use its political and economic might to pressure other countries to follow its example.

Despite increasing the domestic prison population to levels well beyond those of countries at a similar stage of development, and despite increasing interference in the affairs of other countries for the professed purpose of crime control, the US continues to make little progress in dealing with its own crime problem. And yet the country with the gravest crime problem tends to claim a proficiency in crime control and continues to set the agenda for international crime control.

We do not believe that the US provides the best example for other countries to follow – the agenda for national and international crime control needs to be reset. There is a need to take another look at the problem and to dispense with demologies and any other inadequate and interest-serving analytical frameworks. Criminals have never operated in the vacuums assumed by most government officials and media commentators. The chapters in this book provide radically different accounts of crime and law enforcement by contextualising both.

Michael Woodiwiss confronts the still-prevalent view that one can explain organised crime in terms of the 'Mafia' or Mafia-type groups. In challenging this view he shows how it has been of a piece with other alien-conspiracy theories and just as wide of the mark. Still, whilst such misrepresentations may do little to combat organised crime, they fit in very well with other US foreign-policy objectives. This theme is taken up by Bruce Bullington who shows how American military interests have often been served by, but have sometimes compromised the effectiveness of, the international war on drugs. He also documents how little concern there often is for the well-being of many of those involved in this war. For example, after all the evidence of the dangers of dioxins in Agent Orange, the US supplied the defoliant 2,4-D to the Burmese government for use in opium poppy eradication programmes as late as 1985. It has also recently become clear that the workers involved in the Colombian programme designed to substitute for coca cultivation – the production of flowers for the North American market – routinely get covered with biocides, many of them banned in the US. The dangers faced by people because of state and business activity rarely get mentioned in the hysteria about social problems within the US and other advanced Western democracies. Yet, as will become clear throughout this book, these pose some of the most serious dangers facing individuals.

Nicholas Dorn and Nigel South address the question of the influence of the US on national drug policies in the European context. They show that this influence has rarely been beneficial and that it has, if anything, exacerbated drug use and restricted the ability to offer more constructive, creative and effective policies. They also challenge the highly punitive reaction to drug traffickers as excessive and argue that this policy itself tends to contribute to the escalation of violence with which such trafficking is increasingly associated. These articles all suggest that crime is endemic to advanced industrial societies and particularly to the US and that if we want to understand criminal activity we must look to organisational and environmental factors to explain its prevalence.

Alan Block's discussion of a controversy in Pennsylvania about the disposal of hazardous waste provides us with a valuable account of the linkages between organised crime and certain seemingly legitimate businesses. Vincenzo Ruggiero provides a detailed analysis of the activities of a notorious but inadequately researched criminal phenomenon in Southern Italy, the *Camorra*. Whilst *camorristi* are involved in most forms of criminal activity in Naples, the actual organisation of this activity is very loose and there is tension between an 'old' *Camorra* and a 'new' *Camorra*. Further, many *camorristi* activities take place in association with legitimate businesses and in these arrangements the *Camorra* is typically in a subordinate position. These examples bring into focus the issue of commercial crime – illegal activities engaged in by business organisations in pursuit of their goal of maximising profit. Michael Clarke documents the prevalence of this in Europe in his exploration of agricultural fraud in the EEC. Farmers, owners of slaughterhouses, wine merchants, exporters and importers all play their part in a 'scam' costing taxpayers some £6 billion per annum. Frank Pearce and Steven Tombs provide an even more poignant example of the high cost of commercial crime in their analysis of the Bhopal disaster, with over 3000 fatalities, and its legal aftermath. The case involves a US subsidiary in a Third World country. Finally, Laureen Snider poses the question: why is there so much commercial crime and why is so little done about it? Despite the undeniably destructive impact of much corporate activity, corporations, through their economic power and political influence, have defeated or circumvented previous reform efforts with ease. She stresses the necessity to identify the factors responsible for the defeat of these reform efforts before meaningful change can be achieved.

This volume, then, is integrated by a number of themes. A major focus is on organisational crime, illegal acts which must be understood in the context of continuous enterprises pursuing their goals in relatively unpredictable social, political and economic environments. These environments are national, transnational and global. All need to be examined carefully. It is also important to recognise that law-enforcement activities often cause as many problems as they are designed to solve. Sometimes this is accidental and unrecognised, at other times there is a certain indifference to negative consequences, but there are also times when governments act in ways which are diametrically opposed to their stated intentions. The volume as a whole challenges the simplistic assumption that crime is caused by bad individuals, acting alone or conspiring together, and that crime can be adequately controlled simply by increasing conventional police activity. The articles show that this assumption does not square with the available empirical evidence.

Notes on the Contributors

Alan A. Block is a Professor in the Administration of Justice at Pennsylvania State University. He is the author of seven books on organised crime, the latest being *Masters of Paradise: Organized Crime and the Internal Revenue Service in the Bahamas*. He is also the editor of *Crime, Law and Social Change: An International Journal*.

Bruce Bullington is a Professor in the Administration of Justice at Pennsylvania State University. He has written widely on drug use and drug users including a book on *Heroin Use in the Barrio*.

Michael Clarke is a Lecturer in Sociology at the University of Liverpool. He has published articles and books on the practice and regulation of commercial crime including *Regulating the City* and, most recently, *Business Crime*. He is currently researching the regulation of estate agents in England and Wales.

Nicholas Dorn is Development Director at the Institute for the Study of Drug Dependence in London. He is the co-editor with Nigel South of *A Land Fit for Heroin?* and co-author with Nigel South and Karim Murji of *Traffickers: Policing the Drug Distribution Business*.

Frank Pearce is a Professor in Sociology at Queen's University in Canada. He has written on sociological theory, including a book, *The Radical Durkheim*, and on organised and corporate crime, notably in *Crimes of the Powerful*. He is on the editorial boards of *Economy and Society* and the *Journal of Human Justice*.

Vincenzo Ruggiero completed his doctorate at the University of Bologna and is a Visiting Lecturer in Sociology at the London School of Economics. He has published articles on Italian organised crime and two books on the prison system, *Il Carcere in Europa* and *Il Carcere in Materialle*. He is now based at the School of Social Work at Middlesex Polytechnic.

Laureen Snider is an Associate Professor in Sociology and Associate Dean at Queen's University in Canada. She has published many articles on the political economy of corporate crime and on women and the legal system. She is on the editorial boards of the *Journal of Human Justice* and the *Canadian Journal of Sociology*.

Nigel South is a Lecturer in Sociology at the University of Essex. He is the co-editor with Nicholas Dorn of *A Land Fit for Heroin?*, co-author with Nicholas Dorn and Karim Murji of *Traffickers: Policing the Drug Distribution Business* and author of *Policing for Profit* on the private security sector.

Steven Tombs is a Senior Lecturer in Sociology at Liverpool Polytechnic. His many publications have focused on issues of health and safety, particularly in the chemical industry.

Michael Woodiwiss is a Lecturer in American Studies at the University College of Swansea. He is the author of *Crime, Crusades and Corruption* and the forthcoming *Crime and the American Century*.

1

Crime's Global Reach

MICHAEL WOODIWISS

On 20 December 1946 Colonel Garland Williams of the Federal Bureau of Narcotics (FBN) gave Americans a new way to understand organised crime. He announced that the Mafia 'is a very dangerous criminal organization that is being used to undermine the principles of American ideals of law enforcement'. He then elaborated: 'The organization is national in scope. . . . [Its] leaders meet annually, usually in Florida, and there agree upon policies for the control and correlation of their various criminal enterprises.'[1]

Williams had introduced the public to his agency's interpretation of organised crime and an idea that gained in momentum during the following decades, eventually dominating national and international perception of organised crime. It still provides the framework for the official US interpretation of the problem. This idea was that a conspiracy with Sicilian origins was centrally organised and dominated organised crime nationally and internationally.

I intend to trace the development and consequences of this idea and then turn it around to show that the dominant forces behind the growth of significant national and international organised criminal activity since the Second World War emanated from within the most powerful country in the world and not from one of the most backward parts of Europe or any other part of the developing world.

The first book to popularise and elaborate on the FBN's analysis was *Chicago Confidential* published in 1950. The Mafia in this is 'the supergovernment which now has tentacles reaching into the Cabinet and the White House itself, almost every state capital, huge Wall Street interests, and connections in Canada, Greece, China and Outer Mongolia, and even through the Iron Curtain into Soviet Russia'.

The authors of this book were two newsmen on the New York tabloid, the *Daily Mirror*, and they kept coming back to the Mafia

1

idea in a series of sequels. The organisation is 'run from above, with reigning headquarters in Italy and American headquarters in New York'. It 'controls all sin' and 'practically all crime in the United States', and is 'an international conspiracy, as potent as that other international conspiracy, Communism, and as dirty and dangerous, with its great wealth and the same policy – to conquer everything and take over everything, with no scruples as to how'.[2]

A Senate committee investigating crime in 1950 and 1951 acknowledged the influence on its conclusions of these two newsmen as well as the FBN. This committee chaired by Senator Estes Kefauver of Tennessee gave prestigious support to the idea of the Mafia as a centralised, supercriminal, international organisation. The committee's report traced the history of the Sicilian Mafia and its 'implantation' into America and made a number of often-repeated assertions: 'There is a nationwide crime syndicate known as the Mafia, whose tentacles are found in many large cities. It has international ramifications which appear most clearly in connection with the narcotics traffic. . . . Its leaders are usually found in control of the most lucrative rackets of their cities. There are indications of a centralized direction and control of these rackets.'[3]

The only evidence the report offered for its Mafia conclusions were a number of drug trafficking stories involving Italian-American gangsters. Neither these stories nor any testimony at the hearings were at all convincing about the idea of a centralised organisation dominating or controlling organised crime.[4]

The committee's funds had been limited and Senator Kefauver expressed his gratitude to the FBN after the hearings: 'Our greatest help in tracking down the trail of the Mafia came from the Federal Bureau of Narcotics. . . . Because of the Mafia's dominance in the dope trade, the Narcotics Bureau has become the leading authority on this sinister organization.'[5]

The head of the FBN was Harry J. Anslinger, who dominated his agency in much the same way as J. Edgar Hoover dominated the FBI. Anslinger had ensured that the Kefauver Committee came to conclusions that were acceptable by lending them one of his top agents, George White. In the early months of the investigation White was particularly influential, briefing the committee's members and counsel. His help was frequently acknowledged during the hearings and he was referred to as 'one of the great experts on the Mafia'.[6] White was a former newsman and knew how to work journalists. He continually talked up his arrests and, like Anslinger, the Mafia conspiracy theory. Many crime writers of the 1950s acknowledged their debt to him.

Colonel Williams, Commissioner Anslinger and Agent White were not only drug-enforcement officials who helped give Americans a new way of understanding organised crime. They were also actively involved in the implementation of war-time and postwar American foreign policy, through the Intelligence Services.

Recent research by Alan Block and John McWilliams has revealed that the FBN's Commissioner and agents significantly influenced the formation and development of American Intelligence: the FBN provided a convenient and 'legitimate' cover for subsequent counter-espionage and counterintelligence activities in the post-war era'. The authors document Anslinger's early intelligence activities from the time of the First World War to the establishment of the Office of Strategic Services (OSS) to meet the emergency of the Second World War. Anslinger was also responsible for shaping the FBN into 'one of America's premier foreign intelligence agencies'. Garland Williams had become the New York District Supervisor for the FBN in 1936, but drug enforcement during the war took second place to intelligence duties. Among these he became the Director of Special Training for the OSS. The training programme Williams designed covered 'demolitions, weapons, close combat, silent killing, physical conditions and fieldcover', plus undercover work, sabotage and guerrilla warfare. George White also managed to combine drug enforcement activities with his country's other foreign-policy objectives. During the war he was an enthusiastic trainer for the OSS in the type of skills mentioned above.[7]

According to Anslinger and his agents, the main peril faced by the country was foreign conspiracies. Journalists were fed many stories about the FBN standing alone in brave defiance not only of the Mafia but of the People's Republic of China. The intention of both was to speed up the moral degeneration of the United States. Anslinger himself co-authored a book published in 1954 which claimed that most of the illegal drug supply was grown and processed in communist China, from where it was spread 'with cold deliberation' to free countries, notably the United States. He had previously provided a link between the two conspiracies by explaining that, although the Chinese Communists were making the major profits, the Mafia was distributing the Chinese-manufactured heroin in the United States.[8] Drug trafficking, it was said repeatedly, provided China with dollars for war, and weakened the health and moral fibre of its enemies.

Few chose to challenge Anslinger's absurd ideas at the time.

From time to time during and since Anslinger's reign evidence has indicated that some individuals and officials from communist countries have been involved in international drug trafficking but this has never been on the same scale as the friends and allies of the United States. Drug-trafficking routes tend to follow established trading routes.

Commissioner Anslinger, on his own admission, helped to cover up the personal fallibilities of America's most visible Cold Warrior on the home front. A book called *The Murderers* which he co-authored in 1962 described this man as 'one of the most influential members of the Congress of the United States. He headed one of the most powerful committees of Congress. His decisions and statements helped to shape and direct the destiny of the United States and the free world.'

Anslinger had learnt that this leader was a morphine addict who had no intention of fighting his habit:

It was a delicate moment in world affairs. The situation presented by the morphine-addicted lawmaker presented a precarious problem. There was imminent danger that the facts would become known and there was no doubt that they would be used to the fullest in the propaganda machines of our enemies. Such a scandal could do incalculable harm to the United States and the free world.

The Commissioner then admitted that he helped the legislator obtain regular supplies of morphine to prevent him going 'to the pushers'. The addict was later revealed to be another of America's postwar conspiracy theorists, Senator Joe McCarthy.[9]

Anslinger and his agents were more directly involved in the Cold War in other ways. Recently released Freedom of Information Act documents, for example, have detailed the FBN's involvement with Central Intelligence Agency (CIA) efforts to develop mind manipulation with drugs for interrogation purposes. In 1947 the CIA had replaced the OSS as America's premier foreign intelligence agency. During the early 1950s the CIA, fearing the Communists were getting ahead of them, intensified their research into behaviour control. Anslinger co-operated and supplied the services of some of his agents plus amounts of heroin and marijuana for research purposes. In 1953 project MKULTRA began to explore the potential of a newly invented hallucinogen, LSD. In one equipment, Frank Olsen, a researcher employed by the CIA, was spiked and subsequently jumped from a tenth-floor window in circumstances that were covered up for more than two decades.

With Anslinger's permission, George White was seconded from the FBN on a part-time basis to set up safe houses for drug experiments. In 1955 White took over the running of one of the CIA's most bizarre programmes. The San Francisco safe house was a plush apartment, decorated in the style of a film-set bordello and wired for sound. Drugs were served to unwary victims in food, drinks and cigarettes in crude efforts to elicit information. Most of White's subjects were addicts, small-time dealers or prostitutes, who would be unlikely to complain if they found out what was being done to them or who could be blackmailed into compliance. White would also hire prostitutes to pick up men in bars, bring them back to the apartment, spike their drinks and take them into the bedroom. White would then watch the proceedings through a two-way mirror. As the various branches of the CIA obtained or developed new chemicals they were taken to White for such clandestine testing. After White retired he wrote his own epitaph for his role with the CIA, possibly only half in jest, in a letter to a former colleague: 'Where else could a red-blooded American boy lie, kill, cheat, steal, rape and pillage with the sanction and blessing of the All-Highest?'[10] White, like Anslinger and Williams, was a committed Cold Warrior.

Anslinger's stories about gigantic foreign conspiracies made him the first head of a US federal agency to 'globalise' discussion of organised crime. Hundreds of books and articles repeated variations on his themes in the style of Lait and Mortimer. As 'proof' of the supercriminal Mafia crime combine all that editors required were unrelated anecdotes about Italian-American gangsters, mainly from New York, with the narrative livened up with words like 'godfather', 'tentacles' and most essentially 'omerta', the 'secret and unwritten' code of silence of the Mafia. These were mythical interpretations, magically stringing together disconnected fears, prejudices and hatreds about drugs, communism and foreigners. Anslinger had found a way to absolve the United States from any responsibility for its drug and organised crime problems.

The FBN sponsored the all-powerful Mafia idea during a period aptly called *The Great Fear* by David Caute. Legions of informers were organised by J. Edgar Hoover's FBI to report on the movements and activities of communists or alleged communists. The House Committee on Un-American Activities forced thousands of journalists, diplomats, authors, trade unionists and scientists to testify against themselves. If they exercised their Fifth Amendment rights and refused to answer questions, this was interpreted as admitting guilt and many lost their jobs as a result. Individual states and cities emulated the federal government and instituted loyalty programmes and demanded loyalty oaths from employees. Local interrogation bodies and private vigilante groups also hounded suspected communists.

The famous Hollywood blacklist was only one of many. Hundreds of academics and journalists lost their jobs for 'un-American' thinking. In most cases, however, American intellectuals, journalists and film-makers wanted to keep their jobs. Academics retreated to the specialist journalists to publish; frequently caution and qualification obscured critical analysis. Journalists and film-makers stayed with safe subjects and patriotic themes within strictly circumscribed limits. It was a time most people kept their heads down, fearful of producing anything that could be considered out of line.[11]

Out of all this came a mythological and fundamentally faultless America. Problems such as organised crime and corruption were either minimalised, or externalised as the result of foreign influences. The FBN's Mafia stories and analysis were simply aspects of Cold War mythology. Myths, of course, need to contain some truth to be at all convincing and we shall return to this later. But all the concentration on the Mafia concealed more than it revealed. During the 1950s American capacity to analyse crime regressed.

The idea of the Mafia as central to understanding organised crime was a new variant of an old nativist and xenophobic theme. For over a century American politicians and opinion-makers had been blaming immigrants for all sorts of social problems, not just crime. Journalists churned out ethnic-conspiracy articles and ethnic stereotypes were established in people's minds. The word 'Mafia' entered the American vocabulary in the late nineteenth century but not in the cohesive, organisational sense of the post-Second World War era. Up to that time Jews were more frequently scapegoated as a sinister people, prone to conspire against an otherwise pure system.

Ethnic-conspiracy theories and stereotyping were an important part of the propaganda accompanying America's early twentieth-century moral crusade. This crusade put tens of thousands of federal, state and local laws on the statute books in an attempt to enforce morality by prohibitions on alcohol, gambling, prostitution and drugs, plus strict censorship and a host of more trivial restrictions. Only total suppression of 'vice' would do; the idea of regulating and controlling gambling, medicalising drug addiction or tolerating recreational drug or alcohol use was as unthinkable as licensing murder or robbery. With business support American moralists had the finance, commitment and organisation to persuade, cajole, bribe and bully enough people to ensure that virtue and abstinence became official state policy.

Of all the laws passed during these years the Harrison Narcotic Act of 1914 turned out to have the most significance in the long term. Although the intention of the Act was chiefly to prohibit the use of drugs for recreational purposes, Treasury agents were able to exploit its ambiguous wording to prohibit certain drugs totally. There was an intense campaign to prevent doctors treating drug users: between 1914 and 1938 some 3000 doctors served penitentiary sentences for this offence. Doctors were effectively prohibited from dispensing heroin or morphine to addicts or to ease the pain of the terminally ill. A major black market soon developed as criminals moved in to supply both addicts and users with a variety of the newly illegal drugs.[12]

The intoxicant that most worried Americans during the 1920s was alcohol. In 1919 the Volstead Act had been passed, providing for enforcement of the 18th Amendment to the Constitution. The Amendment prohibited the manufacture, transportation, sale and importation of intoxicating liquor within the United States. Rumrunners, bootleggers, gunmen, speakeasy operators, graft-seeking politicians, corrupt judges and bribe-taking cops and coastguards all shared in this immense new potential for easy money.

During Prohibition ethnic stereotyping and alien-conspiracy theories temporarily went out of fashion as explanations for crime. In part this was because bootlegging was the main criminal enterprise and not many thirsty Americans could be persuaded that bootleggers were un-American. Al Capone, Dutch Schultz, Waxey Gordon and the rest were simply gangsters who took the opportuni-

ties that a foolish law and a corrupt system gave them; they were
never alien intruders or members of ethnically exclusive conspiracies. Prohibition did, however, give Jewish- or Italian-American
gangsters their first chance to match and often surpass WASP or
Irish-American competitors in profiting from crime.

The term 'organised crime' was first commonly used by academics
and commentators during the 1920s to describe a distinctly American type of social, economic, legal and political problem. Prohibition-
era analysis of organised crime tended to accept that there might be
something wrong with American laws and institutions and the way
the country had developed.

In 1929 John Landesco produced a report for the Illinois Crime
Survey on organised crime in Chicago. Landesco's survey did not
seek to lay the blame for organised crime on any identifiable ethnic
or social group; he made no clear distinction between 'underworld'
or 'upperworld' responsibility for successful organised crime.
Throughout his survey, Landesco emphasised the importance of
political corruption: 'Organized crime and organized political corruption have formed a partnership to exploit for profit the enormous
revenues to be derived from law-breaking.' He concluded that
an understanding of organised crime 'should make possible a
constructive program that will not content itself with punishing
individual gangsters and their allies, but will reach out into a frontal
attack upon basic causes of crime in Chicago'.[13]

The extent and success of organised crime during Prohibition was
seen by most commentators as an American problem that involved
society and government as much as the individual criminal or criminal
syndicate. In 1931 Walter Lippmann argued this most lucidly in an
article entitled 'The Underworld as Servant'. The underworld for
him was significant because it serviced the outlawed desires of the
American people, drink, sex, gambling and drugs: 'The high level of
lawlessness is maintained by the fact that Americans desire to do so
many things that they also desire to prohibit.' He concluded with a
dilemma:

> Sooner or later the American people will have to make up their
> minds either to bring their legislative ideals down to the point
> where they square with human nature or they will have to estab-
> lish an administrative despotism strong enough to start enforcing
> their moral ideals. They cannot much longer defy the devil with a
> wooden sword.

The effective enforcement of morality laws required, in Lippmann's words, 'the establishment of the most despotic and efficient government ever seen on earth', 'thousands and thousands of resolute and incorruptible inspectors, policemen, prosecutors, and judges', 'the expenditures of enormous sums of money', and finally 'the suspension of most civil rights'.[14]

By the 1930s the weight of academic, political and journalistic opinion favoured the repeal of the Prohibition Amendment. Most thought that Prohibition had created or worsened a situation of widespread and systematic lawlessness in the country's cities and states. The vast resources of publisher William Randolph Hearst, plus those of several dozen millionaires, ensured that the Wets won the propaganda battle. Nothing could help the cause of the 'Dry' supporters of Prohibition in their despairing efforts to slow the momentum towards repeal. The Drys were reduced to arguing that the 'noble experiment' was not working because foreign rumrunners and conspirators were 'attacking the global prohibition revolution by trying to wreck it in the country of its birth'.[15] Few people took them very seriously at the time but the argument resurfaced in the postwar era, resuscitated by the likes of Colonels White and Williams and most notably Commissioner Harry J. Anslinger. For them the prohibition to be protected was that of drugs.

Anslinger had been appointed Commissioner of the Federal Bureau of Narcotics in 1930. According to Douglas Clark Kinder's research, his anti-communist, prohibitionist and global outlook were already well established. As a State Department official he had been stationed in Europe, the Caribbean and South America during the 1920s. From Europe he submitted reports which expressed fear of the Soviet Union and the Third Communist International. From the State Department he moved to the Treasury and as an assistant commissioner of Prohibition he had advocated harsh punishment for liquor-law violators. His international experience and prohibitionist commitment qualified him for the FBN job. Anslinger held his position from 1930 until his retirement in 1962, during which time his agency lobbied energetically for drug-prohibition policies at home and abroad.[16]

Using or selling drugs was for Anslinger 'civic corruption' and 'murder on the instalment plan'. His approach to drug control was

simple: 'Get rid of drugs, pushers and users. Period.'[17] But his belief
that effective enforcement and draconian penalties were the only
answers to drug use and addiction began to be challenged. Some
doctors and academics argued for medical- rather than police-based
drug-control policies and they got some support from within the
law-enforcement community. One crime commission asked whether
the country really should pursue a drug-control policy that was
ineffective and fabulously profitable to drug traffickers.[18] August
Vollmer, the foremost police reformer of the day, wrote:

> Stringent laws, spectacular police drives, vigorous prosecution,
> and imprisonment of addicts and peddlers have proved not only
> useless and enormously expensive as a means of correcting this
> evil, but they are also unjustifiably and unbelievably cruel in their
> application to the unfortunate drug victims. Repression has driven
> this vice underground and produced the narcotics smugglers and
> their supply agents, who have grown wealthy out of this evil
> practice and who by devious methods have stimulated traffic in
> drugs.

For Vollmer drug addiction was not a police problem: 'it never has
been and never can be solved by policemen. It is first and last a
medical problem, and if there is a solution it will be discovered not
by policemen, but by scientific and competently trained medical
experts.'[19]

Anslinger responded to such challenges by developing self-serving
distractions, one of which was to blame aliens for America's drug
problems. Dwight Smith has argued that the Bureau could therefore
justify the importance of its task and explain its lack of success
without having to inquire more deeply into the problem of addiction
itself.[20] Just as anti-gambling campaigners were asserting that the
legalising of gambling, its regulation and control, would be a
capitulation to criminal interests, Anslinger used similar arguments
to justify calls for yet more penalties against drug users and traffickers
and for increased yearly budgetary appropriations.

The FBN's indispensability was firmly established by the 1950s,
its wisdom about organised crime rarely challenged. The rest of the
law-enforcement community, with the temporary exception of
the FBI, came to accept and elaborate on its all-powerful Mafia
interpretation.

The FBN continued to set the agenda on drug control, easily seeing off the few challenges it faced from the medical and academic community. Anslinger remained adept at steering public opinion, as well as state and federal lawmakers, in the direction he wanted: more laws and more repressive powers; drug addiction in the United States was to be a police problem not a medical problem; draconian sentences would deter both use and sale. Federal legislation passed in 1951 sharply increased penalties for drug offenders, both users and suppliers. And in 1956 the peak of federal punitive action against drugs was reached when sentences for some offences were raised to five years on the first conviction, and the death penalty could be imposed for selling heroin to anyone under 18 years old.

Anslinger also made a significant impact on international drug control. He dominated the deliberations over the appropriate course of action against narcotics after the war. A study of Anslinger's reports for the United Nations Economic and Social Council's Commission on Narcotic Drugs (CND) 'indicated the growth of his control over narcotic foreign policy and provided a basis for future antidrug activities by the CND and by the United States governments through bilateral diplomacy'.[21] The peak of Anslinger's international career was reached in 1961 when the UN's Single Convention on Narcotic Drugs brought under one instrument all the prior international antinarcotics pacts, except one which Anslinger did not approve of. Current international drug-control policies are built on the Commissioner's framework and the UN now plays host to rapidly expanding drug-control bureaucracies from every part of the world. This system still follows a line dictated from Washington.

Anslinger was a loyal servant of his government. He was able to make a significant impact domestically and internationally because his beliefs and policies fitted well in the framework of US foreign and domestic policy, and the United States, more than any other country shaped the world after the Second World War.

The 1960s, however, ushered in a period of unprecedented popularity for heroin, cocaine, marijuana and every variety of proscribed substances, all of which became vastly profitable to produce and distribute. There were unprecedented opportunities for the development of significant international organised crime. Some of these opportunities were, of course, taken by groups of Italians, Sicilians and Italian-Americans.

The existence of the American Mafia as a centralised organisation dominating organised crime could not be proved, but incidents and revelations involving Italian-American gangsters continued to give some substance to the FBN-sponsored concept.

In 1957 a convention of about 60 suspected Italian-American racketeers was disrupted by state police at Apalachin, New York. Most of these had legitimate 'fronts' in a variety of businesses ranging from taxicabs, trucks, and coin-operated machines to olive oil and cheese. No useful information came from the police action, but it gave a much-needed boost to the alien-conspiracy theory at a time when interest was dwindling.

But 1963 was the conspiracy theorists' most significant year. Another congressional committee, this time chaired by Senator John McClellan of Arkansas, held televised hearings before which a small-time New York criminal, Joseph Valachi, revealed that he was part of something he called 'Cosa Nostra' or 'Our Thing'. Valachi had been arrested by the FBN but FBI agent James Flynn spent eight months with him helping him to develop his final story. The agency switch has symbolic significance because from that time onwards the FBI led professional and public perception of organised crime. The Valachi show was put on to mobilise support for increased federal involvement in the war against organised crime.

Although some of Valachi's testimony does ring true in the light of later events and revelations it was certainly not enough to justify the assertions about the structure of US organised crime that were based on it. However, by the end of the 1960s, as a result of these assertions, most Americans saw the Mafia as a monolithic, ethnically exclusive, strictly disciplined secret society, based on weird rituals, commanding the absolute obedience of its members and controlling the core of the country's organised crime.

Back in the late 1940s when the FBN first began to talk up their discovery, very few people would have associated organised crime exclusively with Italian ethnicity. By the 1960s the words 'Mafia' and 'organised crime' had become virtually synonymous.[22] Government officials were more than happy to supply journalists with the 'facts' to support this explanation for the country's organised-crime problem.

It is worth noting at this point that the FBN had to be abolished in 1968 when it was found to be riddled with corruption. Almost every agent in the New York office was fired, forced to resign, transferred or convicted, and this constituted about one-third of the agency's total manpower – a staggering proportion. Congressional testimony later revealed that FBN agents had taken bribes 'from all levels of traffickers', had sold 'confiscated drugs and firearms', had looted 'searched apartments', had provided tipoffs 'to suspects and defendants' and had threatened 'the lives of fellow agents who dared to expose them'.[23] This scandal attracted minimal press attention and it failed to make an impact on legislators then deciding how best to control organised crime. By then corruption had been effectively excluded from any influential analysis of organised crime. By then the problem had been reduced to 'The Mafia v. America' on the cover of *Time* magazine.

The conception of organised crime as an alien and united entity was as vital for the law-enforcement community as the conception of communism as an alien and united entity was for the intelligence and foreign-policy-making community. Organised crime, like communism, was presented as many-faced, calculating and relentlessly probing for weak spots in the armour of American morality. Morality had to be protected from this alien threat. Aliens were corrupting the police; therefore the police had to be given more power. Compromise, such as reconsideration of the laws governing gambling and drug-taking, was out of the question – the only answer was increased law-enforcement capacity and more laws to ensure the swift capture of gambling operators and drug traffickers behind whom the Mafia was always supposed to be lurking. (The Cosa Nostra label did not catch on with most journalists and fiction writers, but federal officials still use it.)

Members of Congress were convinced enough by the Mafia's 'threat to the nation' to enact a series of measures long sought-after by the federal law-enforcement and intelligence community. Or ganised crime-control provisions in the 1968 and 1970 omnibus crime-control acts included: special grand juries; wider witness immunity provisions for compelling reluctant testimony; extended sentences for persons convicted in organised-crime cases; and the use of wire-tapping and eavesdropping evidence in federal cases. Such major alteration in constitutional guarantees was justified by the belief that the problem was a massive, well-integrated, international conspiracy. The measures gave unprecedented head-hunting powers to federal police and prosecutors, tipping the balance away from such civil liberties as the right to privacy and protection from unreasonable search and seizure, and towards stronger policing powers.

These laws and concurrent anti-drug legislation had a great potential for abuse which was soon fulfilled. This abuse was not restricted to financial corruption and police brutality; much of it was politically motivated. Federal policemen were given more scope to do what Hoover's FBI had been doing illegally for years – spy on and suppress political dissent. The Nixon administration used its new powers more actively against anti-Vietnam war protestors than Italian-American gangsters. Between 1970 and 1974, in particular, grand juries, along with increased wiretapping and eavesdropping powers, clearly became part of the government's armoury against dissent. A list of abuses during these years would include: harassing political activists; discrediting 'non-mainstream' groups; punishing witnesses for exercising their Fifth Amendment rights; covering up official crimes; enticing perjury; and gathering domestic intelligence.[24] By the time of Nixon's 1974 resignation in the wake of the Watergate scandal it was clear that Congress has bestowed an armoury of repressive crime-control laws on people who were themselves criminally inclined.

More recently, in 1984, Reagan administration officials used organised-crime control powers to infiltrate church meetings and wiretap church telephones in Arizona and Texas. The intention was to monitor the efforts of some churches to provide 'sanctuary' to Central American refugees. These refugees were primarily from El Salvador and Guatemala, countries whose regimes had the active support of the US government despite much documented evidence of violent suppression of dissent and 'death squad' activity. For a single set of indictments, 40,000 pages of secretly taped conversations involving priests and nuns were compiled. No prison sentences resulted but the harassment had successfully impeded the work of the sanctuary movement.[25] In the meantime the extent of organised crime in America was not significantly affected. The 1968 and 1970 organised-crime control measures were, as constitutional scholar Leonard Levy put it, 'a salvo of fragmentation grenades that missed their targets and exploded against the Bill of Rights'.[26]

The FBI's concentration on the twenty-plus Italian-American crime syndicates that undoubtedly exist has shown that some of them swear blood oaths of allegiance, form inter-state or regional alliances to try and regulate competition, and use murder and intimidation to protect territory, markets and operations.

But the history of Italian-American organised crime has been more notable for savage internecine struggle against other groups than for the mutual enrichment, discipline and codes of absolute obedience described in most accounts. Criminal syndicates are powerful in the United States and they are often based on such unifying factors as religion, kinship, ethnicity and prison experience, just as racially exclusive, old-school or masonic networks exist in other businesses. They are necessarily secretive, all have 'omerta-like' codes; criminal activity is not something that it is intelligent to talk about.

Thanks to wiretaps, bugs and informants, American mafiosi have been talking to the federal authorities for the past three decades. But no evidence has ever been produced to show that one organisation or cartel was or is capable of exercising effective control over illegal markets. Out of a mass of contradictory evidence came an organised-crime control strategy that has not controlled organised crime. No neat and tidy hierarchy of capos, consiglieres and soldiers can explain the tidal wave of crime and systematic violence associated with organised-crime activities.

Italian-American career-criminals will continue either to operate separately or to compete or co-operate on occasion. They will also continue to be collectively called the Mafia and be much overrated in films and newspaper articles. In 1986, for example, 'Fat Tony' Salerno and Tony 'Ducks' Corallo were the most notable gangsters convicted of racketeering in a series of dramatic court cases that made the name of US Attorney, Rudolph Guiliani. An editorial in the *New York Times* reflected the government's view with the claim that: 'Society, at last is organized. With convictions like these, it's the mob that's coming apart.'[27] Similar claims had been made 50 years earlier when Manhattan prosecutor Thomas E. Dewey also convicted some New York gangsters. The organised-crime situation in the meantime has become much more pervasive and destructive.

There is no doubt that Italian-American gangsters have made a significant contribution to American organised-crime activity in the twentieth century but by making an Italian conspiracy central to organised-crime analysis Americans have only been led further away from understanding it and reducing its impact.

In 1945 Anslinger wrote in a letter to an associate: 'The world belongs to the strong. It always has, it always will.'[28] The world that emerged after the Second World War belonged mainly to the United

States of America. The Germans, Italians and Japanese had been beaten. The war had accelerated the process of French and British imperial collapse, and only the Soviet Union represented a serious threat to American interests and ambitions.

At the end of the war only the United States of all the powers had a functioning physical plant capable of the mass production of goods, and excess capital. Only the United States had become richer rather than poorer because of the war. It possessed gold reserves of $20 billion, almost two-thirds of the world's total of $33 billion. The United States had a monopoly on the atomic bomb and the American Navy dominated the Pacific and the Mediterranean. American troops occupied Japan, the only important industrial power in the Pacific, and Americans dominated France, Britain, Western Germany and Italy.

'The Pax Americana had come of age.' As Paul Kennedy has argued, new overseas markets had to be opened up to absorb the flood of US products. Americans had to stay in control of strategically critical materials such as oil, rubber and metal ores, or have unrestricted access to these materials. Such considerations combined to make the United States committed to the creation of a new world order beneficial to the needs of western capitalism in general and to the needs of the United States in particular. The International Monetary Fund, the International Bank for Reconstruction and Development and, later, the General Agreement on Tariffs and Trade were the international arrangements to secure the compliance of most countries to this new world order. Countries wishing to secure some of the funds available for reconstruction and development under these arrangements were obliged to conform to American requirements on free convertibility of currencies and open competition. The system eventually worked to the advantage of corporations in a reconstructed Western Europe as well as in the United States itself. *Laissez-faire* conditions tend to favour strong, technically advanced countries. But countries less well equipped to compete – in particular developing countries in Asia, Africa and South America – were tied into a system that has often proved to be against their long-term interests.[29]

The only significant rival faced by the United States stayed out of these money and trading arrangements. US–Soviet antagonism long preceded the Second World War but intensified as it became clear that the war had torn apart the old international order. The Soviet Union concentrated its resources on maintaining Eastern European satellite states. The United States kept a powerful presence in Western Europe but still had ample resources left over to intervene forcibly in peripheral areas of the world to prevent or impede the establishment of regimes deemed to be incompatible with its interests.

The rationale behind America's postwar foreign policy was first articulated, in 1946, by George Kennan, the State Department's expert on Soviet affairs. According to Kennan, the Soviet Union was an imperial empire, expansionist and hostile; but an all-out clash for the United States could be avoided through 'containment'. Containment required 'the adroit and vigilant application of counterforce at a series of constantly shifting geographical and political points'. Hardliners in the Truman administration interpreted containment as a justification for the use of a wide variety of clandestine warfare tactics, ranging from radio propaganda to sabotage and murder, to 'contain' left-wing initiatives virtually anywhere in the world.[30]

The CIA emerged as the agency that directed the covert side of containment. It was established in 1947, first as a fact-finding agency but soon afterwards as one authorised to carry out secret operations abroad. These operations were to be kept secret from both Congress and the public. The process had begun before 1947 but after that year it expanded and accelerated. The idea was to learn and then practise effective espionage and counterespionage techniques, and, according to a secret commission, 'to subvert, sabotage and destroy our enemies by more clever, more sophisticated, and more effective methods than those used against us'.

The CIA was a young agency, the American foreign secret-service community as a whole was relatively inexperienced. The idea was to subvert, sabotage and destroy communism, and none knew better how to do this than Nazis and Nazi collaborators. The American anti-communist crusade has justified alliances with criminals of all sorts; in the immediate postwar years the first alliance was with Second World War criminals.

In 1988 Christopher Simpson published a meticulously researched book that began to uncover US political-warfare practices of the early postwar era. In *Blowback: America's Recruitment of Nazis and its Effects on the Cold War*, he describes these practices and their consequences. Simpson shows how the United States recruited Nazis, ex-Nazis and Fascist collaborators from Eastern Europe and the Soviet Union, many of whom were war criminals responsible for the massacre of thousands, to serve as intelligence analysts, spies, covert operations specialists, guerrilla warfare candidates and assassina-

tion experts, all in the name of the anti-communism. This recruitment process was effectively ignored or covered up by the media.
On the US payroll during these years were, for example, Klaus
Barbie, the 'Butcher of Lyons', Reinhard Gehlen, Hitler's most senior
military intelligence officer on the eastern front, and Otto von
Bolschwing, who had once instigated a massacre of Jews in Bucharest and served as a senior aide to Adolf Eichmann. Barbie's career
progression is particularly relevant to this discussion and I shall
return to it.

American intelligence covert activity has also involved collaboration with less ideologically motivated gangsters and drug traffickers. During the war the gangsters who controlled waterfront
labour had been co-opted by Naval Intelligence to prevent sabotage.[31]
After this had been achieved the gangster-run unions were left free
to perform their more traditional role, which was to run rackets and
keep the workforce cheap and docile, using violence if required.
After the end of the war the CIA felt that a similar arrangement was
necessary in France. In the late 1940s the Agency feared that socialist
waterfront unionists, active in the key port of Marseilles, would
come to an alliance with communist political movements. According
to Alfred McCoy, the CIA believed that communist control of the
docks 'might threaten the efficiency of the Marshall plan and any
future aid programmes' and increase the political chances of the
communists nationally. And so:

> The CIA . . . sent agents and a psychological warfare team to
> Marseilles, where they dealt directly with Corsican syndicate
> leaders through the Guerini brothers. The CIA's operatives sup-
> plied arms and money to Corsican gangs for assault on Communist
> picket lines and harassment of important union officials. During
> the month-long strike the CIA's gangsters and the purged CRS
> police units murdered a number of striking workers and mauled
> the picket lines.[32]

The State Department had funded this successful operation with the
help of large American corporations. Marseilles docks were, like
New York's, left in the control of gangsters and smugglers. Before
long, laboratories and packaging plants were set up around the
French port to package heroin for export to the United States.
The heroin pipeline later known as 'the French Connection' was
established.

The opium processed in France had been grown in Turkey, Iran and southeast Asia, converted into a gooey paste known as 'morphine base', brokered by Turkish businessmen and Lebanese warlords, and transferred at sea for transport to Marseilles and then on to New York, hub of the richest drug market in the world. In New York it would be taken on by bulk-buyers, often Jewish- or Italian-Americans, before being repackaged and adulterated for final sale. By the 1950s Sicilian mafiosi began to form business alliances with Italian-American gangsters to exploit the American market.

Southwest and southeast Asia opium remains an important cash crop for impoverished tribal peoples. As Roger Lewis has written: 'With its high price, high yield per acre, labour-intensive nature and inaccessibility on high, rugged hard-to-control terrain . . . [i]t is a low-bulk, high value, non-perishable commodity.' Eradication efforts are fiercely fought off. The peasant farmer only receives a tiny fraction of the eventual value of his crop. But the people who control the refining process, those who ship the refined product to the market and, finally, those at the top of the consumer distribution system make fortunes by exploiting golden entrepreneurial opportunities to buy cheap and sell dear.[33]

The US government's promotion of the drug traffic in the cause of Asian anti-communism can be traced back at least to the early 1950s when Chiang Kai-shek's Kuomintang government was evicted from mainland China by Mao Tse-tung's communists. Part of Chiang's army ended up in an opium-growing area of neighbouring Burma, where they used American-supplied weapons to organise and extort from the trade. McCoy also found Burmese intelligence reports which revealed that the CIA planes bringing in military supplies for the Kuomintang loaded up with opium for the flights back to Taiwan or Thailand.

CIA involvement in the drugs business in southeast Asia intensified when the Americans invaded Vietnam in the 1960s. The area now known as the 'Golden Triangle' which stretches across 150,000 square miles of northeast Burma, northern Thailand and northern Laos rapidly became the world's main source of supply for heroin. The former French rulers had collaborated with corrupt local élites in the export of opium through Saigon. American involvement opened up a much larger market as GI demand for heroin supplemented the growing demand from addicts and users at home.[34]

Jonathan Kwitny's research has revealed that restrictions on drug enforcement made sure that this traffic could continue unhindered and be profitable to US allies and particularly co-operative US offi-cials. One gruesome smuggling practice was to cut open, gut and fill GI corpses with heroin before flying them back to the United States. 'Witnesses were prepared to testify that the heroin-stuffed soldiers bore coded body numbers, allowing conspiring officers on the other end, at Norton Air Force Base in California, to remove the booty – up to fifty pounds of heroin per dead GI.' The army covered up this discovery and sent the investigators to combat duty.[35]

During the war, opponents charged that the CIA was knowingly financing its operations from opium money. This implausible-sounding conspiracy theory has been confirmed by Orrin DeForest who from 1968 to 1975 was one of the Agency's chief interrogation officers. DeForest writes in a recently published book that the South Vietnamese trade in opium was 'a fine, cut-rate way of financing operations. . . . And so we bought billions and used the money to finance operations. None of us felt there was anything immoral about this.'[36]

The North Vietnamese victory in 1975 was accompanied by a wave of South Vietnamese immigration to America – over 200,000 initially. Among these was Nguyen Cao Ky, a former leader of the Saigon regime. General Ky made alliances with other former South Vietnamese officers and established an anti-communist organisation in exile. A former member has testified that this group of about 1000 members had an organised-crime division with branches in major American cities. Ky's operation recruited recently arrived Vietnam-ese immigrants and trained them to rob and kill to protect drug trafficking and extortion rackets, mainly in Asian communities.[37]

US involvement in Central and South America followed a course similar to that followed in southeast Asia. Anti-communism justified alliances with corrupt rulers, or deposed rulers wanting to return to power, or any variety of expedient entrepreneurs wishing to cash in on chaos. US involvement has again been accompanied by significant international organised-crime activity with negative consequences for the American people.

One major difference is that US consumer demand for South American cocaine far exceeds that for southeast Asian heroin. This feeds the growth of 'narcocracies' in countries like Peru, Bolivia and Colombia whose financial power continues to have a destructive impact on these countries.[38] Private armies wage war against each other or against the state on a scale far beyond that of the Chicago bootleg war of the 1920s but basically for the same reasons: protection or expansion of businesses whose massively inflated profits derive from US prohibition laws.

The story of Klaus Barbie and other intelligence entrepreneurs connects the cocaine trade with postwar US recruitment and protection of Nazis and with US-supported military regimes in South and Central America. As chief of the Gestapo in Lyons, France, Barbie's war crimes included torturing and murdering captured resistance fighters and deporting Jews to death camps. In 1945 he was put on the US Army intelligence payroll to mould clandestine Nazi cells in Eastern Europe into anti-communist spy rings. In 1951 he was given a new identity and sent to join the US anti-communist crusade in Latin America. Research by Linklater, Hilton and Ascherson led them to conclude that Fascist ideals and methods found 'fertile soil' in Latin America.

Barbie settled in Bolivia where he advised the country's rulers on torture, the setting-up and running of concentration camps and the organisation of squads whose main purpose was killing and intimidation. In 1978 Barbie became security consultant for Roberto Suárez, Bolivia's most notable drug trafficker of the day. For Suárez he helped to organise a paramilitary squad to protect operations. This squad became known as the Fiancés of Death and played an active part in the campaign of terror initiated by the leaders of a 1980 military coup, one of whom was Colonel Luis Arce Gómez, a cousin of Suárez. The new regime immediately murdered many of the trade union leaders who had led the opposition to their takeover. With the help of the Fiancés they also took virtual control of the cocaine trade, driving the smaller operators out of business and 'taxing' the shipments of Suárez and other major traffickers.[39]

The rise of the cocaine trade since the early 1970s has been accompanied by a confusing mixture of violence, corruption and political expediency. The forthcoming trial of former CIA employee General Manuel Noriega of Panama may reveal more about US involvement in this mixture but there is already no disputing CIA knowledge of the large scale trafficking operations of many of its friends and collaborators in South and Central America. A Senate subcommittee has, for example, confirmed that the US-supported Contra rebels used drug money to support their fight against the Nicaraguan government:

it is clear that individuals who provided support for the Contras were involved in drug trafficking, the supply network of the

Contras was used by drug trafficking organizations, and elements of the Contras themselves knowingly received financial and material assistance from drug traffickers. In each case, one or another agency of the US government had information regarding the involvement either while it was occurring, or immediately thereafter.[40]

All this was known to US government agencies while the country was officially engaged in the war against drugs mentioned earlier. On 18 March 1986 President Reagan brought his administration's main domestic and foreign concerns together when he announced that: 'Every American parent will be outraged to learn that top Nicaraguan government officials are deeply involved in drug trafficking. There is no crime to which the Sandinistas will not stoop. This is an outlaw regime.'[41] Reagan made this statement to support his request to Congress for $100 million more in aid to the Contras. The priority was to bring down the Nicaraguan government. He spoke on prime-time television and his words were reported uncritically by most of the media. Much less exposure was given to both State and Justice Departments' rebuttals of Reagan's assertion. The Sandinista drug-connection story was in fact largely fiction which makes it representative of the misinformation that has characterised American government announcements on international crime since the Second World War.

This account of postwar US foreign policy does not mean to suggest one big US conspiracy controlling international crime but an American-influential global system which has allowed for and often encouraged the proliferation of numerous networks that successfully and illegally pursue power or profit. The CIA could no more control international organised crime than the Mafia. But the CIA has operated in ways that either included or protected criminal activity and has covered up this involvement. In the final analysis, all the rhetoric and mythmaking of American bureaucrats and politicians simply obscured the fact that the war on crime and drugs has always occupied a lowly position on the list of the nation's priorities.

On 14 October 1982 President Reagan announced a plan intended to 'end the drug menace and cripple organized crime'.[42] Part of the plan was the establishment of a task force, nominally headed by Vice-

President George Bush, which deployed everything from destroyers and helicopter gunships to a balloon-shaped radar device nicknamed Fat Albert to intercept smugglers in South Florida waters. A year later an enlarged task force was expanded into a national narcotics interception system. The tens of millions of dollars spent achieved little. Smugglers were perhaps inconvenienced and required to use more ingenuity, but the new elaborate and expensive surveillance techniques failed to stop them bringing drugs into the country. The rest of the plan, similarly, was mainly for public-relations purposes and failed to make an impact on the extent and success of organised crime.[43]

Reagan's advisers were probably well aware that organised crime would not be crippled by the plan and therefore a crime commission was also thought necessary to maintain public support for prevailing organised-crime control policies. On 28 July 1983 Reagan formally established the President's Commission on Organized Crime to be chaired by Judge Irving R. Kaufman and composed of eighteen other men and women, mainly from the law-enforcement community.

After three years' selective investigation the Commission concluded that the government's basic approach to the problem was sound but needed a harder line on all fronts: more wiretaps, informants, undercover agents in order to get more convictions which would require more prisons. Witnesses who might have pointed out the deficiencies of this approach were not consulted. Corruption within the system was scarcely considered as part of the problem. Otherwise, people might have questioned the wisdom of this solution.

The only recommendation to attract much attention was a call for a widespread national programme to test most working Americans for drug use; in effect, to force most Americans to submit to regular, observed urine tests. The tests require supervision because people might be tempted to bring in someone else's clean urine. At a news conference Judge Kaufman explained the recommendation. The investigation had convinced him that 'law enforcement has been tested to its utmost. . . . But let's face it, it hasn't succeeded. So let's try something else. Let's try testing.'[44] The immense problem of drug-related gangsterism and corruption was to be tackled by examining urine. Even Walter Lippman could not have imagined a more bizarre wholesale invasion of privacy.

A small number of liberals objected to the Commission's urine-testing recommendation but a poll taken after the Commission's report was issued showed that nearly 80 per cent of Americans did not oppose drug testing; in fact, many already worked for corporations that regularly tested their personnel. The law-enforcement community had announced that testing people's urine would reduce the demand for drugs and therefore hit organised crime in the pocketbook, so millions of Americans were prepared to line up and give their samples. Although the results of these tests have often been shown to be wrong, the business of urine-testing laboratories and equipment manufacturers is booming. Five companies made around $173 million in 1989 from the testing of American workers. Projected profits in 1990 were expected to be $340 million.[45]

In January 1990 President George Bush announced a new $10 billion anti-drugs package. This included an extra $1.2 billion to the Pentagon to finance the military prohibition of drug imports, with a radar 'picket fence' across the Caribbean, backed up by naval and air patrols to investigate suspicious boats and planes. Bush's plan also called for: an end to 'frivolous appeals' by drug convicts; restrictions on the use of plea-bargaining in drug cases; allowing the use of evidence even if questionably or illegally collected; and an expansion of the use of undercover and entrapment operations by police and customs.[46] All this will further stretch America's prison system but is no more likely to control organised crime than previous initiatives.

Contrary to the Mafia interpretation, not much about organised crime fits into a neat and tidy pattern. Not much conforms to the ethnically exclusive formulas most popular writers and journalists still follow. Americans from every ethnic group and from the lowest to the highest levels of society and government have always been involved.

There is a never-ending supply of recruits for the lower levels of organised crime and the source is not restricted to the ghettoes and housing projects of the cities, where youth gangs compete violently for territory and to protect drug-distribution networks. Outlaw motor cycle gangs, for example, are mainly groups of white Protestants from rural and suburban areas. Only a minority of biker gangs are involved in criminal activities but there are still hundreds of individual gangs heavily involved in organised-crime activities. Their record ranges from drug distribution and extortion to the use of violent tactics to muscle in on legitimate businesses.[47]

Thousands of career criminals do eventually get caught, convicted and sentenced to time in prison, but imprisonment has proved to be part of the problem of organised crime rather than its solution. In many US prisons gangs fight to establish control over prostitution, protection and drug-trafficking rackets in systems based on brutality, informants and staff corruption. Prison gangs tend to be organised along racial and ethnic lines and some, like the Aryan Brotherhood, the Black Guerrillas and La Nuestra Familia, have state-wide and even inter-state influence. They run rackets and assassinate competition on the outside as well as on the inside.[48]

The demand for drugs in the United States fuels organised crime. Sources of raw material exist throughout the world, including the United States. Organizations, large and small, buy and process the raw materials and distribute the product through a host of retail outlets. Although some operations have lasted for decades, organisation in the drug business is largely spontaneous, with anyone free to enter it at any level if he or she has the money, the supplier and the ability to escape arrest or robbery.

There has never been an ethnically based monopoly in the drug business. There are many thousands of distribution and smuggling networks – decentralisation characterises the industry with a high turnover of personnel. Smuggling organisations tend to restrict their operations to importation, leaving distribution within the United States to indigenous groups.

If increased drug-law enforcement has done anything over the past two decades it has been to create competitive advantage for criminal groups which have the skills, connections and capital to nullify enforcement by corruption, and the firepower to resist theft and takeover bids. Violence in the drug trade today far exceeds anything experienced during the bootleg wars of the 1920s, but the motives are generally the same: protecting territory or goods from rivals, discouraging informants, or stealing money or drugs from other traffickers.

Organized-crime activity involves the whole system of law enforcement and criminal justice, but not in the simple 'Good Guys versus Bad Guys' scenario that the US government control strategies require to be effective.

In 1967 President Johnson's Crime Commission had de-emphasised corruption in its analysis of organised crime but at least it made the unequivocal statement that 'All available data indicate that organized crime flourishes only where it has corrupted local offi-

cials.'[49] Corruption has continued to characterise drug law enforcement well into the 1980s. The cities of Detroit, Chicago, Miami and
Portland have all experienced major scandals in recent years. The
offences uncovered include: 'skimming' cash and drugs from seizures;
pocketing money earmarked for informants; lying to obtain search
warrants; committing perjury in court to obtain convictions; selling
drugs and guns; accepting bribes and protecting drug syndicates.

Higher-level officials have often been found to be corrupt. In 1982
the sheriff, chief of police, a judge and another person from Henry
County, Georgia, were convicted of aiding and abetting smugglers
when landing at an airstrip and 'providing an escort service' into
Atlanta. Southern sheriffs, in particular, have been revealed to be as
involved in drug trafficking as their predecessors were in bootlegging.
Most notable is Sheriff Leroy Hobbs of Harrison County, Mississippi,
who was sentenced to 20 years in prison in May 1984 for drug-
trafficking offences. Hobbs had been elected on a promise to crack
down on drugs and corruption.[50]

For Lippman, America's ambitious moral reform programme
implied 'the establishment of the most despotic and efficient government ever seen on earth' and 'thousands and thousands of resolute
and incorruptible inspectors, policemen, prosecutors and judges to
enforce it'. The US government may have despotic tendencies but is
no nearer efficiency, resolution and incorruptibility than during
Prohibition. Defence lawyers take their share of the proceeds of
organised crime. Defence fees are often so high that career criminals
have to step up their illegal activities while on bail to keep up the
payments. The lawyers make sure that their clients know that there
is a firm connection between fee payment and the zealous exercise of
professional expertise, secret knowledge and organisational 'connections' on their behalf.[51]

Banks, most noticeably in Florida, have boomed in recent years by
laundering vast amounts of drug money. In Miami so many drug-
trade dollars have flowed through the city's branch of the Federal
Reserve system that it did not need to issue any new currency for
some years and even exported used dollars to other Federal Reserve
districts. Since 1970 the city has become an international banking
centre, rivalling London and New York, and no one seriously disputes
that dollars generated by the trade in marijuana and cocaine account
for this rapid rise to prominence. The problem, as Senator William
Proxmire has put it, is that 'Many banks are addicted to drug money,
just as millions of Americans are addicted to drugs.'[52]

In order to be useful, organised-crime money has to be made legitimate and untraceable. Banks can do this, but money in banks is idle money and few entrepreneurs can resist opportunities to make money active. Investment in legitimate business gives a successful criminal a base in the mainstream of American economic life. The amounts involved undoubtedly make organised crime an important source of investment capital. Hot money has been particularly welcome in high-risk operations where venture capital is hard to come by – one successful precedent was the setting up of gambling casinos in the Nevada desert in the 1940s and 1950s. But organised-crime money has also found its way into corporate farming, computer manufacturing and, above all, real estate.[53]

There are few significant areas of American life that have not affected or been affected by organised crime. Organised crime is an essential feature of the American social, economic and political systems, but the experts and commentators who stick to the Mafia framework manage to disguise this fact by representing it as something alien and distinct from American life.

US governments continue to refuse to re-examine an analysis which conceals more than it reveals, and American people continue to accept organised-crime control policies that undermine civil liberties more than organised crime. Ageing Italian-American gangsters are incarcerated from time to time in a blaze of publicity and exaggerated claims about their significance, but any vacuums created are soon filled. There are stronger forces around than the force of law. social, economic and political forces which often combine to make the law at best inadequate, at worst counter-productive.

The organised-crime control strategy that evolved in the postwar era can guarantee short-term, publicity-laden successes in the war against crime. It can promise success in public relations terms for policing agencies, enhance the career prospects of ambitious prosecutors and provide opportunities for presidents to posture against crime. However, it will continue to fail because the thinking behind it has always denied American responsibility for American problems. The FBN, the FBI and the legions of journalists who feed off these agencies for their stories had everybody looking in the wrong direction. People were being distracted by Mafia stories while an ideal environment for the growth of significant crime on a global scale was taking shape.

Al Capone was a nightclub bouncer before Prohibition. By 1924 he was in control of a large and growing business, more by luck than talent. Bootlegging profits enabled him to expand and diversify operations; illegal rackets were complemented by semi-legal and legal enterprises. Breweries, distilleries, speakeasies, warehouses, fleets of boats and trucks, nightclubs, gambling houses, horse and dog racetracks, brothels, and numerous small but legitimate businesses together produced a yearly income of hundreds of millions of dollars.[54] But Capone would have remained an insignificant thug without an alcohol control policy that vastly inflated the prices for a product that was easy to produce, and without the nullification of the law that only money can achieve. Thanks to the export of US-style drug control policy these conditions now extend the world over.

Gangsters do not operate in a vacuum. They need the right environment to survive and prosper. This environment is one of market opportunity for illegal goods and services, accompanied by government helplessness or complicity. Among the negative and unintended consequences of postwar US foreign and domestic policy have been unprecedented opportunities for significant, international organised crime. This process has been perpetuated rather than tackled by other countries, most of which tend to go along meekly with the United States on the drugs issue. The situation now is best described as a global fix. This type of fix is not synonymous with drug taking nor with bribery and corruption, but it has involved all these. The fix in this case involves worldwide networks of alliances, commitments and obligations, all mutually reinforcing, of such a nature as to move much of the rest of the world towards the condition of many US cities, where there is an almost complete paralysis of law enforcement and observance.

Americans will make no progress towards reducing the destructive impact of organised crime until they can accept it as an American problem and not an alien intrusion. To do this they would need to dispose of Cold War Mafia mythology and rethink an analytical framework that whitewashes a flawed system. However, the capacity of the US government to analyse crime has regressed to a point that looks to be beyond redemption. A multi-ethnic assortment of gangsters and criminal opportunists will continue to take their chances.

Notes

1. Quoted in D. Smith, *The Mafia Mystique* (New York: Basic Books, 1975) pp. 123–4.
2. L. Mortimer and J. Lait: *Chicago Confidential* (New York: Crown, 1950) pp. 176–7; *USA Confidential* (New York: Crown, 1952) p. 15; *Washington Confidential* (New York: Crown, 1951) p. 178.
3. US Senate Special Committee to Investigate Crime in Interstate Commerce (hereinafter called the Kefauver Committee), 82nd Congress, *Third Progress Report* (Washington, DC: Government Printing Office, 1951) p. 147.
4. W. Moore, *The Kefauver Committee and the Politics of Crime* (Columbia: University of Missouri Press, 1974) pp. 114–134.
5. E. Kefauver, *Crime in America* (London: Victor Gollancz, 1952) p. 28.
6. Kefauver Committee, *Hearings*, Part 10 (Washington, DC: Government Printing Office, 1951) p. 501.
7. A. Block and J. McWilliams, 'On the Origins of American Counter-intelligence: Building a Clandestine Network', *Journal of Policy History*, vol. 1, no. 4 (1989).
8. D. C. Kinder, 'Bureaucratic Cold Warrior: Harry J. Anslinger and Illicit Narcotics Traffic', *Pacific Historical Review*, 50 (May 1981) p. 171.
9. H. J. Anslinger and W. Oursler, *The Murderers* (London: Arthur Barker, 1962) pp. 172–3; B. Fremantle, *The Fix: The Inside Story of the World Drugs Trade* (London: Michael Joseph, 1985) pp. 73–4.
10. J. Marks, *The Search for the 'Manchurian Candidate': The CIA and Mind Control* (London: Allen Lane, 1979) pp. 20, 88–99, 101, 199, 220; A. W. Scheflin and E. N. Optom, *The Mind Manipulators* (London: Paddington Press, 1978) pp. 134–41.
11. D. Caute, *The Great Fear: The Anticommunist Purge Under Truman and Eisenhower* (London: Secker and Warburg, 1978). For the purge of academics during these years, see E. W. Schrecker, *No Ivory Tower: McCarthyism and the Universities* (New York: Oxford University Press, 1986).
12. F. Browning and J. Gerassi, *The American Way of Crime* (New York: G. P. Putnam's Sons, 1980) p. 467.
13. J. Landesco, *Organized Crime in Chicago*, (1929; rept. Chicago,: Ill.: University of Chicago Press, 1968) pp. 189–221.
14. W. Lippmann, 'The Underworld as Servant', in G. Tyler (ed.), *Organized Crime in America* (Ann Arbor, Mich.: University of Michigan Press, 1967) pp. 58–69.
15. A. Sinclair, *Prohibition: The Era of Excess* (London: Faber and Faber, 1962) p. 349.
16. D. C. Kinder, op. cit., pp. 172–3.
17. Quoted in Anslinger's obituary notice, *New York Times*, 18 November 1975, p. 40.
18. State of California, Special Crime Study Commission on Organized Crime, *Third Progress Report* (Sacramento, Cal., 31 January 1950), p. 100.

19.   A. Vollmer, *The Police and Modern Society*, (Berkeley, Cal.: University of California Press, 1936) pp. 99–118.
20.   D. Smith, op. cit., pp. 184–8.
21.   D. C. Kinder and W. O. Walker III, 'Stable Force in a Storm: Harry J. Anslinger and United States Narcotic Foreign Policy, 1930–62', *Journal of American History*, 72 (March 1986): 922. See also K. Bruun, *The Gentleman's Club: International Control of Drugs and Alcohol* (London, University of Chicago Press, 1975) pp. 132–48.
22.   For the most thorough and insightful analysis of Valachi's testimony see Smith, op. cit., pp. 218–40.
23.   US Senate hearings before the Permanent Subcommittee on Investigations of the Committee on Government Operations, *Federal Drug Enforcement*, 94th Congress, 1st Session, 9–11 June 1975, Part I, pp. 134–44.
24.   See A. Block and W. Chambliss, *Organizing Crime* (New York: Elsevier, 1981) pp. 194–211.
25.   S. Shapiro, 'Nailing Sanctuary Givers', *Los Angeles Daily Journal*, 12 March 1985, p. 4.
26.   Leonard Levy quoted in S. Pizzigati, 'The Perverted Grand Juries', *Nation*, 19 June 1976, pp. 743–6.
27.   Editorial, *New York Times*, 24 November 1986, p. 18.
28.   Anslinger to R. W. Kauffman, 19 March 1945, Box 3, Harry J. Anslinger Papers, Historical Collections and Labour Archives, Pattee Library, Pennsylvania State University.
29.   P. Kennedy, *The Rise and Fall of the Great Powers* (London: Unwin Hyman, 1988) pp. 358–60.
30.   This section relies heavily on C. Simpson, *Blowback: America's Recruitment of Nazis and its Effects on the Cold War* (New York: Collier, 1988) pp. 83–4, 127, 135, 199–201, 223. See also W. Blum, *The CIA: A Forgotten History* (London: Zed Books, 1986).
31.   See A. Block and John C. McWilliams, 'All the Commissioner's Men: the Federal Bureau of Narcotics and the Dewey–Luciano Affair, 1947–1954', *Intelligence and National Security*, vol. 5, no. 1 (January 1990) pp. 171–92.
32.   A. W. McCoy, *The Politics of Heroin in Southeast Asia* (London: Harper and Row, 1972) pp. 44–9; F. Pearce, *Crimes of the Powerful* (London: Pluto Press, 1976) pp. 141–52.
33.   R. Lewis, 'Serious Business: the Global Heroin Economy', in A. Henman, R. Lewis and T. Malyon, *Big Deal: The Politics of the Illicit Drugs Business* (London: Pluto Press, 1985) pp. 10–11.
34.   McCoy, op. cit., pp. 85–91; J. Kwitny, *The Crimes of Patriots* (New York: Touchstone, 1988) p. 47.
35.   Kwitney, op. cit., p. 52.
36.   O. DeForest and D. Chanoff, *Slow Burn: The Rise and Bitter Fall of American Intelligence in Vietnam* (New York: Simon and Schuster, 1990), reviewed by J. Mirsky in the *New York Review of Books*, 16 August 1990, pp. 29–36.
37.   President's Commission on Organized Crime (Kaufman Commission),

Record of Hearing III, Organized Crime of Asian Origin (Washington, DC: Government Printing Office, 1984) pp. 328–42.

38. R. T. Naylor, *Hot Money and the Politics of Debt* (London: Unwin Hyman, 1987) pp. 165–86.

39. M. Linklater, I. Hilton and N. Ascherson, *The Fourth Reich: Klaus Barbie and the Neo-Fascist Connection* (London: Hodder and Stoughton, 1984) pp. 16–19, 215–319; N. Chomsky, *Turning the Tide: US Intervention in Central America and the Struggle for Peace* (London: Pluto Press, 1985) pp. 198–207.

40. US Senate, Subcommittee on Terrorism, Narcotics and International Operations of the Committee on Foreign Relations, *Drugs, Law Enforcement and Foreign Policy* (Washington, DC: Government Printing Office, 1989) p. 36.

41. Bernard Weinraub, 'Reagan Condemns Nicaragua – Plea for Aid to Rebels', *New York Times*, 17 March 1986, p. 1; Joel Brinkley, 'Drug Agency Rebuts Reagan Charge', *New York Times*, 19 March 1986, p. 3.

42. Quoted in Leslie Maitland, 'President Gives Plan to Combat Drug Networks', *New York Times*, 15 October 1982, p. 1.

43. For a more detailed evaluation of Reagan's war on drugs see M. Woodiwiss, *Crime, Crusades and Corruption* (London: Frances Pinter, 1988) pp. 197–226.

44. Quoted in Joel Brinkley, 'Meese Supports Drug-Testing for U.S. Employees', *New York Times*, 5 March 1986, p. 47.

45. M. Freudenheim, 'Booming Business: Drug Use Tests', *New York Times*, 3 January 1990, p. D1.

46. Richard L. Berke, 'Bush to Seek $1.2 Billion for a Bigger Drug War', *New York Times*, 25 January 1990, p. 20.

47. *Narcotics Control Digest*, 20 February 1985, p. 1.

48. For an analysis of prisons and prisons gangs see L. Caroll, 'Race, Ethnicity, and the Social Order of the Prison', in D. Kelly, *Criminal Behaviour: Text and Readings in Criminology* (New York: St Martin's Press, 1990), pp, 510–27.

49. President's Commission on Law Enforcement and the Administration of Justice, *The Challenge of Crime in a Free Society* (Washington, DC: Government Printing Office, 1967) p. 446.

50. *Narcotics Control Digest*, May 1984, p. 12.

51. For an analysis of 'the practice of law as a confidence game' see A. S. Blumberg, *Criminal Justice* (Chicago: Quadrangle Books, 1967) pp. 110–15.

52. Quoted in P. Lernoux, 'The Miami Connection', *Nation*, 18 February 1984, p. 198.

53. For the investment of organised-crime money, see K. Sale, *Power Shift: The Rise of the Southern Rim and its Challenge to the Eastern Establishment* (New York: Vintage Books, 1976) pp. 80–8.

54. J. Kobler, *Capone* (London: Coronet, 1972) pp. 10–11.

2

All about Eve
The Many Faces of
United States Drug Policy

BRUCE BULLINGTON

INTRODUCTION

This paper describes the multifaceted nature of US drug policy as it functions both in the United States and in other nations. On the one hand, the policy claims a hard-line approach to the domestic drug problem through a confounding variety of programmes orientated to eliminating drugs at their source, interdicting shipments from producer-nations to the US, rigorous enforcement of the criminal statutes regulating such use, and convincing the young not to use illicit substances in the future. These diverse efforts are generally discussed within the context of two dominant categories, supply- and demand-reduction strategies. Most supply-reduction strategies have been directed at producer countries, in recent times focusing on the Central and South American nations of Panama, Nicaragua, Colombia, Bolivia and Peru, the major source and transhipment nations for marijuana and coca, North America's preferred illicit substances. In contrast, demand-reduction efforts target domestic users and potential users, utilising the combined resources of the federal, state and local governments.

There is another aspect of drug policy that is neither openly discussed nor publicly recognised by most US officials. This involves the use of narcotic operatives stationed in foreign nations in supply-reduction efforts to provide intelligence to the US State Department, the Department of Defense and the Central Intelligence Agency regarding a number of areas of concern that are by no means drug-related. An example of this occurred in April 1989 when the Colombian government accused the US Defense Department of using the ruse of the drug-trafficking fight to install a sophisticated radar system on a Colombian island that they said was actually intended to monitor activities in Nicaragua.[1] Such hidden agendas of drug policy can be used to explain many of the obvious inconsistencies and erratic enforcement practices related to the War on Drugs, for, on balance, drug policy has consistently been treated as secondary to other foreign-policy concerns, and especially the perceived threats posed by communism in this hemisphere and throughout the world.

The following chapter describes and discusses the significance of each of the different faces of contemporary US drug policy. This account begins with a description of the contours of the current manifest policy, identifying the diverse programmes geared to supply and demand reduction. The relative effectiveness of each of these approaches is evaluated in light of the articulated goals that public officials and other supporters have claimed for them. Finally, a brief case-study of drug enforcement and US foreign-policy initiatives as they impact on the group of islands comprising the nation of the Bahamas is presented. This example clearly demonstrates how the US government has allowed other foreign-policy concerns to take precedence over drugs.

The War on Drugs was given new meaning with President Bush's expanded use of the military in the 1989 invasion of Panama. In this action the administration demonstrated an eagerness to employ the military in drug interdiction activities and in assuring the capture of General Noriega. This occurred at the same time as the warming of western relations with communist countries around the world posed a serious threat to the military establishment. With Mikhail Gorbachev's achievements leading to the demilitarisation of Eastern Europe, the US military has been forced to locate new enemies.[2] The 1989 incursion into Panama signalled that Latin American drug barons and their collaborators may be one group selected for this dubious honour. Thus, escalating the involvement of the military role in the drug war allows Pentagon strategies to blunt some of the budgetarily damaging effects of the new East–West détente and the so-called 'peace dividend' that it is thought will follow from sharply reduced military budgets.

President Bush's invasion of Panama could have proved politically problematic for him, especially if General Noriega had escaped capture. In this instance the gamble paid off, however, and Bush's popularity soared as a result of Operation Just Cause's success. The results of three different opinion polls conducted in late January 1990 indicated that Americans overwhelmingly approved of the

President's actions in Panama. Respondents were equally pleased with Bush's overall performance during his first year in office (the approval ratings in the three polls ranged from 76 to 80 per cent, the highest popularity rating of any US president since John F. Kennedy faced down the Soviets in the 1961 Cuban missile crisis).[3]

Understandably the President's actions raised familiar suspicions in Latin American and other nations. The Organization of American States, for example, voted overwhelmingly to condemn the US for the assault as a clear violation of Panama's sovereign status.[4] OAS member-countries were extremely concerned that their own sovereignty could as easily be violated by the American military in what they see as the United States' hegemonic efforts to go to extremes in order to thwart drug production and trafficking.

Vice-President Dan Quayle was sent on a goodwill tour of Latin America in late January 1990 to repair strained relations and alleviate Latin American anxiety over the sovereignty issue. Mexico, Venezuela and a number of other OAS member-nations requested that the Vice-President cancel his planned appearances there because of hostile public relation to the invasion.[5] Ultimately Quayle desisted, limiting his visit to Honduras, Jamaica and Panama, and not stopping in those nations most concerned about the American military action. While in Honduras for the installation of the new president, he also conferred with the leaders of several other Latin American nations and, based on these talks, concluded: 'The Central American presidents understand why the President did it and that he had no other viable option. . . . Operation Just Cause was a non-issue. There was more concern about economic development and how we can help the [Panamanian] Endara government than there was criticism of the United States.'[6]

A second and clearly related Latin American concern developed after the US State Department announced a planned naval blockade of Colombia designed to intercept shipments of cocaine and marijuana in transit to the United States. An immediate Latin American outcry led the policy-makers to change their inflammatory language, dropping the term 'blockade' and explaining that they only planned to conduct routine military manoeuvres in the area. Of course, suspicious craft would be routinely stopped and searched but normal shipping and commerce through the region would not be disrupted.[7]

During the month of January 1990 a Colombian group, probably composed of several drug smugglers, calling itself the Extraditables released a number of hostages and called for a truce with the government.[8] Press releases indicated that this somewhat mysterious out-law group had declared President Barco's administration the victor in Colombia's internal drug war and that they (the drug barons) were now willing to dismantle their organisations in exchange for amnesty for past crimes.[9] As a token of their good faith they also turned over three large drug-processing laboratories which had allegedly produced as much as 20 tons of cocaine per month. Despite these overtures, sceptics doubted the group's sincerity about quitting the business permanently.[10] At the time President Barco refused to grant any concessions to the Extraditables and until recently the group remained in hiding.[11]

On 31 January 1990 a US Coast Guard ship precipitated an incident in international waters off the coast of Mexico by firing on a boat of Cuban registry flying a Panamanian flag. The American captain explained the ship fitted a 'profile' used to identify vessels that were likely to be carrying drugs. He ordered it to stop and submit to a search. When the captain of the Cuban ship ignored these demands, warning shots were fired across his ship's bow. Following this, the suspect vessel continued on and was fired upon and hit. Despite extensive damage the ship was able to limp into Mexican waters and docked safely at Tampico. The justification provided by the Coast Guard for firing at the ship was that they had obtained 'permission' to do so from the recently installed Endara government in Panama. The US vessel did not follow the ship into Mexican waters but requested that the Mexican government search it for them. This request was rejected.

On 15 February 1990 a much-heralded one-day summit of Latin American leaders was held in Cartagena, Colombia. The meeting was called by President Bush, ostensibly to 'co-ordinate' anti-drug efforts between the United States and the 'big three' Latin American nations of Bolivia, Colombia and Peru. A very substantial military presence accompanied the conference; US warships lay off the shore of Cartagena to 'supplement' the protection provided by massive Colombian forces (more than 5000 troops).[12] In the United States the media warned of an alleged threat to the President posed by the narcoguerrillas. At one point it was reported that these groups were attempting to obtain SA-7 shoulder-fired anti-aircraft missiles which could be used to shoot down the President's plane.[13] Despite the clamour, the actual conference was conducted without disturbance.

It was clear from the outset that the meeting would be little more than a photo opportunity for the leaders in attendance. The accord, which had been drawn up in advance by the US State Department, promised the three South American leaders up to $2.2 billion in foreign aid over a five-year period in exchange for co-operation with US initiatives in the current drug war.[14] That sum appeared inadequate to outside observers who estimate that the coca industry generates in excess of $4 billion per year in revenues for these three nations alone; the Bush proposal would provide them with only $424 million in foreign aid during the coming years.[15] A closer look at the agreement also reveals that about 80 per cent of the aid would be used to fund police and military activities rather than to provide much-needed economic support and incentives.[16] Bush's idea of stationing US warships off the coast of Colombia was sternly rejected at Cartagena by President Barco, who indicated that his nation would view such an action as a violation of their sovereignty.

THE CONTOURS OF US DRUG POLICY

Throughout this century, from the time of the passage of the first national anti-narcotic legislation, the Harrison Act of 1914, US government leaders have periodically taken up the issue of illegal drug use and successfully brought it to the forefront of public consciousness, usually creating a 'moral panic' in the process. In most instances these efforts resulted in the mobilisation of powerful support for programmes designed to suppress the drug traffic and severely punish those who participate in it. The most notable feature of US policies has been their total reliance on criminalisation of the drug problem. This approach contrasts sharply with those utilised by some other industrialised nations, such as the Netherlands, the United Kingdom and the Scandinavian countries, which have all adopted policies based on a public-health approach that excludes or minimises any criminal justice intervention with drug users.

The war metaphor has frequently been employed in domestic US anti-drug efforts. The warriors' targets usually include those involved in the production of plants and chemicals that comprise natural and synthetic psychoactive drug substances, those who process and transport these materials from their countries of origin into the United States, and street-level sellers and consumers. Underlying the prevailing philosophy and social policy is the moral conviction that certain chemical substances must not be ingested because they are inherently 'evil' and/or harmful, certain to lead users into lives of degradation, debauchery and ill-health. The inflammatory rhetoric accompanying the war claims that those said to be making fortunes from the drug trade 'despicable vermin' selling 'poison and death' to otherwise innocent American youth. Based on the results of many public opinion polls, this powerful hyperbole has had a significant impact on public attitudes toward the drug issue.[17] If we strip such statements of their value judgements, however, we are left with the observation that the real villains are actually inert pills and potions, vegetable matter, powders and liquids that have the capacity to alter human sensation and thought processes in ways that many people find quite pleasant. Seen from this perspective, those who grow or manufacture, process, ship and sell these commodities are little more than merchants responding to the demand created by willing users, much as modern gun manufacturers and sellers simply provide a desired commodity, despite its undesirable relationship to needless violence and death.

None the less, for several decades now US presidents have re-peatedly invoked the war metaphor in their battle against the supply and use of illicit substances. It is noteworthy that none of the many different drug wars has been successful in coming close to curtailing either availability or use in this country. This abysmal record no doubt reflects the fact that these policies have all been based on unreasonable expectations and flawed logic.

In identifying and discussing the most significant core elements of contemporary US drug policy, it may be useful to categorise them under the two general headings described earlier. The first includes those efforts that are directed at the supply side of the drug problem; these are concerned with reducing or eliminating the availability of illicit substances. With regard to supply-side issues we shall briefly discuss: (a) crop substitution and eradication programmes; (b) extradition agreements and kidnapping; (c) law-enforcement interdiction activities; (d) military support activities; (e) economic pressure on drug-producing and transhipping nations; and (f) property seizure and asset-forfeiture laws.

The second general heading includes those policies that focus on demand reduction. These approaches are primarily concerned with deterring the user from wanting and seeking the illicit substances. They include: (a) penalty enhancement for drug use and related activities; (b) drug testing as a condition of employment; (c) primary prevention through drug education; (d) drug-user rehabilitation;

and (e) propagandising through the media in order to reduce drug demand.

The point of this discussion is to evaluate the impact these supply- and demand-reduction tactics have had on the current domestic drug market and its customers.

SUPPLY SIDE EFFORTS

Crop Substitution and Eradication Programmes

Crop Substitution

One important component of US drug policy has been directed at reducing the land area devoted to the growth of coca and marijuana, the plants from which the most popular illicit drug substances are derived. In many cases drug-producing plants are cultivated in other nations, often in the most economically depressed regions of under-developed countries. The plants have been grown in most of these areas for millennia and often serve as the basic economic staple for growers. Many of these plants have traditionally been used in an instrumental sense as well, to provide energy for work, as an appetite suppressant and to prevent fatigue. There is also a substantial legal outlet for derivatives of these plants in the market for modern medicines.

Beginning with Richard M. Nixon's attempts to convince the Turkish government to put pressure on farmers to reduce their opium poppy production in the early 1970s, we have seen a number of crop substitution programmes introduced during the last two decades. The Nixon administration initially announced that their attempts had been successful: the Turkish government had agreed to reduce the cultivation of opium poppies and to promote their replacement with other cash crops. It was subsequently learned, however, that the programme had only a brief, ephemeral, inconsequential effect. After several years under the substitution programme, Turkish growers returned to poppy cultivation in order to recoup lost income. It was clear from this experiment that legal crops simply cannot be expected to compete favourably with illegal ones in terms of the magnitude of financial benefits derived by their growers.

More recent crop substitution efforts of the Reagan and Bush administrations have focused on the growth of coca plants in South America, especially in Bolivia and Peru. These two nations are thought to be responsible for nearly all of the world's coca leaf production, although many other nations now produce small amounts and plantings of a new low-altitude variety of coca has recently been reported in Brazil.[18] Under the US plan Latin American farmers have been urged to substitute approved agricultural crops such as tomatoes and potatoes for coca. If successful, this would lead to a sharp reduction in the number of illegal plants grown and consequently in the volume of coca leaf processed into cocaine.

There is abundant evidence that these crop substitution efforts have been spectacularly ineffectual. In fact, the volume of land currently under coca cultivation has steadily increased in the largest producer-nations, most recently at a very rapid rate. Many peasants have been encouraged by the relative prosperity offered by coca cultivation and have left the economically depressed urban centres for rural areas in order to initiate new plantings. A 1987 State Department progress report by the Bureau of International Narcotics Matters (INM) states: 'Optimism about the future must be tempered by the reality that has actually occurred in Bolivia since 1980. "Voluntary" campaigns . . . have not worked. Far from reducing total hectareage, Bolivia's coca cultivation expanded during 1986 by at least 10 per cent'.[19] A State Department report released in March 1990 noted an even greater rise in coca production the previous year.[20]

One US observer, Major Clarence Merwin, had been sent to Bolivia in 1983 on a civilian contract to train the Mobile Rural Patrol Unit (UMOPAR), an élite anti-narcotic law-enforcement group known popularly as the 'Leopards'. Merwin found that corruption and staggering inefficiency plagued 'voluntary' crop reduction plans. After two years of first-hand experience observing the abortive implementation of these plans, a frustrated Merwin was convinced that such measures could never yield satisfactory results.[21]

Based on the pathetic record of US attempts to influence the agricultural activities and crop preferences of drug-producer countries, there is little cause for optimism regarding future crop reduction efforts. On rare occasions this policy has resulted in very short-term 'gains', such as when the Turkish government co-operated with the plan in exchange for short-term increases in foreign aid. The reduction in opium poppy production lasted only until local farmers discovered that the new cash crop represented a significant decline in their incomes, however.

In order for any substitution plan to work effectively it would first be necessary for the US to encourage consistently the production of legal crops through some kind of price-support structure. To date this has not occurred. One recent case makes the point very well. On 3 July 1989 the United States refused to vote for continuation of an international trade agreement that had for 27 years maintained high price levels for coffee. As a result coffee prices plummeted overnight by 50 per cent and the crop threatened to cost Colombia (coffee is that nation's most valuable legal export) more than $400 million year.[22] Of course, coffee is one of the acceptable cash crops that United States policy-makers have encouraged these same nations to cultivate instead of coca. The sudden drop in coffee prices will hardly induce sceptical Andean farmers to take up the suggestion: they find coca plantings much more profitable than other cash crops.[23] In the same 'Alice in Wonderland' way, at the Cartagena drug summit President Bush supported an increase in the export of cut flowers from these nations, promising to consider reducing the domestic duties charged for such imports. Predictably, United States growers reacted angrily, saying that this would flood the market with inexpensive flowers and severely affect their business.[24] Thus, domestic economic interests have always deterred the implementation of such promises made to other nations.

Eradication Programmes
US drug policy has strongly supported the implementation of eradication programmes in conjunction with crop substitution efforts. As noted above, the latter have been remarkably unsuccessful. Similarly eradication programmes have had chequered careers. Since the early 1970s the US has funded the purchase by the governments of producer-countries of herbicides and the equipment with which to apply them (including the helicopters). Richard Nixon was the first American president to approve such action during his infamous 1969 Operation Intercept/Operation Co-operation programme with Mexico. At that time Mexican officials were provided with helicopters and the defoliant paraquat for use on marijuana and opium poppy fields. As knowledge of the eradication programme was made public, there was a substantial outcry in the US regarding the potential health hazards that this programme might pose to domestic users who consumed the contaminated plants. These fears were

exacerbated when it was reported that Mexican growers had been quickly harvesting the sprayed marijuana and shipping it north to be sold in the States. Many assumed that severe, perhaps lethal, health consequences would follow. It must be added that at least one US official responded to the clamour over this potential public-health disaster by stating that smoking marijuana was against the law and consequently these consumers would be voluntarily poisoning themselves.

Despite such temperance puffery, there was little question that publicised accounts of the hazards of smoking tainted marijuana had an effect, although not the one which eradication enthusiasts wished for. Serendipitously, the volume of marijuana brought in from Jamaica and South America increased dramatically, while that imported from Mexico dwindled. Finally and perhaps most significantly, after the paraquat scare a very large domestic growing industry developed. Today it is estimated that nearly one-quarter of all marijuana consumed in the United States is domestically produced.[25] Thus, the origins of this new multi-billion dollar marijuana-growing industry can be traced directly to Operation Intercept, an outcome not anticipated by government anti-drug planners.

Another example of the failure of eradication policies is provided by Burma, which has long been the source for a significant amount of the raw opium that ultimately finds its way onto the world heroin market. In 1985 the United States provided the Burmese government with hundreds of millions of dollars-worth of the chemical herbicide 2,4-D, and also loaned to that nation helicopters for its application.[26] It was intended that the 2,4-D would be used to eliminate the illicit poppy crops. Despite the well known dangers associated with the use of this chemical defoliant (2,4-D is one, although not nearly the most toxic, of the ingredients in the infamous Agent Orange used in Vietnam), in the first three years of this programme's operation there was no American oversight of the project's implementation.

Recent accounts of the eradication programme's effects indicate that the Burmese army has used the herbicide to defoliate the crops of political enemies in an internal war that has been raging there for three generations, and those of remote hill tribes who refuse to pay tribute. In addition, 2,4-D has been applied indiscriminately; consequently the chemical has contaminated water and food supplies, resulting in severe medical problems for local populations. An observer notes:

Saturation spraying appears prevalent, far above the amount needed for opium eradication. Redeployment of spraying helicopters for other military usage such as evacuating wounded troops from battles, has been common. . . . The 2,4-D spraying program appears to be carried out in a manner that endangers civilians in the spraying areas. The herbicide and spray drift have ruined and contaminated food crops as well as opium crops. Spraying has been done close to inhabited areas. Illness and deaths due to ingestion of sprayed food, contact with spray and inhalation of spray, have been reported. Both humans and livestock suffer adverse health effects from the herbicide.[27]

Once this critical information was made public in 1988, several US politicians belatedly developed an interest in the Burmese programme. Ultimately the Burmese government suspended all opium control programmes and during 1989 opium production there doubled.[28]

The latest eradication programme undertaken in Bolivia with US support is also revealing. There, despite abundant evidence of eradication's futility, the United States has remained committed to a policy that relies heavily on this unpopular and unsuccessful approach, including aerial defoliation, burning of coca fields and the manual removal and destruction of individual plants. Given the significant resistance to these methods presented by the coca-growing farmers in the region, the most recent US plans have included the promotion of biological methods; the most significant of these has been the proposed use of a larva that would eat the leaves of the coca plant.[29]

Despite good intentions, these actions have proved counterproductive and serendipitously appear to have stimulated the production of coca in the Chapere growing region (which produces coca with the highest alkaloid content, preferred for conversion to cocaine hydrochloride).[30] The reasons for this unanticipated result are clear. First, the eradication programme has sprayed both coca and other agricultural crops which are grown in the same vicinity; often these other legal crops are grown between the rows of coca plants. In these instances the approved plants have been found less able to resist the defoliant than coca which is 'extremely resistant to such chemical agents'.[31] Consequently, the peasants have lost their legitimate crops to eradication defoliants and then recouped their losses by planting even more of the hardy coca shrubs. A second reason for the increase in coca production is that growing the plant is easier and much more profitable than raising tomatoes, potatoes or any other acceptable (to the US) cash crop. Unlike these approved vegetables, the coca plant grows quickly and in poor-quality soil (it can be harvested for the first time within one year of planting) requires little care, is disease- and bug-resistant, can be harvested three or four times each year and will produce for 40 years or more. Bolivian peasants are neither fools nor interested in losing marginal livelihoods to satisfy United States moralists.

One final concern should be noted before leaving the Bolivian example. The US money provided to eradicate coca crops largely goes to military and law-enforcement units, just as in Burma. In 1984 the US convinced the Bolivian government to move its army into the Chapere growing region at harvest-time, in order to physically prevent cocaine producers from harvesting and selling their crop. Since more than one-half of the foreign exchange of Bolivia is derived from the coca trade, this military action had immediate and grave economic consequences. The following observation about these events was made by an American writer:

> The Bolivian peso was devalued by two thirds overnight, and the nation (which has changed governments about once a year for the past decade) was left in near collapse. In addition, cocaine production wasn't upset at all; it was merely postponed, and not by much. Bolivia received millions in American aid for drug eradication, yet coca production was unaffected. The American effort there has left Gestapo-like antidrug strike forces trained by the DEA and a lot of ill will.[32]

These examples demonstrate how United States drug policy has willy-nilly caused catastrophic changes in the economies of target nations, while actually stimulating poppy and coca plantings. Administration 'free-enterprisers' ironically enough, seem to lose sight of exactly how entrepreneurs act and markets grow.

A final observation should be added for those who remain committed to policies directed at the elimination of drug plants at their source. It has been estimated that only about 50 square miles of land are required to produce all the coca needed to supply the entire US market, and 5000 acres of opium poppies to supply the heroin market.[33] Surely it is wishful thinking to presume against all the contrary evidence that the United States can stop the production of these plants.

Extradition Agreements and Kidnapping

A second US drug policy strategy implemented in Latin America has been to push for the development and enforcement of extradition agreements with the governments of producer countries, encouraging them to turn over suspected drug racketeers for trial in this country. A built-in assumption of such proposals is that 'justice', however defined, cannot be assured or provided in the defendant's native country. This could be due to a corrupt or weakened central government, the relative strength of criminal factions or a host of other reasons. Whatever the justification, however, extradition efforts have generally proved futile, for Latin American and other nations have typically refused to extradite their nationals for trial elsewhere. Colombia, for example, first signed an extradition treaty with the US in the late 1970s. Despite the agreement, few defendants were ever sent to America for trial and for long periods of time the treaty was held to be invalid by that nation's Supreme Court. For several years in the late 1980s there was a change of sorts in Colombia's stance, however, for at that time they extradited 26 persons for prosecution in the United States.[34] The reason for this apparent policy reversal was generally thought to have been the wave of bombings and killings of government officials, educators, reporters, editors and seemingly countless innocent bystanders attributed to narcotraffickers operating with impunity in that country.

While extradition has been of great symbolic importance for US policy, when its use is not available kidnapping has sometimes been used with legal impunity. Perhaps the most notorious example of this occurred last year with the US invasion of Panama designed to depose Manuel Noriega and to bring him to trial in the US on drug-trafficking charges. This extreme military action demonstrated to the world the Bush administration's willingness to go so far as to wage war in order to enforce domestic drug laws. There is little doubt that Noriega's fate was tied to US concern over the Panama Canal treaty rather than with drug policy *per se*. Yet – and perhaps this is the most important point – US drug policy provides a 'false front' vocabulary in which many foreign policy actions are covered by the omnipresent War on Drugs. We shall return to this subject later.

Interdiction Activities

An important component of US drug policy consists of the actions of federal law-enforcement organisations directed at the interdiction of drugs either at the US border, in international waters or at the foreign source of production or refining, and destined for the street market in the United States. During the early days of drug enforcement and up until the 1960s or so, most interdiction activities conducted outside the country were directed by the Federal Bureau of Narcotics. In 1968 this federal drug agency was reorganised and renamed the Bureau of Narcotics and Dangerous Drugs (BNDD). Later, in 1975, the BNDD was once again reorganised and renamed the Drug Enforcement Agency (DEA).

In recent times many different federal organisations have been assigned separate, and in some cases overlapping, responsibility for drug interdiction efforts abroad. At present, for example, there are more than 30 agencies involved in a variety of US-sponsored interdiction efforts in Latin America.[35] They include the Drug Enforcement Agency, US Customs, the US Information Agency, the Bureau of International Narcotic Matters, the Federal Bureau of Investigation, the Central Intelligence Agency, the Agency for International Development, various US military organisations and a host of others.

Given the panoply of different bureaucracies involved in these interdiction programmes, jurisdictional squabbles have been commonplace. Despite such organisational problems, however, some common themes can be deduced.

A substantial proportion of DEA time and effort is spent gathering and acting on intelligence information regarding international smuggling efforts. In addition, the agency conducts joint operations with some foreign governments and DEA agents serve as educators and supervisors, training members of foreign narcotic squads and helping them to launch attacks on the producers and traffickers in a number of critical regions. In Bolivia these activities have led to the formation and training of the élite Leopards (see p. 39). This US-trained unit has conducted a number of source interdiction raids. The Leopards best-known and allegedly most-successful mission took place in 1986 in a joint effort called Operation Blast Furnace. This involved a four-month series of raids in which 160 US soldiers and civilians transported the Leopards on 260 forays against suspected drug laboratories.[36] Ever since the completion of this enforcement effort, United States government officials have claimed that the programme 'disrupted cocaine trafficking in Bolivia'. This is typical government hyperbole. In fact, Operation Blast Furnace had at best a very short-term effect and not one significant trafficker was arrested in the raids.[37]

An impressive array of 'high-tech' equipment has been designed for and utilised in the War on Drugs by the law-enforcement groups involved in interdiction activities. For example, state-of-the-art radar planes (AWACS) and tethered radar balloons and blimps have been used to identify suspicious planes and ships that may be carrying drugs into the Unites States. Space satellite technology has been employed for some time to determine the size of coca- and marijuana-growing regions in South America. Military planes have also been loaned to the drug-enforcement groups and military personnel have flown missions that combine routine training functions with inter-diction surveillance activities.

Even though the technology implemented by criminal-justice agencies has been steadily improving. It has been suggested that those who traffic in drug substances possess modern equipment that rivals, if not exceeds, that possessed by enforcement personnel. This observation is reported in, among other places, a 1986 Comptroller General's report to the Subcommittee on Government Operations.[38] Even more telling, this document also reveals that much of the highly touted interdiction paraphernalia, including many different land- and air-based radar systems, high-speed boats, Cobra helicopters and the like have been neutralised by the traffickers, who simply adjust their operations to accommodate the schedule of enforcement activities. The report cites the following examples of how even relatively unsophisticated espionage undermines the effectiveness of such interdiction programmes:

1. The traffickers may determine the duty hours of Customs radar watch personnel by observing their arrivals and departures at their duty sites or by obtaining copies of their work schedules (these are not classified information). Based on such information the smugglers may choose appropriate times to move their goods when the risk of detection is minimal.

2. Schedules of Customs jet interceptors maintenance and operation may be determined through direct observation of their home base or by obtaining copies of maintenance records. This would give smugglers the opportunity to cross the border

with the aircraft even when the radar detection system is active and to be through the net before any interception could take place.

3. Air surveillance of Coast Guard cutter operations in various marine 'chokepoints' (such as through the Bahamas) allow smugglers to avoid or at least minimize the probability of an apprehension.

4. Radar surveillance along most of the US land border and coastline, except for Florida, are meager at best. Traffickers have access to information about the location of this equipment and can thus avoid detection. In one instance the most vulnerable areas along the Southwestern border were identified in a major newspaper, and, according to public officials, smugglers quickly took advantage of this information.[39]

In addition to the difficulties identified above, the specialised interdiction equipment also presents maintenance and repair problems which sharply reduce its effectiveness. The GAO study revealed that this equipment is often out of service due to occasional breakdowns and routine maintenance; the Customs aerostat radar balloon in the Bahamas, for example, was out of service 49 per cent of the time when the air interception branch was staffed.[40] On other occasions, weather conditions prove disabling and prevent interception equipment from operating; and at times there are no trained crews available to work the equipment. Taken together, all these difficulties have severely hampered the effectiveness of federal interdiction efforts. The established system is by no means comprehensive and is vulnerable to all the vicissitudes of individual and equipment frailty. Those who are moving drugs into the country have made it their business to learn the operating schedules of personnel and equipment, and quickly adjust their activities to minimise the risks of detection and apprehension. Although many loads of contraband are discovered and impounded, most get through the protective net. Government spokespersons claim that as much as 11 per cent of the drugs being brought into the country are interdicted, although many experts contest this figure. The US Customs Service, for example, has estimated that it only interdicts about 1 per cent of all drugs smuggled by air and 6 per cent of those transported by water.[41]

The net effect of the totality of interdiction activity is very difficult to ascertain. There is no question that there has been a dramatic increase in the total volume and value of drugs confiscated through the efforts of US Customs at various points of entry as well as by other law-enforcement groups. For example, the annual volume of cocaine and marijuana seized by US law-enforcement agencies increased dramatically throughout the 1980s.[42] These figures undoubtedly reflect the increases in time, money and personnel that have been directed at this aspect of drug interdiction. Despite such accomplishments, however, few law-enforcement representatives claim that there have been any real or substantial effects on the domestic drug markets produced by these often record seizures. It would seem, too, that there are limited returns that can be expected from the enhancement of US Customs port-of-entry personnel and operations. The volume of traffic, both human and goods, that passes through regular Customs inspection areas located at the borders prohibits any large-scale intervention measures. They would impose intolerable delays on travellers and would prove destructive to legitimate commerce.[43]

Military Support Activities

The involvement of the Unites States military in the drug wars was either non-existent or minimal until the late 1980s, at which time the policy was adjusted significantly; during the last few years the military role in the drug-interdiction arena has precipitously increased. The examples provided by the recent invasion of Panama and the proposed flotilla off the coast of Colombia demonstrate that United States troops are likely to be used in future drug-interdiction activities at levels never before imagined.

The explanation for the previous 'hands-off' approach related to the original 1878 Posse Comitatus Act, which forbade the military from enforcing federal, state and local civilian law and from supplementing civilian law-enforcement efforts. Despite the law there were a number of occasions when Congress authorised the use of federal troops to quell civil disorders, as occurred during the 1968 Democratic National Convention riots, and earlier in labour–management battles.[44]

In 1981 the Posse Comitatus Amendment was passed, an act which allows the use of the military to support civilian law-enforcement activities.[45] Since that time there has been a dramatic increase in the use of military personnel to assist civilian law-enforcement in drug interdiction. Military equipment and personnel are now routinely made available to drug-enforcement agencies, although exact figures on the volume and value of these resources is difficult, if not impossible, to establish. (For example, when a military fighter plane is sent on a training flight that also includes drug surveillance, the costs of this equipment and personnel are not likely to be calculated in drug war expenditures.[16])

It should be noted that these recent changes in the roles and missions of various military organisations were neither sought nor even supported by military authorities. Now it is clear that they will play such a role in the future, however, their enthusiasm for participation in drug-interdiction activities has increased dramatically. It seems likely that the collapse of communist regimes in Eastern Europe and consequent reductions in military appropriations have been responsible for this sudden change of heart.

Economic Pressure on Drug Producing and Transhipping Nations

Throughout the last two decades the United States government has repeatedly threatened to impose, or has in fact imposed, economic sanctions on those nations implicated in some way in the domestic drug-supply problem. This policy is usually described using the metaphor of the 'carrot and the stick': the 'carrot' of foreign aid is offered for those who are co-operative; the 'stick' of economic sanctions is threatened if they fail to comply with US drug-control plans.[47] Most, if not all, of these nations are economically underdeveloped, some are overwhelmingly impoverished. Hence, the supposed usefulness of this policy.

The threat of withdrawal of US monetary support has led many foreign government officials to pay lip service to, and in some instances to actively attempt to impose, US anti-drug values on their indigenous populations. Conforming to these external demands has resulted in increasing violence in these regions. In Colombia, for example, the Barco government was earlier 'encouraged' to pursue aggressive drug-trafficking organisations, with the US threatening to implement economic sanctions if they failed to do so. The resulting crackdown by the Colombian government, with the assistance of US DEA agents, military personnel and equipment, led to a wave of retaliatory bloodshed in which innocent civilians, police officials, government leaders, judges, newspaper editors and others were gunned down.[48]

Bolivia's experiences are also illuminating. That nation has suffered a near-total collapse of its formal economy during this century, due to devaluation of mineral deposits (especially tin and lead) and endemic political instability (there have been more than 100 different governments there during this century). As the economy has deteriorated, unemployment and underemployment rose (the figures for 1989 indicate a 20 per cent unemployment rate), resulting in extensive poverty among very large segments of the population. This downturn in the formal economy has led to a concomitant surge of participation in, and spectacular growth of, the informal economy which includes such activities as home industries, handicrafts and the production of coca. Coca labourers receive as much as US$20 per day in wages, an amount equal to the average monthly family income for a Bolivian peasant family.[49] These factors, coupled with increased US demand and the development of an entirely new market for cocaine in Europe, have led to rapid proliferation of this component of the informal economy. The annual revenues from coca production in Bolivia are known to be greater now than the total generated by the formal economy.[50] Under such circumstances one might ask of what value, then, is the 'carrot and stick'?

Property Seizure and Asset Forfeiture Laws

During the last two decades US drug warriors have enthusiastically utilised the provisions of property seizure and asset forfeiture laws to deprive drug traffickers of their ill-gotten gains. The relevant statutes that allow for this confiscation include the 1970 Bank Secrecy Act (and its 1978 amendment), the 1970 Organized Crime Control Act particularly its RICO (Racketeer-Influenced Corrupt Organizations) provisions subsequently amended, and the CCE (Continuing Criminal Enterprise) statutes.[51] These laws were intended to deny both suspected and convicted drug traffickers of their assets, including cash, bank accounts, real estate, automobiles, jewellery, art and any other goods derived from drug profits.

Today many prosecutors and drug-enforcement units consider the forfeiture laws among their most effective tools in combating the drug trade. Since the enactment of these statutes the federal government has assumed ownership of thousands of planes, ships, automobiles, real estate parcels, homes and other property owned by drug traffickers or those charged with drug crimes. One intended benefit of asset-forfeiture statutes was to provide an opportunity for government officials to plough the profits derived from the resale of confiscated items back into the War on Drugs programme, thereby financially rewarding law enforcement for aggressive anti-drug activities. Police agencies could then use these assets to purchase needed equipment and supplies to be used in future interdiction efforts; some promoters of the plan have even contended that the drug police could eventually become totally self-sustaining.

The promise of a 'free ride' on the backs of drug suspects has proven to be extremely attractive to the police. Federal, state and local agencies are now generously treating themselves to the assets of such defendants. One Boston DEA representative recently claimed that his agency had doubled its annual budget of $500 million through drug seizures and asset forfeiture provisions. It has been noted by observers that in some locales polices are actually delaying arrests and 'following the money' rather than the drugs in order to ensure that they confiscate a commodity that can be converted to the police's own use, as a portion of the cash recovered in this way comes back to them while the drugs are simply destroyed.

Recent evidence suggests that at least some federal asset-forfeiture programmes have not worked as intended. A 1989 GAO investigation of the US Customs' programme revealed that the agency was losing money on the programme despite taking in more than one billion dollars-worth of property! The explanation for this extraordinary finding was this: the federal agency contracted out the handling, storage and disposal of the confiscated property to a private vendor, Northrop Worldwide Aircraft Services, Inc. of Burbank, California; this firm charged the government exorbitant rates for storage of these goods and then sold them at auction at cut-rate prices.[52] Consequently a programme that in theory could not lose money became a financial disaster in practice. The firm responsible for this financial débâcle has been charged with criminal fraud. During the same period the Justice Department made $270 million on its forfeiture programme, demonstrating that turning a profit on this confiscated merchandise is at least possible.[53]

One particularly disturbing recent development, which is an extension of the asset-forfeiture statutes, provides that attorneys' fees may not be paid in cash with drug monies. The 1984 Comprehensive Crime Control Act and the Tax Reform Act allow for the seizure of all a defendant's assets, including fees paid to attorneys. The new law requires attorneys to report all fees involving cash payments of $10,000 or more, and also forces them to reveal fees and other formerly privileged information if called to testify before grand juries.[54] One anticipated consequence of this provision will be that those charged with drug-trafficking offences will not be able to find competent private attorneys who are willing to defend them. Consequently, private attorneys will refuse to take these cases and defendants will be forced to depend on the wiles of public defenders. Again, the Noriega case provides a clear illustration of this practice as the government has refused to allow his private attorneys to be paid from his frozen assets, despite the fact that it is known that at least $1 million of these funds was earned as 'legitimate' payment for 'work' he did for the Central Intelligence Agency over the last fifteen years or so. Predictably, the American Bar Association reacted angrily to these new provisions, its members arguing that they will severely undermine the integrity of the Sixth Amendment's right to counsel.[55] One recent report indicates that the IRS is now pursuing approximately 90 attorneys who have refused to provide the information required under the law. In response to such practices the American Bar Association recently approved an ethics amendment that states: 'the war on drugs cannot and must not become a war on lawyers . . . and a war on the Bill of Rights'.[56]

It is most important to note that asset forfeiture can occur independently of a defendant's conviction. Indeed, forfeiture proceedings can be brought without a defendant even being charged with any crime. In other instances, defendants acquitted of drug crimes still have had their assets seized in separate civil proceedings. The underlying justification in legal theory for such a procedure is that 'guilt' attaches directly to the property itself.[57]

Asset-forfeiture programme proponents claim the provisions have armed law enforcement with the necessary tools to put a real dent in the rewards realised by those participating in the illegal drug market. These claims are generally thought to be supported by figures which demonstrate that the number of property seizures have been increasing and that the value of the goods derived in this manner has been substantial. Sociologist James Inciardi asserts that the programme has been effective and that it would be even more so if forfeiture provisions were even more aggressively pursued.[58]

Despite their intended purpose to deprive those who traffic in drugs from enjoying the rewards of their risks and labours, the seizure and forfeiture of assets seem unlikely ever to have more than a minimal potential impact on drug dealers. As noted above, since the initiation of these efforts there has been a steady increase in the value of goods seized by various police agencies. At the present time, some twenty years after the passage of the first of these laws, the Customs programme has resulted in the seizure of goods valued at $1 billion. But given that the illegal US drug trade is estimated to generate more than $150 billion per year, and that most of this revenue represents profit (an IRS study estimates that drug profits are 50–90 per cent of revenues), the relatively modest seizures that have been achieved to date compromise an insignificant proportion of the total.[59] As such they are not likely to have any substantial general deterrent effect.

There are several other difficulties with asset forfeiture provisions that are consistently mentioned by critics. One of these has been what many scholars call their savaging of constitutional guarantees; a second is that they are a clear enticement to law-enforcement corruption. They argue that by enhancing the significance of arrest, the probability of traditional corruption occurring is increased, as well as the proliferation of new forms based on law enforcement's newfound financial interests.

DEMAND-REDUCTION POLICIES

Penalty Enhancement

During the last two decades the penalties attached to conviction for various drug crimes have undergone dramatic changes. The most recent trend has been a marked increase in the numbers of drug users brought into the justice system through arrest and incarceration, and increases in the penalties prescribed for specific violations. The policy of the earlier period (the late 1960s and early 1970s) had at least rhetorically emphasised enforcement efforts directed at the lobby side including drug smugglers and sellers; it had conspicuously downplayed the significance of criminal justice sanctions for individual users. A brief review of the arrest statistics for that period, however, reveals that the largest number and proportion of police arrests were of drug users for personal possession, even while the government was claiming that pushers were the primary targets of their enforcement activity. Given the difficulty of making good cases against large-scale dealers and the relative ease of making low-level user busts, one could hardly have expected anything else.

Under Presidents Reagan and Bush national policy has been redirected to unabashedly promoting demand-reduction strategies, particularly by 'enhancing' the penalties for personal possession and use of drug substances. Administration spokesmen argue that without such a 'scorched earth policy' little can be accomplished in the drug war. What is needed, they say, is 'zero tolerance' of drug use based on the belief that deterrence can work if violators are aggressively sought out and prosecuted. Shortly after the zero tolerance notion was first articulated, the US Coast Guard seized a number of luxury yachts after stopping and searching them and discovering minute amounts of marijuana on board. In several of these cases the owners of the vessels were not even on their boats, yet the vessels were seized and were to have been sold at public auction. Complaints by the yachts' owners and their influential friends led to a quick reassessment of the zero-tolerance notion, however, at least as it applied to the wealthy. The ships were returned to their owners.

There can be little question that recently penalty enhancements for drug crimes have led to marked changes in the performance of justice agencies, and especially of the police. The policies have affected police officers by rewarding them organisationally for pursuing even the smallest, most inconsequential drug offender. Thus, any drug arrest is now considered a 'good bust', and police around the country have responded to the incentive by making hundreds of thousands of arrests of these minor offenders who previously would have been counselled and released, or simply ignored. (Approximately three-quarters of all drug arrests each year are for simple possession of drugs, and not for more serious drug crimes.[60])

The increase in drug-user arrests that occurred because of the current law enforcement orientation of national drug policy have quickly resulted in gaol overcrowding, court backlogs and major difficulties in appropriating prison space to hold those convicted and sentenced for these crimes. During the last decade, for example, the United States prison population has doubled and is expected to do so again during the 1990s.[61] Most of this increase can be attributed to the arrest and convictions of drug users who now comprise a far higher percentage of the total number convicted than ever before. In the federal system, for example, approximately one-third of 44,000 current prisoners have been incarcerated for drug offences; within fifteen years it is anticipated they will comprise more than one-half of the 100,000 or more prisoners who will at that time be housed in the federal system.[62] Also, there is a clear trend toward longer sentences, which means that prisons will experience less inmate turnover than before.

The patterns identified above have resulted in calls for many new correctional institutions to be built and monies have been regularly appropriated by both state and federal legislatures for this purpose. These practices ensure that the 'warehouse' effect on a generation of drug users will be an incontestable and undesirable outcome of the current drug war.

Drug Testing and Employment

A second notable feature of contemporary demand-reduction strategies has been the promotion of widespread drug testing in the workplace, both private and public. The calls for such tests have been accompanied by fantastic and untenable claims that drug use in the workplace has been responsible for almost all recent on-the-job accidents, worker absenteeism and production problems: the total cost of these difficulties has been routinely estimated at more than $100 billion per year. These figures have never been empirically substantiated, however. They are accepted as matters of faith. Recently a short essay in *Scientific American* pinpointed the absolutely chimerical nature of such claims.[63]

Workplace drug testing has been strongly supported by the business community, the present national political administration and others who argue that it is an essential component of programmes aimed at reducing workplace accidents, employee sick days, absenteeism and lost productivity. In a 1989 speech, for example, President Bush argued that 'drug use among American workers costs businesses anywhere from $60 to $100 billion a year in lost productivity, absenteeism, drug-related accidents, medical claims and theft'.[64] Since that time this claim has been repeatedly used to justify further intrusions into employees' rights to privacy.

When subjected to rather elementary scientific scrutiny, Bush's claims were found to be gross distortions of the findings of a single study completed in 1982 by the Research Triangle Institute. In this survey of 3700 households, investigators discovered the average reported income in homes where at least one person admitted to *ever* using marijuana for at least 20 days in any 30 day period was 28 per cent less than for households where no one had used the drug regularly. Then, without any scientific justification, the researchers defined the income difference as 'loss due to marijuana use', and projected these figures to the entire US population. This foolish survey then added $47 billion in estimated costs of drug abuse to society, adjusted the figures for inflation and population increases and thereby arrived at the figure the President presented as fact![65]

Despite the outcries raised by some trade unions, civil libertarians and others, routine drug-testing procedures have been fully implemented in many private and public workplaces. Recent figures indicate that during 1989 more than eight million Americans had their urine tested while at work; this year it is thought that more than fifteen million will be tested.[66] The percentage of companies requiring such tests has dramatically increased: 21 per cent in 1986, and more than 50 per cent in 1989.[67] In addition, the Supreme Court has consistently allowed such tests. Their reasoning has been based on a 'balancing of interests', a pseudo-scale the Court has devised to weigh the varying interests involved. Based on these evaluations it is now evident that, at least in the private sector, the Court views a worker's right to privacy as less important than an employer's right to know. In civilian occupations the Court has allowed urine testing of employees in the transportation industry and in federal and metropolitan police work. Widespread court-approved urine testing to detect drug use raises many important questions ignored by policy planners and the judiciary. Perhaps nothing is quite so fundamental as the fact that the test results may be inaccurate; in fact, recent studies indicate a wide variance in test accuracy between different testing methods and laboratories.

Seldom mentioned in the current testing fad has been the huge industry that has quietly developed to provide analysis of urine samples and test results. Many different laboratories are currently handling these samples and are charging very substantial fees for their services. The most sophisticated (and accurate) methods of analysis cost more than $100 per drug in order to detect accurately the presence of the drugs, and even these results may be fallible. The powerful private security industry (staffed in many instances by retired law enforcement officers) has also been handsomely profiting from its participation in drug-testing and screening programmes, and has thus become a formidable lobbying presence for their expansion. One must never underestimate private interests' stake in public policy.[68]

An extremely important question raised by the burgeoning adoption of drug testing is whether or not this intrusion/indignity should be tolerated in a 'free' society. Traditional individual protections have certainly been undermined in the rush to apprehend drug users by chemical analysis performed on their urine and very often against their will. Furthermore, even in the eventuality that the presence of illicit substances is detected, there is no test that can indicate whether the drug actually affected the person's work performance at the time. Given the lengthy half-life of many psychoactive substances and the fact that some drugs like marijuana remain present in detectable amounts for up to two months after they are initially ingested, the mere presence in the body of trace amounts of a drug does not demonstrate that the person's work-performance was actually impaired by it.

A society that requires routine involuntary tests of bodily wastes in order to determine their chemical composition and then allows such information to be used as a basis for refusing to hire, firing or punishing someone, can hardly claim to be free in any traditional sense of the word.

Primary Prevention: Drug Education

Along with all the new law-enforcement programmes funded by the current drug war, the architects of the policy have also put some new monies into the area referred to as 'drug education'. It should be noted at the outset that the funds set aside for this purpose comprise a very small percentage of the total budget for the anti-drug effort. In the Bush proposal for drug war spending in 1990–1, the $10.5 billion package allocated only 30 per cent of the total for all non law-enforcement activities; these include rehabilitation, treatment, education and other programmes.[69]

An evaluation of the structure and content of the funded drug-education efforts reveals their ideological, anti-scientific bias. Under this administration drugs can only be discussed in the ideological context of 'Just say no', the slogan first developed and promoted by Nancy Reagan. (Ironically, the Reagan drug war budgets actually imposed severe cuts in the funds made available for educational and treatment purposes while providing generous increases for law enforcement agencies.) Nearly all current 'drug education' programmes sponsored by the government present a prohibitionist value-system as fact, thereby promoting ideology as science.

In 1986, under the leadership of William Bennett (until recently the so-called drug czar), the United States Department of Education published and disseminated a lengthy tract titled *What Works – Schools without Drugs*.[70] At the time administration officials urged schools, parents and other interested parties to obtain copies of this educational material and to put the federal recommendations into action at the local level. The following are a few of the recommendations:

- Teach standards of right and wrong and demonstrate these standards through personal example . . .
- Help children to resist peer pressure to use drugs by supervising their activities . . .
- Implement security measures to eliminate drugs on school premises and at school functions . . .
- Implement a comprehensive drug prevention curriculum from kindergarten through grade 12, teaching that drug use is wrong and harmful and supporting and strengthening resistance to drugs . . .
- Develop collaborative arrangements in which school personnel, parents, school boards, law enforcement officers, treatment organizations, and private groups can work together to provide necessary resources.[71]

In order to implement these ideas the government publication suggests that parents establish groups to lobby for anti-drug and anti-paraphernalia laws; look for drug-related magazines, jokes and slogans; 'look for "warning flag" phrases and concepts', such as 'There are no "good" or "bad" drugs, just improper use'. This is, the tract notes, a popular semantic camouflage in pro-drug literature which merely confuses young people. Finally, it is suggested that parents should support schools in their right to search students and their lockers for drugs.[72]

It is now apparent that much of the government 'advice' has affected the practices of schools and parents in many communities. For instance, in one Virginia school a third grade pupil who brought a sealed can of 'Billy Beer' (part of her parents' collection of rare beer) to present to her class during 'show and tell' was suspended for three days and forced to undergo drug counselling, due to the school's inflexible drug policy.[73] This disturbing incident is symptomatic of one result of current drug policy – the vilification of euphoria, the triumph of temperance ideology.

Drug User Rehabilitation

One policy option that could have a significant impact on the popular demand for illicit drugs would be the funding of a variety of efforts aimed at the rehabilitation of addicted users. But as most know, the federal government has been traditionally hostile to such rehabilitation programmes. This official attitude is reflected in the oft-expressed view that drug users are almost all addicts and that addicts commit innumerable violent crimes in order to feed insatiable drug appetites. Under these circumstances it is not surprising to find user rehabilitation is the last policy option to receive drug war funding, and that the amount allocated for this purpose is slim indeed.

Under the Reagan administrations, drug rehabilitation was paid lip-service when drug budgets were discussed. During his eight-year tenure, however, federal monies allocated for this purpose were slashed. The most recent proposal by the Bush administration has recommended an increase in the funds set aside for drug user rehabilitation programmes, but once again the amounts prescribed are not nearly sufficient to meet current demands. The costs of many drug rehabilitation programmes are exorbitant, as private vendors have discovered and taken advantage of this highly lucrative market. The United States is now awash with 28-day programmes cunningly designed to reap the short-term treatment benefits provided by many health insurance programmes. Since most such policies cover no more than 29 days of treatment, that is what is provided. Patient costs in many of these facilities range from $100 to $1000 per day! Under such circumstances it is small wonder that these efforts seldom work although their many failures are hidden, for it is not to the vendors' advantage to keep and publicise outcome statistics.

At the other extreme, the public programmes are forced to operate with minuscule budgets and thus are predetermined to fail. Nearly all have very large numbers of street clients and long waiting-lists for assistance of any kind. In addition, their clients are disproportionately 'hard-core' addicts requiring expensive, lengthy treatment with little likelihood of success. Public programmes also suffer very high staff 'burnout' rates. These features of public-sector rehabilitation efforts have contributed greatly to their dismal outcome statistics. These programmes are most often found in the poorest urban communities and can provide little hope to individuals who genuinely need substantial social, economic, and legal assistance.

Finally, there are a number of treatment programmes that are modelled on the self-help philosophy pioneered by Alcoholics Anonymous. We now find specialised groups to treat and support the spouses, children and families of drug users. Most operate on shoestring budgets and can do little more than provide moral support to the suffering.

Media Manipulation and Reduced Drug Demand

The government effort to convince the public to support present policies has been well funded, unlike the treatment programmes described above. In the United States today one can hardly turn on a television set without being treated to a picture of eggs frying in a pan while an announcer intones that this is what happens to your brain when you try drugs, or a personal anti-drug testimonial presented by an athletics hero or some other well-known personality. Many of these individuals, it turns out, were users who were caught and sentenced to complete such 'public service commercials' as a way of avoiding or reducing their prison terms.

The various media are constantly bombarding the public with government anti-drug messages and have, for the most part, enthusiastically taken up the pitch. Their net effect in fuelling public concern is obvious. According to media-sponsored polls, the 'drug problem' is now mentioned by more Americans than any other issue as the most serious problem the country faces: 'it is THE problem, thought more important than anything else.[74] Nearly every evening television newscasts feature stories on drugs. In addition, the major networks produce a drug 'specials'. These presentations are notable for their uncritical acceptance of the law-enforcement perspective. Commentators follow federal, state and local law-enforcement officers on raids of 'crack houses', focus their cameras on the miseries experienced by addicts, and resolutely announce that these are daily incidents in the lives of the heroic enforcers. The now famous CBS special '48 Hours on Crack Street', originally broadcast in 1987, presented viewers with a classic case of cognitive dissonance reinforced by a multi-hour follow-up, 'Return to Crack Street', which was shown in 1989. Both programmes puffed official pronouncements of drug felons as sophisticated master-criminals while showing more often than not very young children, mostly black, unarmed, brutally forced to the ground in front of cameras with guns pointed at their heads, while their homes were dismantled by vigilant cops searching for dope.

The print media, too, have contributed significantly to the 'moral panic' reactions of many Americans to the drug problem. All the major news weeklies have featured special reports on the latest battles in the drug war. *Time, Newsweek* and *US News and World Report* for example, have each presented drug topics as front-cover subjects on many occasions during the last four or five years. The intent of these articles seems to be to remind Americans that drugs are always demonic. In doing so there is seldom a mention of the fact that most people who use illicit drugs do so recreationally and occasionally, or that the overwhelming majority of users are not addicted to the substances in question and do not look like the 'down and outs' presented in the broadcasts or printed accounts. These persons' lives are not dominated by the need to obtain drugs; they voluntarily control their use of the substances and they seldom get into any trouble with them, yet they are rarely mentioned in the alarmist publications.

ASSESSING THE EFFECTS OF THE DRUG WAR

Drug Availability

If the present approach had been effective, the amounts of illicit drugs reaching the street market in the United States should have been reduced significantly. This would have been reflected not only in increases in seizures in producer countries and along the US borders, but in shortages of these substances on the streets and escalating prices for those which were available as well. There is no question that the generous funding for hiring new federal, state and local law-enforcement interdiction personnel has resulted in a substantial increase in the amounts of illicit drug substances that have been confiscated. Despite record seizures, however, there have not been any significant long-term shortages in illicit drugs which remain widely and generally available throughout the nation. In addition, the street prices for some drugs, and particularly cocaine, have fallen dramatically during the last decade, due to an apparent glut on the market. Today's cocaine sells for a fraction of its price in 1980, suggesting that the increased amounts confiscated may in part reflect trafficker response to the escalating enforcement pressure; they simply compensate for their losses by bringing more of the drug in.[75] Given coca's relatively low cost at its source, this seems a likely explanation.[76]

Incidence of Use

A second goal of US drug policy (and one that has been especially aggressively pursued by the Bush administration) has been to reduce domestic demand. At present the estimated patterns of use are determined largely on the basis of the responses to three surveys of unique populations. The Institute for Social Research located at the University of Michigan is perhaps the most important single source of such information. Each year the Institute collects drug-use data from a sample of high-school seniors throughout the United States. The Institute has been gathering and compiling this annual data on student self-reported drug use since 1975. They publish their annual findings in a National Institute of Drug Abuse (NIDA) report titled *National Trends in Drug Use and Related Factors among American High School Students.*

A careful review of the trends suggested by the summary statistics compiled from these surveys indicates that there have been some notable changes in high-school student's reported drug use each year since the survey began. Since 1979 these changes have generally been downward, although there have also been reported increases in the use of some drugs. One of the most interesting and well-publicised trends has been a reported dramatic decline in marijuana use for over a decade.[77] Before we can confidently accept the survey's conclusion there are several issues needing resolution. The fact that the study does not include high-school dropouts (who tend to be far more involved in drug use than regular students) and those who are absent from class on the day when the self-report form is administered (also a group more likely to be involved with drugs than are regular attenders), leads one to question its accuracy.

Perhaps even more importantly, public attitudes toward drug use have certainly hardened significantly during this time period, due to the success of governmental anti-drug propaganda campaigns and a host of other factors. It would be naïve to think that high-school seniors are totally unaware of this growing intolerance and that when asked about their personal drug use that they would accurately report it, especially if they were active users. It seems much more likely that some of the reported reduction in personal use may actually be a reaction to public condemnation of any drug use, and not necessarily a real decrease in such use. For these reasons it is not at all certain that the reported reduction is an accurate reflection of actual use by the high-school-aged population.

The second bell-wether for tracking North American drug-use patterns is the Drug Abuse Warning Network (DAWN) database, which is presented in a semi-annual report consisting of drug-overdose and death statistics submitted by a sample of hospital emergency rooms and medical examiners' offices around the country. Although this data represents only the emergency room admissions at selected locations (about 679 facilities located in 27 different metropolitan areas), it is used as an indicator for the entire country.[78] A careful review of these statistics would only convince an objective observer that our domestic drug problem, as measured by emergency room 'episodes', overdoses and deaths is ever-changing. As with the high school surveys, increases in one area are often counterbalanced by decreases in another; for some categories there is simply no change during the time period covered.

It can be argued, too, that hospital and coroner data should not be used as valid indicators of the volume of drug use in a community, except in the crudest sense. Given the nature of the illicit drug market, many, if not most, of the substances sold on the streets are cut with any number of contaminants. When purchasing street drugs there is no consumer protection as is provided in the purchase of legal drugs through the federal Pure Food and Drug Act and its product-labelling requirements. A bad 'batch' of heroin, for instance, can lead to an epidemic of overdoses in a given community and distort that locale's statistics for that year. An example of this was provided when police reported a dramatic increase in overdoses due to the recent importation of an especially potent form of Asian heroin called 'China White', which was said to be much more lethal than the street heroin available earlier.[79]

It should also be noted that there are vast differences between communities in terms of the drug preferences of local users, patterns and forms of acceptable use, and the like. These distinctions can also lead to confusion when trying to make sense of data for the entire country. Other difficulties with the DAWN data include: these reports only include those who seek assistance for a drug problem; no names are used and therefore a single person may be counted multiple times during a study period; most users report the use of more than one drug at a time (referred to as drug mixing or polydrug use), making it extremely difficult to determine which substance caused the medical problem for which treatment was sought; the drug counts are based on the verbal statements of the user and/or his friends and not on scientific analysis of blood or urine (users are often unaware of the actual content of the drugs they are taking); alcohol-only incidents are not counted in the survey – alcohol is included only when it has been used in combination with other substances; there are no data presented for New York City as that city's medical examiner's office does not participate in the DAWN system; and non-urban areas are not covered by the survey.[80] These serious constraints should lead those who use such data to do so only with extreme caution.

The third major source of information commonly used to estimate the parameters of the US user population is the *National Household Survey on Drug Abuse* produced by the National Institute on Drug Abuse.[81] This survey has been conducted ten times, beginning in 1971 and 1972 with two studies sponsored by the National Commission on Marijuana and Dangerous Drugs. The last eight studies were completed by NIDA, the most recent in 1989. For these surveys a national probability sample is taken of households in the coterminous United States. In selected households a roster of residents is prepared, including all those present who are age 12 or older. A sampling of these residents is then taken and respondents are asked to fill out a self-administered answer sheet regarding their personal drug use.[82]

The most recent *Household Survey* results were euphorically described by President Bush at a press conference held in December 1990. The President announced that the survey revealed a dramatic 45–70 per cent reduction in the recreational use of cocaine and marijuana between 1985 and 1989. Critics quickly challenged the President's interpretation of this data, however, noting among other things that problematic, hard-core use was unchanged and that a significant reduction in middle-class recreational use should hardly be seen as a major victory of the War on Drugs.

The *Household Survey* approach presents a number of methodological difficulties. As noted above, a central concern is the validity of the figures obtained from any self-reports of drug use. Undoubtedly some respondents overestimate while others underestimate their personal use and one cannot assume that the two groups will cancel out one another. Another problem is that this survey excludes groups known to have relatively high use rates, including those living in college dormitories, in prisons and gaols, in military installations, and homeless and transient populations.[83]

In order to supplement these three major sources of information on the parameters of current drug use, one can utilise data obtained from a number of recent studies of street users, participants in a variety of treatment programmes, surveys of the general population, studies of offender populations and others. Each of these sources of information is useful to some degree in attempting to piece together a profile of contemporary drug use in the United States. But they all have inherent statistical and methodological problems.

An example may prove helpful in understanding some of these difficulties. In a number of selected urban areas random urine tests are given to some criminal arrestees upon admission to gaol. The test results are collected, counted and analysed by researchers in an attempt to describe contemporary patterns of use and their relationship to the commission of criminal acts. Although these studies are not comprehensive, they do indicate that well over one-half of those charged with non-drug crimes in the studied areas had some amount of illicit chemical in their bodies at the time of their arrest.[84] Of course, the tests do not and cannot tell whether the use of a particular drug is causally connected to the commission of these crimes. Additionally, one should not prematurely conclude that these data reveal a recent increase in drug use by criminal offenders as this information has only been collected for a few years and there are no base years for comparison. We must also take note of the fact that the simple presence of these substances in measurable amounts does not mean that an offender was under a narcotic's influence at the time a crime was committed, for, unlike alcohol, we have not yet established for illicit drug substances, except in the grossest sense, the amounts necessary to alter reasoning ability and human performance.

Given the limitations of the various sources of information available for determining contemporary drug-use patterns, any claims about actual drug-use trends must be highly qualified. It is evident that domestic policies aimed at reducing or eliminating illicit drug use have not had their desired effect; although public attitudes toward these drugs have hardened, there has been no really significant reduction in their use, except for non-problematic, recreational use by middle-class Americans.

CONCLUSION

The focus of this chapter has been to present an overview and evaluation of the key elements in contemporary US drug policy. It was noted that current approaches can generally be categorised as either supply- or demand-oriented strategies, that the former have dominated federally sponsored programmes, and that recently critics have argued convincingly that the balance between them has been skewed in the wrong direction. In fact, the 1988 Omnibus Drug Law requires that in the future 60 per cent of federal funding will be spent on demand-reduction and the remaining 40 per cent on supply reduction-programmes. Reviewing federal expenditures, however, reveals that the Congressionally mandated changes have not yet materialised; supply concerns still preoccupy federal officials.

The continuing failure of efforts directed at drug interdiction, crop eradication and reduction, pressuring foreign governments and other supply-side approaches is now abundantly clear. It must be noted that illicit drugs are now produced in record quantities and that they are available throughout the United States at relatively low cost. These facts demonstrate that the drug war is not being won with regard to significantly reducing drug supplies. On the contrary, there are not even demonstrable inroads being made despite record expenditures and commitments.

With regard to demand-side issues, US policy has been both underfunded and internally inconsistent. On the one hand, some suggest we should concentrate on apprehending and punishing users, while promoting ideological 'Just Say No' campaigns as the preferred form of drug 'education'. These notions represent yet another extension of the criminalisation model that dominates our international policy orientation. On the other hand, there are a few who argue that we need to provide treatment for users and to jettison or downplay our criminal justice approach in favour of the adoption of a public-health model of our drug problem. Clearly, this would call for a conceptualisation of the drug problem totally different from the dominant criminal model that has guided US policy for the last 75 years. One thing is certain, however. It is absurd to keep up the charade of claiming simultaneously to treat and to punish users.

The ambiguities built into United States drug policy abroad have been revealed in a number of recent investigations. For example, in 1986 the Congress mandated that the President must 'certify' that foreign nations implicated in the drug trade have co-operated fully with the US in its War on Drugs activities. Without such certification foreign aid monies were to be reduced or withheld, and other sanctions imposed against those who failed to co-operate. In practice, the process has not worked because Presidents Reagan and Bush have both been reluctant to de-certify those nations that are central to the drug trade but seen as crucial to other US foreign-policy interests. Thus, when President Reagan certified five nations in 1988, including Mexico, Bolivia, Peru, Paraguay and the Bahamas, Congressman Larry Smith of Florida proposed a 'resolution of disapproval'. Smith was at the time Chairman of the House of Foreign Affairs Committee Task Force on International Narcotics Control and urged his colleagues to find, as he had, that these countries were doing virtually nothing to stem the flood of drugs into this country. The Bahamas, for example, was characterised as extremely corrupt, providing a 'low-risk environment for drug smugglers'.[85] In 1988 President Reagan finally de-certified four nations including Iran, Syria, Afghanistan and Panama, but this action amounted to little more than a symbolic gesture, as they were not receiving any US foreign aid or military assistance at that time.[86]

The example presented by the Bahamas is especially informative.[87] The current Prime Minister, Lyndon Pindling, has long been accused of complicity with drug traffickers. Several members of Pindling's cabinet were forced to resign in 1983 following the revelations of a Royal Commission of Inquiry which found that they had accepted bribes from drug smugglers and participated in smuggling conspiracies. The evidence against Pindling was not found to be sufficient to warrant an indictment, but many called for his resignation anyway. At the very least, he participated in some very shady dealings, banking more than $3.5 million in a five-year period *above and beyond his official salary*.[88] The Bahamian investigation found that Pindling had received a great deal of money in the form of loans, gifts and the like which were provided by friends who asked nothing in return – an unlikely scenario.

The Bahamas' strategic location has made the islands popular with drug smugglers bringing contraband into the United States. During the last ten or fifteen years the area has become widely known in US intelligence circles as the last stopover for most of the cocaine and much of the marijuana brought into the Unites from Latin American nations. Despite this knowledge, nothing has been done to de-certify the Bahamas or to pursue aggressively prosecutions of Bahamian politicians known to be involved in the drug traffic. As was the case in Panama, Honduras and a number of other conspicuous examples, apparently the Bahamas are seen as strategically essential to US security interests and therefore drug activities are accepted as one cost of doing business with that government. Clearly, the message this conveys to other nations is that drug concerns are not as important to the US as are the suppression of communism and rural radicalism in general in the western hemisphere.

Notes

1. Michael K. Frisby, 'Colombia: Drug Fighting Radar Used to Monitor Nicaragua', *Knight-Rider Newspapers*, 9 April 1989.
2. Editorial, 'Notes and Comments', *New Yorker*, 1 January 1990, p. 21.
3. Owen Ullmann, 'White House Concerned by Cartel Threats', *Knight-Rider Newspapers*, 24 January 1990.
4. Rita Beamish, 'Quayle to Meet 6 Latin Leaders', *Associated Press*, 15 January 1990.
5. Owen Ullmann, 'Quayle Brings Bad News on Trip', *Knight-Rider Newspapers*, 28 January 1990.
6. Cal Thomas, 'Quayle a Worthy Emissary of Bush in Latin America', *Los Angeles Times*, 3 February 1990.
7. Mark Thompson, 'Skeptics Say Blockade No Drug Solution', *Chicago Tribune*, 9 January 1990.
8. Tom Wells, 'Drug Cartel Offers Peace for Pardon', *Associated Press*, 18 January 1990.
9. Ibid.
10. Andres Oppenheimer, 'Cartel Surrenders 3 Drug Labs as Peace Offering to Summit', *Knight-Rider Newspapers*, 15 February 1990.
11. In December 1990 the newly elected Colombian government struck a deal with the outlaws promising that they would not be extradited if they turned themselves in for trial in that country's courts. Major trafficker Fabio Ochoa and several other narcotics kingpins quickly took advantage of the offer.
12. Stephen Kurkjian, 'Kidnappings Protect Bush Drug Summit', *Knight-Rider Newspapers*, 14 February 1990.
13. Owen Ullmann, 'White House Concerned by Cartel Threats', *Knight-Rider Newspapers*, 24 January 1990.
14. Kevin Merida, 'Anti-Drug Pact OK'd', *Dallas Morning News*, 16 February 1990.
15. Ibid.
16. Editorial, 'A Summit with Little Substance', *Centre Daily Times*, 20 February 1990.
17. The drug problem has been repeatedly identified in recent public opinion polls as the most significant problem facing America. See, for

example, Marsha Rosenbaum, *Just Say What?* (San Francisco, Cal.: National Council on Crime and Delinquency, 1989) p. 3.
18. Steven Wisotsky, *Breaking the Impasse in the War on Drugs* (New York: Greenwood Press, 1986) p. 59.
19. David Kline, 'How to Lose the Coke War', *Atlantic Monthly*, May 1987, p. 27.
20. Elaine Sciolino, 'World Drug Crop Up Sharply in 1989 Despite U.S. Effort', *New York Times*, 2 March 1990.
21. Kline, op. cit., pp. 22–7.
22. Liz Sly, 'U.S. Coffee Blunder Could Harm War on Drugs', *Chicago Tribune*, 11 November 1989.
23. Farmers Urged to Switch from Coca Leaves to Coffee', *Associated Press*, 12 December 1989.
24. 'Bush Plan Worries Pennsylvania Flower Growers', *Knight-Rider Newspapers*, 17 February 1990.
25. Jerome H. Skolnick, 'A Critical Look at the National Drug Control Strategy', *Yale Law and Policy Review*, 8(36) (1990) p. 86.
26. Edith Mirante, 'The Victim Zone: Recent Accounts of Burmese Military Human Rights Abuse in the Shan State', *Contemporary Crises*, 13(3) (September 1989) p. 210.
27. Ibid., p. 211.
28. Sciolino, op. cit., p. A2.
29. Associated Press, 'Bolivia, Peru Rap Coca-eating Bugs', *Centre Daily Times*, 22 February 1990.
30. Gustavo Vladymir Garcia Hinojoza, 'An Analysis of the Relationship Between the Aggregate Value of Cocaine and the Bolivian Formal Economy', Master's thesis, Pennsylvania State University, December 1989, p. 47.
31. Ibid., p. 61.
32. Laurence Gonzales, 'Why Drug Enforcement Doesn't Work', *Playboy*, December 1985, p. 104.
33. Wisotksy, op. cit., p. 178.
34. Bruce M. Bagley, 'Colombia and the War on Drugs', *Foreign Affairs*, 67(1) (Fall 1988) p. 87.
35. David Kline, op. cit., p. 23.
36. Ibid., p. 27; also see Peter Andreas, 'The U.S. Drug War in Peru', *The Nation*, 13/20 August 1988, p. 14.
37. Ibid.
38. Statement of William J. Anderson, Assistant Comptroller General, 'General Government Programs', before the Subcommittee on Government Information, Justice, and Agriculture Committee on Government Operations, United States House of Representatives, *Hearings: Federal Drug Interdiction Efforts* (9 September 1986).
39. Ibid., pp. 19–21.
40. Ibid., p. 12.
41. US Customs Service, *Customs U.S.A.* (Washington, D.C.: Government Printing Office, 1981) p. 14.
42. Florida Department of Law Enforcement, *Drug Abuse in Florida: Summary of the Problem and Statewide Initiatives* (17 February 1987) p. 1.

43. Steven Wisotsky, *Beyond the War on Drugs* (Buffalo, N.Y.: Prometheus Books, 1990) p. 65.
44. James Inciardi, *The War on Drugs: Heroin, Cocaine, Crime and Public Policy* (Palo Alto, Cal.: Mayfield, 1986) pp. 208–9.
45. Ibid.
46. William Anderson, op. cit., p. 24.
47. Frank Greve, 'American Presence in Drug War to Escalate', *Knight-Rider Newspapers*, 11 February 1990, p. A8.
48. E. J. Hobsbawm, 'Murderous Colombia', *New York Review of Books* 20 November 1986, pp. 27–35.
49. Gustavo Hinojoza, op. cit., p. 44.
50. Ibid.
51. Inciardi, op. cit., p. 208.
52. Michael Isikoff, 'How to Lose Money on a '57 Chevy', *Washington Post Weekly Edition*, 4–10 December 1989, p. 33.
53. Ibid.
54. Linda P. Campbell, 'Lawyers Wary of Clients Paying Fees with Tainted Money', *Chicago Tribune*, 2 November 1989.
55. Ibid.
56. Aaron Epstein, 'American Bar Rebuffs Thornburgh', *Knight-Rider Newspapers*, 13 February 1990.
57. Wisotsky, op. cit. (1990), p. 79.
58. Inciardi, op. cit., p. 213.
59. Ethan Nadelmann, 'U.S.: Drug Policy: a Bad Export', *Foreign Policy*, no. 70 (Spring 1988) p. 88.
60. Ethan Nadelmann, 'Drugs: the Case for Legalization', *Washington Post*, 8 October 1989.
61. Ethan Nadelmann, 'U.S. Drug Policy', op. cit., p. 99.
62. Ibid.
63. John Horgan, 'Test Negative: a Look at the "Evidence" Justifying Illicit-Drug Tests', *Scientific American*, March 1990, pp. 18–19.
64. Ibid.
65. Ibid.
66. Ibid.
67. Ibid.
68. See, for example, *Seminar Program and Exhibits Directory*, 35th Annual Seminar and Exhibits, American Society for Industrial Security, 11–14 September 1989.
69. Peter Reuter, 'Quantity Illusions and Paradoxes of Drug Interdiction: Federal Intervention into Vice Policy', *Law and Contemporary Problems*, 51: 1 (Winter 1988) p. 247.
70. William J. Bennett, *What Works: Schools without Drugs* (Washington, DC: US Department of Education, 1986).
71. Ibid.
72. Ibid.
73. '3rd Grade Student with Beer Suspended: Mother "Furious" ', *Associated Press*, 29 January 1990.
74. Charles M. Madigan, 'Opinion Hardens against Drug Abuse', *Chicago Tribune*, 5 September 1989.

75.   Bruce Michael Bagley, 'US Foreign Policy and the War on Drugs:
      Analysis of a Policy Failure', *Journal of Interamerican Studies and World
      Affairs*, 30(2–3) (Summer/Fall 1988) pp. 189–212.
76.   Nadelmann, 'US Drug Policy: a Bad Export', op. cit. p. 88.
77.   Lloyd Johnston, et al., *Drug Use, Drinking, and Smoking: National Sur-
      vey Results from High School, College, and Young Adult Populations, 1975–
      1988* (Rockville, Md: US Dept of Health and Human Services, 1989).
78.   National Institute of Drug Abuse, *Semiannual Report: Trend Data from
      the Drug Abuse Warning Network*. Series G, no. 21 (Rockville, Md: NIDA,
      1988) p. 2.
79.   Erich Goode, *Drugs in American Society*, 3rd edn (New York: McGraw-
      Hill, 1989) pp. 229–30.
80.   Oakley Ray, *Drugs, Society and Human Behavior*, 3rd edn (St Louis, Mo.:
      C. V. Mosby, 1983) p. 28.
81.   National Institute on Drug Abuse, *National Household Survey on Drug
      Abuse: Population Estimates, 1988* (Rockville, Md: NIDA, 1989).
82.   Ibid., p. 2.
83.   Ibid.
84.   Anonymous, 'Attorney General Announces NIJ Drug Use Forecasting
      System', *NIJ Reports*, Washington, DC: U.S. Department of Justice
      (March/April 1988).
85.   US House of Representatives, *Congressional Record*, 134: 42 (March 1988)
      p. 2.
86.   Bruce Michael Bagley, 'The New Hundred Years War: US National
      Security and the War on Drugs in Latin America', *Journal of Interamerican
      Studies and World Affairs*, 30(1) (Spring 1988) p. 9.
87.   For an excellent discussion of the role of the Bahamas in the contem-
      porary drug trade, see Alan A. Block, 'Ambiguities in U.S. Caribbean
      Policy: the Bahamas, Narcotics, and American Foreign Policy', paper
      presented at the Southwestern Political Science Association meeting,
      Dallas, Texas, March 1987.
88.   *Report of the Commission of Inquiry Appointed to Inquire into the Illegal
      Use of the Bahamas for the Transhipment of Dangerous Drugs Destined for
      the United States of America* (Washington, DC: Government Printing
      Office, December 1984), p. 99.

3

After Mr Bennett and Mr Bush

US Foreign Policy and the Prospects for Drug Control

NICHOLAS DORN and NIGEL SOUTH*

JUST CAUSE

Probably the most extraordinary international political statement of Christmas 1989 was US Secretary of State James Baker's invitation to the Soviet Union to intervene militarily in Romania. As US ground forces followed F-117 fighter-bombers into America's own backyard, opening up the first sizeable military engagement since the failure of the Contras to topple Nicaragua, the Bush administration scrambled for legitimation of its Panamanian adventure – code-named, almost defensively, Operation Just Cause. Other Latin American countries were not amused and, in the European community, only stalwart Britain came out in support, her Prime Minister citing cocaine trafficking. And indeed, had not Noriega's 1988 indictment on racketeering charges softened up public opinion (particularly in the US) then the invasion would have been even more difficult to defend whilst the Soviets were letting history take its course on their side of the Yalta settlement divide.

The metamorphosis of the issue of 'drugs' from the domestic spheres of medicine and petty crime, through a 'War on Drugs' in which police officers in US inner cities found themselves described by Bush as 'freedom fighters', had by the end of the decade became the linchpin for a revival of the Monroe Doctrine.

The drug-control histories of the United States and Britain, to be referred to in this chapter, are close and intertwined in this development as in others. As we shall attempt to show, the British system of drug control has been much more similar to that of the United States than many American commentators[1] assume, most notably since the early 1980s. Although the British cocaine problem in the 1980s was very minor and the extent of any dealing in 'crack' minimal before extensive publicity in 1989, the *threat* of crack (and the coded reference to race in so far as it was seen as a problem among blacks) helped to mobilise consent for realignment of British drug control along North American lines. Internationally, Britain and the US worked together to get support for conventions on the exchange of drug intelligence, anti-money-laundering strategies, extradition and, symptomatically, mutual assistance – for example, procedures for the enforcement agencies of one country to work in others.

These are important developments from the point of view of criminology and it is important that they are not obscured by recent, more dramatic and illegal actions. As international drugs control conventions and their domestic enabling laws lay the basis for a global police concerned with new areas of international financial crime, the question arises as to whether this new internationalisation can represent the just causes of the poor and weak as well as those of the rich and powerful. The following paragraphs inscribe this question in the recent history of drug control policy in the United States and Britain.

THE BENNETT DOCTRINE

As the 'evil empire' of the Soviet Union conceded economic defeat and turned through *glasnost* to *perestroika*, the United States found its own economic position assailed by its free-market allies. It is within a general understanding of the US strategic response to these changing conditions that recent innovations in drug-control policy can be located.

Faced with increasingly competitive Japanese and other Far Eastern and European producers of industrial goods, the Reagan administration had responded by increasing its military and allied high-tech industrial spending,[2] paying for this by cuts in social programmes and by allowing the terms of trade and the federal budget to become increasingly unbalanced. The resulting devaluation of the dollar bolstered US competitiveness in the short term, but the underlying health of the traditional heavy-industry base declined due to under-investment. The resulting plant closures hit especially the urban areas in which minorities were heavily represented who were simultaneously facing cuts in welfare. The circumstances of blacks, hispanics and poor whites in inner cities across the US worsened appreciably whilst indicators of extreme poverty such as homelessness became ever more visible.[3] It seems probable that existing patterns of involvement in the irregular economy and in crime deepened as legitimate sources of income dried up. Some media representations of inner-city problems certainly magnified such changes: in a replay and deepening of the earlier moral panic over 'mugging', young blacks in particular portrayed as mindless or 'crack-crazed' savages who were themselves responsible for the decline in their circumstances. Special attention was paid to drug dealing and drug use as causes of violence, theft and poverty. The media began to report the American urban scene as if there was nothing wrong that SWAT (Special Weapons and Tactics) teams could not put right, and the new conservative social policy explained all by reference to an 'underclass' now out of control.

As regards foreign policy, the State Department finally overcame the trauma of Vietnam and the isolationism that this briefly encouraged. It gained confidence through the use of proxy armies in Afghanistan and Nicaragua, had mounted the invasion of Grenada, aided a similar exercise in colonial assertiveness in the British actions in and around the Malvinas and was under pressure from an increasingly nationalistic public opinion. Post-Carter, the US government became more cynical of the competence and right of nation-states in its backyard to run their own affairs and the undoubtedly large cocaine trade (which, insultingly, seemed highly profitable to black and Spanish-descent people in Latin America) provided a continual irritant.

Thus, by the late 1980s, drugs (especially cocaine) had became a metaphor for everything that might be wrong both sides of the US frontier – in its inner cities and in Central and South America.

It was the achievement of the Bush administration to articulate and develop these discontents into a major plank for its general foreign and domestic policies for the 1990s. After Bush became President, he eased the unfathomable Quayle away from the drugs policy arena (it was too important to be left to him) and appointed William Bennett to the job of reformulating national policy on drugs and co-ordinating the myriad agencies working in the drugs enforcement field.[4] Little effective progress was initially made on co-ordination and prevention of so-called 'turf wars', so continuing the overlaps, duplication and occasional conflicts of the 1970s and most of the 1980s.[5] But a new and clear strategy *did* emerge. The September 1989 national strategy contained four main propositions:

(a) interdiction of drugs at US frontiers should be de-emphasised, since additional spending at this point would not be cost-effective;
(b) interventions in drug producing countries should be stepped up, directly committing the US military where possible;
(c) drug users themselves should be made 'accountable' for their patronage of the drug trade;
(d) the costs of education and treatment should be localised as much as possible so as to have them fall on cities and states rather than on the federal budget.[6]

On the second point, enquiries made of Colombia and other Latin American countries drew the response that these countries did not wish to take up the kind offer of military intervention. On 15 December 1989, however, General Noriega gave the United States the gift of a hostile speech interpretable as a declaration of war,[7] which, when taken with his indictment on racketeering charges, provided a pretext for implementation of what we might call the Bennett Doctrine. Initially, General Noriega escaped the grasp of the invading US forces – probably to the relief of those concerned about political fallout from a trial at which CIA involvement in bolstering the Noriega regime and its capability to traffic in drugs will come under the spotlight. Nevertheless, the primary purpose of the invasion – to prove to anybody not convinced by Grenada that the US was still willing to assert itself by military invasion – had indeed been achieved.

The third plank of the Bennett strategy – that drug users should be made 'accountable' for a consumer choice that benefits drug traffickers – represents a creative reformulation of socio-legal discourse. Previously drug users had been seen, at least in part, as victims: weak and inadequate individuals softened up by peer pressure and exploited by pushers. Such a characterisation served to keep decriminalisation on the agenda, to redirect law-enforcement efforts away from the user and against the trafficker and to support calls for federal funding of treatment facilities. The kids were sick, not bad. Bennett reversed this. Drug users constituted a consumer market for drugs, hence they kept traffickers in business, hence they were responsible for trafficking and its ills. This reversal of responsibility, represented at the level of rhetoric by the proposition that drug users should be held 'accountable' for the drug trade, makes it reasonable for users to be given the attention of the criminal justice system rather than of medicine. It underpins the drive to drug testing in federally funded institutions. And it undercuts any suggestion that public funding of health and welfare programmes should be increased. After all, if your average drug user is responsible for the emergence of the likes of Noriega, then pampering him or her would obviously be counterproductive.

THE SITUATION IN BRITAIN

From 1985 onwards in Britain, the consensus on drugs shifted from an initial tendency to re-medicalise the issue in response to HIV, through a swing to enforcement against traffickers, and then to a historically unprecedented and overt focus on race and drugs.

From the US perspective, the perception of some link between race and drug problems seems unremarkable – perhaps because North American drug problems have historically been defined by reference to minority groups.[8] But in Britain it has been white youth that has attracted the greatest concern, whether as speed freaks, potheads, multi-drug users, solvent sniffers or junkies (heroin injectors or smokers). This focus of concern on whites was in line with the reality, since white youth were over-represented in all patterns of drug use, with the possible exception of cannabis.

Nevertheless, during summer 1989 the British media, law-enforcement circles and political establishment became seized by the conviction that Britain was about to suffer a major epidemic of crack use – and that black areas of the inner city would be the epicentre. Concerns about drugs and HIV then became appropriated within the discourse. Crack was said to be almost instantly addictive and to be virtually untreatable. Following a series of speeches by a visiting Drugs Enforcement Administration official in 1989 and reciprocal visits by politicians and journalists to the US, British parliamentary reports, TV documentaries and newspapers of all persuasions as well as the popular imagination all radiated an excitable foreboding. By autumn 1989 professionals, parents and schoolchildren throughout Britain were talking about crack. Many senior police officers had been convinced by DEA intelligence reports that Jamaican gangs, 'posses' or 'yardies' were targeting Britain with cocaine and crack, and made resolute statements of their determination to carry out operations in black areas asserting that 'you have got to hit the street dealers' and that 'the dealers tend to be in black areas'. Resources were targeted on crack above all other drugs. As might be expected, the clamour of publicity (including handy hints on how to convert cocaine to crack) and the focusing of law-enforcement efforts did together produce an increase in the number of seizures – from around ten seizures per annum up until 1988 to around 50 by'the end of 1989 (mostly very small amounts).[9]

The 'crack attack', as it has been called, was not without productive consequences. For one thing, it jolted the British drug agencies into a realisation that, in spite of a long history of amphetamine availability and the attendant risk of HIV transmission amongst those users of the injectable form who shared injection equipment, stimulant-related problems had remained largely unaddressed in the British heroin-focused system of drug treatment units.[10]

Rather more telling has been the impetus given by crack to the reorganisation of drugs enforcement and, subsequently, law enforcement generally in Britain. Traditionally, Britain's 52 police forces have been under the control of autonomous chief constables and at the time of writing there is no *operational* centralised or national police agency (although there are police *intelligence* units with a national brief and HM Customs and Excise is a national body). However, in the 1970s multi-force Regional Crime Squads were set up to counter major criminal enterprises and from 1986 these developed 'drugs wings' designed to target wholesale-level dealers.[11] Also in 1986 the then Central Drugs Intelligence Unit of the Metropolitan (London) Police was re-designated the National Drugs Intelligence Unit and staffed by Customs officers as well as police – but it remained an information-collating agency, not operational. From 1989, however, the perceived urgency to counter crack gave impetus to plans to build upon the basis of the NDIU a National Drugs Intelligence Office (or Service, as it was being called by summer 1990), of the kind also called for by William Bennett for the US. This was seen by many senior police officers as a step along the road to a National Detective Agency with operational powers across Britain, along the lines of a combined FBI and DEA.[12] These developments, which are at the time of writing only partially worked through, have a significance far wider than drugs enforcement. Just as Britain's version of US legislation on disclosure of information by financial institutions and on confiscation of the assets of convicted drug traf-

fickers (Drug Trafficking Offences Act, 1986) has quickly been followed by further legislation extending these new powers or variants
of them to all other areas of major crime (Criminal Justice Act,
1988),[13] so it seems that concern over drugs is a major factor in
moves toward the creation of a national police force through the
amalgamation of Regional Crime Squads. Whatever the implications
for drug control, this would *potentially* lay the basis for more
vigorous policing of corporate crime.

POLICING, RACE AND DRUGS

More disturbing are the implications for race relations. 1989 saw a
number of new revelations concerning police fabrication of evidence
and 'planting' of drugs (usually cannabis)) on black people. Such
actions seem to account for only a small proportion of the roughly
24,000 instances of police action in relation to cannabis, and to be
carried out by a majority of disgruntled uniformed officers rather
than plain-clothes detectives. The impact upon the black community
is, however, understandably great. In this context, the apparent consensus between senior detectives, politicians and the media that
crack is (or will be) a particular problem in black communities is
very unhelpful. Such assumptions, whatever their motivation, reinforce existing racist attitudes in the lower ranks and thereby sustain policing practices that range from the dubious application of
police discretion in judging who to search and who to charge, to the
'fitting up' of black people because they are community activists, or
which simply follow from the kind of vicious racism expressed by
one police officer who said to a man he wrongfully arrested: 'You
had to open your fucking black mouth.'[14]

Although the Home Office is known to favour a cautious approach
to race and drugs, media portrayals of crack as a predominantly
black problem[15] can only reinforce existing processes that cause many
black people, particularly the youth, to distrust the police. One
practical response would be for the police to recruit *and retain* more
black and other ethnic minorities. (During the late 1980s greater
numbers of black people were leaving the Metropolitan Police than
were joining it.) A greater proportion of black police officers – including detectives – would also help to reverse a further worrying

trend. Personal communications from officers with first-hand knowledge of several inner-city areas suggest that, from 1988 or thereabouts, the lack of black police officers to carry out surveillance and undercover operations was putting the police in the position of being able to operate much less effectively in areas of black settlement than in white areas. The *relative* success of action against dealers operating in white areas seems in some cases (we propose no general rule) to shift dealing from white areas to black areas even when the dealers themselves remain white.

Due to the lack of black officers to carry out normal detective functions such as surveillance, the police are then left with four options: leave things alone; concentrate on arresting the drug users as they leave the dealing area with their purchases; try to build a case against the dealers by detailed surveillance from a distance; or mount massive 'swamp' operations with scores of officers, searching many homes and people, generally disturbing the peace and generating considerable community resentment. The latter consequences tends to ruin already meagre opportunities for information about drug dealers to flow to the police, and locks them into a cycle of mounting 'fishing trips' with often minor success (such as the appropriate named – whether intended or not – 'Operation Kingfisher' in 1989.[16] An almost totally white police force is sliding into the adoption of assumptions and strategies that can only further distance it from communities with which, on its own reckoning, it needs to improve relations. Perhaps there are positive lessons to be asked of the US experience here?

From 1990 the Home Office began to initiate a number of drug-prevention teams in localities of Britain reckoned to have a serious drug problem and/or to be 'vulnerable' to crack. These are likely to be rather more low-key than the 'high-intensity drug trafficking areas' outlined in principle by the US Anti-Drug Abuse Act of 1988. In these latter areas, authorities may carry out 'a menu of activities' including developing special enforcement task-forces, additional prosecution capacity, drug testing of arrestees, treatment and pre-vention activities. In Britain it seems likely that greater community involvement and the generation of relatively low-level drugs intel-ligence will be sought.

It remains to be seen whether Britain follows the US lead and increases the pressure on drug users (alongside continuing efforts to work 'along the chain' to major traffickers). There are voices calling for a refocusing upon users, encouraging them to take 'early retirement' from their drug-using career[17] and for the criminal justice system to strongly encourage drug users to accept some form of treatment or other assistance. We do not share these views, bearing in mind (a) the fact that most arrests are for cannabis possession, for which there is no treatment of which we are aware; (b) the relatively low chances of success of compulsory treatment and the likelihood of relapse; and (c) the likely disproportionate criminalisation of black people. We suggest that the advocates of the strategy of 'forcing people to be free' have yet to think through the implications of that stance.

What then can be offered as a practical alternative to the WASP-ish violence of the Bennett strategy? Certainly not, in our view, advocacy of legalisation or decriminalisation (that is, legalisation of possession for personal consumption). During the late 1980s virtually the only alternative strategy put forward in the US was decriminalisation.[18] In terms of its own internal logic, the attraction of decriminalisation or legalisation may have increased as drug problems deepened, bearing in mind the argument that a licit market would remove those social costs that derive from illegality rather than being intrinsic in substances themselves. However, a major disadvantage of the legalisation position is that whilst it is perfectly arguable amongst diverse left-liberal and right-libertarian thinkers and intellectuals, it meets with little approval amongst other social groups (notably most politicians) who constitute a consensus that drugs are bad and should remain under prohibition. In terms of the broader moral/political discourse within which it is articulated, the legalisation thesis fails to overcome the difficulty that it appears to involve collusion with drug users and traffickers. Indeed William Bennett's recasting of drug consumers as being responsible for the demand for drugs, and hence for trafficking and all its associate ills, discursively repositions advocacy of legalisation as advocacy of international narco-terrorism. Proselytisation of decriminalisation forms the perfect foil for advocates of the war on drugs, who appreciate the utility of critics who have so little to say about 'fine tuning' of drug-control strategy within the context of continuing *criminalisation*. Indeed, one sometimes gets the impression that administration spokespersons rather value the debate on legalisation as a diversion from more difficult questions.

THE LOGIC OF THE MARKET

In moving towards what we might tentatively call a post-Bennett strategy of drug control – that is, one in which the criminal law continues to play the major part but in ways that are more subtle and effective than at present – it is appropriate to focus upon what we know of the operation of illegal markets.[19]

A useful point of departure is acknowledgement of recent work carried out by the Rand Corporation in the United States.[20] This research can be seen as an exemplar of policy research in two distinct senses: it is clear and well argued in its own terms; and it has political currency because it fits the moment (the late 1980s/early 1990s). In a nutshell, Rand argued that heavy expenditure in an effort to police the frontiers of the US against incoming drugs were doomed to be cost-ineffective. The damage done to federal budgets in keeping an AWACS or other surveillance aircraft in the air is considerable, while the rate of detection remains low and the damage to the trafficking organisation is not very great. At this point of intervention in the market, Reuter and his colleagues pointed out, the *replacement value* of the drugs, plane/boat and couriers is relatively low. Organisers remain largely undetected, can send in another shipment and will easily make up the loss of the shipment seized. This is because the price s/he receives for the shipment once it gets through is many times its cost. Given that most shipments continue to get through unscathed, the occasional seizure – however exciting for enforcement agencies – can be greeted with insouciance by the trafficker. The implication waiting to be drawn from this analysis is that frontier interdiction should be de-emphasised in favour of direct action in source countries, and/or greater policing within the US distribution system.

In a 1989 Rand report, Peter Reuter and John Haaga suggest that, within the United States, the focus upon high-level dealers may not be very productive. They point out: 'The very large numbers of imprisoned high-level dealers in a period in which the price of cocaine has continued to collapse shows that the population of persons competent and willing to fill that role is extremely large, perhaps in the many tens of thousands.'[2] In other words, there will continue to be a ready pool of recruits into high-level trafficking. Even though the price of cocaine (and hence the degree of profit) may decline, dealing in this and other drugs is more profitable (and more pleasant) than other occupations available to the bulk of the population, and the chances of arrest decrease the further one distances oneself from the street level. Basing their remarks on interviews with incarcerated dealers, the authors also suggest that, since high level dealing is more commonly done by individuals, couples or loose networks than by organisations, the strategy developed in the US and largely followed by Britain – the 'immobilisation of organisations strategy' as enshrined, for example, in RICO statutes – may be inappropriate. Here Reuter develops his earlier work[22] in which he criticises the notion of 'organised crime' and suggests that most forms of crime do not involve complex or extensive organisations (such as the Mafia). Our own work within Britain also suggests that drug markets are not highly organised, but are fragmented and fluid, containing many simple structures rather than few fixed ones.[23]

There are several reasons why big trafficking organisations do not arise in Britain and the US, of which one is the multiple and overlapping jurisdiction that William Bennett wishes to abolish. With so many different enforcement agencies falling over each other, the chances for monolithic criminal organisations to evolve are slim, since such organisations can only survive when there is one single enforcement agency within which key individuals can be 'bought off' financially or politically. Examples of such circumstances include the New York Police Department in the 1970s, the CIA in Vietnam, the Metropolitan Police Drug Squad in London prior to 1973, and indeed, the Noriega regime in Panama.[24] Multiple jurisdiction presents barriers to widespread corruption and organised crime. The implication of this is that any moves towards unification of drugs enforcement agencies in Britain or the US would need to be balanced by creating internal divisions within them. Organisational overlap and competition are not simply inefficiencies, they are also safeguards. Whatever our view of drugs enforcement agencies at present, corrupting them in the name of efficiency can hardly be regarded as an improvement.

One final observation spanning the US and Britain concerns violence and retribution. As we argue at greater length elsewhere,[25] there has been an increase in the use of violence in and around drug markets, but this cannot be stripped of its context and presented as a consequence of 'human nature', 'Jamaican posses' or (most vacuously) a sad but inevitable aspect of 'modern society'. One simply has to ask how any rational person would respond to a situation in which the penalty for a highly profitable crime had been increased –

from a fine or brief imprisonment as would be typical in Britain twenty years ago, to the many years (up to life imprisonment) and asset confiscation of today. Whilst previously a dealer would regard apprehension as undesirable but not so damaging when viewed from the position of an early release, today the punishment is so total that a proportion of dealers are prepared to threaten and use violence – against potential informers and against the police – in order to evade arrest.

What we are suggesting here is that, faced with the retributive penalties so beloved of successive US and British governments, a prototypically economically rational person involved in trafficking would be likely to resort to violence. The political implication of this is as politically delicate as it is obvious.

THE DEFINITION OF OBJECTS FOR CONTROL

In our closing pages we try to construct the basic elements of a practical drug-control strategy that transcends both the romanticism of the decriminalisers, and the closet racism of the hard-liners. We address ourselves to three levels of the drug market: (a) drug consumers (or purchasers, as William Bennett has cleverly re-designated them); (b) trafficking within and between countries; and (c) cultivation of drugs plants within the developing world.

Drug Consumers

The language used to describe drug users and to denote the proper means of their control has developed through the years, encompassing concepts of the user as demonic, as sick, as immature or inadequate, as a social-work case (more so in Britain than the US), as a client of services, as a source of infection (HIV), as a mindless animal (crack), and as a customer and patron of the trafficker (the latest, 'demand-reduction' formulation). It is important to see that the drug user may, to varying extents, be each of these things, particularly since his or her self-definitions are largely constructed within the linguistic space of the wider society.

The importance of various descriptions of the drug user and theories of addition lies not in their absolute truth-value (which is extremely difficult to establish[26]) but in the implications that they have for control. In our perspective, the one sure thing to say about users of drugs that are legally proscribed by law is that they are criminals by definition – but we doubt that it is useful to say any more about drug users in general. Drug users come from all sections of society; the ways in which they use drugs, the pleasures that they obtain and the difficulties that their use presents to them and to others are at least partially shaped by their broader social circumstances; and we see little virtue or utility in trying to get them all to sing in the same voice. Indeed it seems to us that attempts to define drug users *per se* or in essentialist terms are doomed to failure.

Within the language of market society so clearly in the ascendancy in the later 1980s and early 1990s, it is entirely appropriate to see drug users as purchasers/consumers and to examine the ways in which they subscribe to identities available within and around drug markets and other markets. In terms of social control of the user, then, it makes better sense to attempt some 'social engineering' on the shape and functioning of the market which provides the environment for the purchaser/consumer, rather than to consolidate various negative role-models by addressing users directly ('hello there, you potential crack users').

Trafficking Within and Between Countries

As regards trafficking, the time is clearly ripe for a reassessment of penalties and their practical consequences. In this chapter we have argued that up-to-life sentences and asset confiscation of potentially all one's assets makes drug markets an environment in which the rational trafficker will play 'double or quits', causing any violence necessary to keep out of gaol (see above). The consequences for an already overcrowded prison system, the fiscal costs to the state and the imbalances that high trafficking penalties pose within the criminal law (in Britain, the average wife-killer can get more sympathetic treatment than middle-ranking traffickers), all add up to the conclusion that the punishments for trafficking are absurdly and counter-productively high.

All of this could perhaps be set aside if there were any reason to think that the escalation of penalties had done anything to restrain the drugs trade. But the exemplary, retributional and righteous approach to punishment seems merely to have shaped drug markets into a mirror image of violence. The European concept of harm-reduction, currently becoming understood by some in the US as providing a rationale for needle-exchange schemes and other services for drug users, needs to be widened to apply to drug markets. Whilst no one knows how to reduce the scope of these markets, consideration needs to be given to the question of reducing the various forms or harm currently associated with them.

It is in this spirit that we flag up the possibility of radical reductions in penalties for drug trafficking. Such a move might be described by some as 'sending the wrong signal' (that is, that drugs trafficking is 'not as bad as all that') but, we would respond, it is no good banging war-drums so loudly that you cannot hear yourself think. A reduction in penalties for trafficking – say, a halving of maximum prison sentences and a restriction of asset confiscation to guarantee a continuing reasonable standard of living for offenders' families – could actually increase deterrence and shrink the market. At present, high penalties make it rational for traffickers to intimidate and use violence against suspected informers (including competitors), as well as against the police to resist arrest. Since 'information received' is the mainstay of traditional detective work, any restriction on the flow of such information – because potential informants are frightened – has serious consequences for trafficking investigators. Only if punishments for trafficking were clearly *below* punishments for serious crimes of violence would it become rational for the trafficker to abstain from threats and use of violence. Hence there is a good case for suggesting that a reduction of penalties for trafficking could reduce both the size of drug markets (through increasing the flow of information to law-enforcement agencies) and reduce the levels of violence currently associated with these markets.

Although we have expressed doubts about the social utility of the successive hikes in penalty over the last decade in Britain and the US, we welcome recent developments in the control of financial crime such as money laundering, and also welcome the development of international conventions and bilateral treaties in this area. In an era in which financial capital is clearly internationalised, it is necessary to develop the legal framework so as to provide some elements, at least, of regulation. There seems no reason why international fraudsters and the like, who operate across national states, should then shelter behind a national boundary. If it has taken the outcry against drug trafficking to provide the impetus towards the more general internationalisation of law on corporate and financial crime, then this seems no reason for complaint. The burgeoning of international agreements around financial crime offers up possibilities for control of many aspects of the operation of transnational corporate bodies – for example, in respect of health and safety, product safety and environmental pollution.[27] Drug-related legislation is currently one of the most dynamic areas of criminal justice, and potentially provides more progressive 'spin-off' opportunities than are recognised. At present most of those of a progressive or liberal persuasion are lined up in truculent opposition to drug laws – this seems rather a wasted opportunity.

Drug Plant Cultivation

Lastly, we turn to control of drug plant cultivation in developing countries. A serious discussion must be located within an understanding of the necessary conditions for resolution of the crisis of debt, as well as in an understanding of the options for future foreign policy of the United States.

One useful point of reference on both counts is the Brady Plan for partial write-offs of much of the debt and conversion of the remainder into equity. IMF loan facilities would no longer be granted to those countries (generally with an authoritarian government) most ready to cut subsidies to the petty production sector of agriculture, and to those willing to encourage large-scale cash cropping for export in order to generate foreign exchange. Instead, financial assistance would be tied to developing countries' commitment to expand subsidies to the indigenous farming sector, improving the viability of food cultivation for local consumption. Such a financial programme – well understood in development studies and in banking – would provide a better chance that drug plants would not be replanted after the passing of short-term incentives offered by specific crop-substitution programmes (typically around five years). Any revision in IMF loan criteria would at present depend on the acquiescence of the US, which has the major say in IMF policy, although this situation is likely to change as the relative economic power of the US wanes.

A further reform that would be equally good for country development and crop substitution is restriction of flight capital. One technical possibility would be an international convention requiring financial institutions to refuse to accept flight capital in excess of aggregate holdings beyond a certain proportion of a country's GNP. This would reduce the rate of devaluation of developing countries' currencies against the dollar and hence reduce the escalation of debt, the acute shortage of foreign exchange and subsequent institutional support for cultivation of exportable cash crops. Such measures would face difficulties, but some of the elements – the Brady Plan (better accepted in London financial circles than in New York), and recent international conventions concerning money laundering and like matters – are already in place. Whilst this is not the policy agenda of the Bush administration, shifts in political balance within the US and between her and her major trading competitors could bring such a genuinely *pro-development* policy into being, with benefits for drug control.

In conclusion: in one sense, the drug-control strategies of the US at the end of the 1990s remind one of Britain's Opium Wars a century earlier. The common factors are (a) the articulation of drug policies on the basis of what fits the broader foreign policy; (b) the collapse of these policies into a débâcle; and (c) useful legacies. After years of military incursion designed to make the then 'backyard' of the Raj an open market for British goods, contradictions in the exercise and pressure from Britain's trading competitors forced withdrawal, signalling the turning point of that country as a world power. In 1989–90, as US spokespersons referred to the 'decapitation' of the Panamanian government and kept their ex-protégé, Noriega, awake at night by playing such tunes as 'I Fought the Law and the Law Won', so the US was described as an 'occupying power' by the Vatican and denounced by the UN General Assembly. The decline of the US provides opportunities for changes in development policy and drug control and, in this emerging context, national laws and international agreements controlling drugs and money flows may attain much broader relevance.

Notes

* The authors would like to thank Jasper Woodcock for reading an earlier draft of this article.

1. For example, J. Wilson, *Thinking about Crime* (New York: Vintage Books, 1985).
2. Most notably, of course, the investment ploughed into the Strategic Defense Initiative, the so-called Star Wars programme.

3. P. Rossi, *Down and Out in America: The Origins of Homelessness* (Chicago, Ill.: University of Chicago Press).
4. For a broader discussion of US drug policy see Chapter 2 by Bullington in this volume.
5. Comptroller General, Office of, General Accounting Office, *Federal Drug Enforcement: Strong Guidance Needed* (Washington, DC: General Accounting Office, 1975); Comptroller General, Office of, General Accounting Office, *Federal Drug Interdiction Efforts Need Strong Central Oversight* (Washington, DC: General Accounting Office).
6. Executive Office of the President, *National Drug Control Strategy* (Washington, DC: Office of National Drug Control Policy, 1989).
7. Writing in the *New York Review of Books* in March 1990, the commentator Theodore Draper observed that many writers, including himself, had accepted that 'one of the reasons for the invasion was Noriega's "declaration of war" against the United States'. This he based on President Bush's speech to a press conference on 21 December 1989. However, after looking at what the text of Noriega's 15 December speech actually said, Draper submits that 'Bush's statement was, at best, a half truth, at worst a flagrant distortion'. According to Draper:

    > The key passage in Noriega's speech on 15 December accused the President of the United States of 'having invoked the powers of war against Panama' and 'through constant psychological and military harassment of having created a state of war in Panama, daily insulting our sovereignty and territorial integrity'.

    Noriega did apparently stress 'the urgency to unite as one to fight against the aggressor' but this was in the context of a claim that the US had initiated open hostilities and aggression. Hence there was nothing unilateral about a declaration of war from Panama, rather there was a declaration that the country found itself in a state of war arising out of the actions of the US. This might be viewed as hair-splitting or the inclination of administrations to be 'economical with the truth', were it not for the very powerful justificatory role played in defending the US action by Noriega's supposed unilateral declaration of war.

8. J. Helmer, *Drugs and Minority Oppression* (New York: Seabury Press, 1975); J. Helmer and T. Vietorisz, *Drug Use, the Labour Market and Class Conflict* (Washington, DC: Drug Abuse Council, 1974).
9. 'Risk of Police Community Conflict'; 'The Stutman Connection'; and 'Government Backs Off Anti-Crack Drive', *Druglink*, 4, 5 (1989); 'Crack Crazy! Evil Gangs Spread Drug Throughout Britain', *Sun*, 25 May 1989.
10. C. Reinarman and H. G. Levine, 'The Crack Attack: Politics and Media in America's Latest Drug Store', in J. Best (ed.), *Images and Issues: Current Perspectives on Social Problems* (New York: Aldine de Gruyer, 1989); SCODA (Standing Conference on Drug Abuse), *Working with Stimulant Users: A Conference Report* (London: SCODA, 1989).
11. ACPO (Association of Chief Police Officers), Final Report of a Working Party on Drugs Related Crime, chaired by R. F. Broome (unpublished report: ACPO, 1985; extracts published as appendix in N. Dorn,

K. Murji and N. South, *Traffickers: Policing the Drug Distribution Business* (London: Routledge, 1991).

12. *Drug Enforcement Report*, 5(22) (23 August 1989): p. 6; P. Imbert,'Do We Need a British FBI?', *Police Review*, 14 July 1989; Home Affairs Committee, *Drug Trafficking and Related Serious Crime*, vol. 1 (London: Her Majesty's Stationery Office, 1989); N. Dorn, K. Murji and N. South, 'Mirroring the Market? Police Reorganisation and Effectiveness against Drug Trafficking', in R. Reiner and M. Cross (eds), *Beyond Law and Order* (London: Macmillan, 1990).

13. The Drug Trafficking Offences Act 1986, *specifically* requires any banks with suspicions about the drug-related criminal nature of deposits to disclose those suspicions and furnish further information to the appropriate authorities. This is usually done by means of the security division at the head office of the bank communicating with the National Drugs Intelligence Unit at Scotland Yard. The Criminal Justice Act, 1988, does not contain the same *requirement* of banks to make disclosures, but it does provide them with legal protection in circumstances where they draw attention to funds or property which they suspect may be linked to criminal activities. Similar provisions were also drafted into the Prevention of Terrorism Act (Temporary Provisions) Act, 1989. See P. Rodgers, 'Small Banks Warned as War on Laundered Drug Money Hots Up', *Guardian*, 14 November 1989, p. 14. For a critical discussion of the evolution and implications of this legislation see N. Dorn and N. South, 'Profits and Penalties: New Trends in Legislation and Law Enforcement Concerning Illegal Drugs', in D. Whynes and P. Bean (eds), *Policing and Prescribing: The British System of Drug Control* (London: Macmillan, 1990).

14. Policy Studies Institute, *Police and People in London*, vols 1–4 (London: Policy Studies Institute, 1983); T. Kirby, 'Police Accused of Planting Drugs on Blacks', *Independent*, 17 June 1989, p. 5; J. O'Sullivan, '"Framed" Club Owner is Cleared of Drug Charges', *Independent*, 17 June 1989, p. 5; B. Levin, 'What More Evidence Must They Have?', *The Times*, 25 January 1990, p. 12; B. Levin, 'Justice under a Blue Cloud', *The Times*, 12 January 1990, p. 14; IRR (Institute for Race Relations), '£100,000 Damages for Victim of Drug Plant by Notting Hill Police', *IRR: Police Media Research Project Bulletin*, 57 (January 1990) p. 1; £100,000 Damages Against the Met.', *Police Review* (8 December 1989) p. 2470; 'PCA (Police Complaints Authority) Investigate Notting Hill Complaints', *Police Review*, 22 December 1990, p. 2570.

15. Such images can be particularly negative when associated with the trappings of violent crime and can be found in the 'quality' press as readily as in the sensational tabloids. For example, in July 1989 the *News of the World* carried a story on yardie gangsters with a photograph of a 'yardie chief' showing off guns and gold. The preceding month the *Observer Magazine* had published a report invoking exactly the same image of black 'gangsters' 'weighed down with gold and brandishing firearms' and likening them to the notorious Kray brothers gang of the 1960s. See J. Sweeney, 'Heirs to the Krays', *Observer Magazine*, 25 June 1989, pp. 27–30.

16. *Observer*, 1 October 1989; *Evening Standard*, 6 October 1989.
17. M. Gilman and G. Pearson, 'Lifestyles and Law Enforcement', in D. Whynes and P. Bean (eds), op. cit.; G. Pearson, 'The Street Connection', *New Statesman and Society*, 15 September 1989, pp. 10–11.
18. E. Nadelmann, 'Drug Prohibition in the United States: Costs, Consequences and Alternatives', *Sciences*, 245 (1 September 1989) pp. 939–47; A. Trebach, *The Great Drug War and Radical Proposals that Could Make America Safe Again* (London: Collier-Macmillan, 1987); M. Woodiwiss, *Crime, Crusades and Corruption: Prohibitions in the United States, 1900–1987* (London: Francis Pinter, 1988).
19. See P. Reuter, *Disorganized Crime: Illegal Markets and the Mafia* (Cambridge, Mass.: MIT Press, 1983); B. Johnson *et al.*, *Taking Care of Business: The Economics of Crime by Heroin Abusers* (Lexington, Mass.: Lexington Books, 1985); M. Moore, *Buy and Bust: The Effective Regulation of an Illicit Market in Heroin* (Lexington, Mass.: Lexington Books, 1977); R. Lewis *et al.*, 'Scoring Smack: the Illicit Heroin Market in London, 1980–1983', *British Journal of Addiction*, 80 (1985) pp. 281–90; N. Dorn and N. South, 'Drug Markets and Law Enforcement', *British Journal of Criminology*, 30(2) (Spring 1990) pp. 171–88.
20. P. Reuter, *Quantity Illusion and Paradoxes of Drug Interdiction* (Santa Monica, Cal.: Rand Corporation, 1989); P. Reuter *et al.*, *Sealing the Borders: The Effects of Increased Military Participation in Drug Interdiction* (Santa Monica, Cal.: Rand Corporation, 1988); P. Reuter and J. Haaga, *The Organization of High-Level Drug Markets: An Exploratory Study – A Rand Note* (Santa Monica, Cal.: Rand Corporation, 1989); Dorn and South, op. cit.
21. Reuter and Haaga, op. cit., p. 56.
22. Reuter, *Disorganized Crime*, op. cit.
23. Dorn and South, op. cit.
24. Knapp Commission, *The Knapp Report on Police Corruption* (New York: George Brazillier, 1972); A McCoy, *The Politics of Heroin in Southeast Asia* (New York: Harper and Row, 1972); B. Cox, J. Shirley and M. Short, *The Fall of Scotland Yard* (Harmondsworth, Middx: Penguin, 1977).
25. Dorn, Murji and South, op. cit.
26. See C. Fazey, *The Aetiology of Non-Medical Drug Use* (Paris: UNESCO, 1976).
27. See in this volume Chapter 7 by Pearce and Tombs, and Chapter 8 by Snider.

4

Defending the Mountaintop
A Campaign against Environmental Crime

ALAN A. BLOCK

This chapter recounts an attempt by a British-based rubbish company, Attwoods, led in part by Denis Thatcher, to open a landfill in
a rural mountain community in Central Pennsylvania. Attwoods
had entered the lucrative American garbage market by acquiring an
American company, Industrial Waste Services Inc., which, it became clear, had been implicated in racketeering activities.[1]

Attwood's entrance into the town of Snow Shoe in 1988 touched
off a small protest movement led by local residents worried about
potential environmental hazards that a new landfill would bring to
the area.[2] Although environmentally sophisticated, the locals were
unaware of the company's background and history. They none the
less were deeply suspicious about the firm and were convinced that
Pennsylvania's Department of Environmental Resources (DER) would
neither properly investigate it nor protect their community from
pollution unless forced to do so by extraordinary means.[3] As a resident of State College, the home of the Pennsylvania State University,
a neighbouring town in the same county, I was concerned with the
issues agitating the Snow Shoe protestors and thus circumstances
drew me into the dispute. Having already spent a decade examining
aspects of the waste disposal industry, particularly organised crime
and the illegal disposal of toxic waste, it seemed reasonably certain
to me that more light could be shed on the British firm than had been
so far provided. But if there was substantial evidence linking it to
either organised crime or illegal practices in general, it wasn't apparent how this information could be used to affect public policy. The
research effort was thus bound with considerations of political effectiveness – what to do if important criminality was found. What

91

follows is an account of both what was found and how the research process was conducted.

SNOW SHOE, 1988

In 1988 the local State College paper, the *Centre Daily Times*, reported that a new British firm, Attwoods PLC, proposed to buy a large portion of land owned by the R. S. Carlin Coal Company.[4] The latter was a strip-mining firm which also operated an out-of-date landfill in Snow Shoe. Carlin's dump was scheduled to close within a year or two because it didn't meet new state rules and regulations. In anticipation of the closing, Attwoods appeared eager to buy about 800 acres of Carlin land adjacent to the operating landfill. Attwood's intention was to construct what they characterised as a modern, non-polluting rubbish heap.[5] Local interest was aroused, and I began a minor study of Industrial Waste Services Inc. (IWS), located in Miami, Florida.

The first research probe seemed easy enough – a review of documents already at hand pertaining to IWS, a name that was not unfamiliar.[6] In this review the most recent documents dealing with IWS were scrutinised first simply because they came most readily to mind. Each reading, however, set off several chains of enquiry which hopped back and forth in time and location. At the start IWS resembled a kind of jigsaw puzzle for which many of the pieces were likely to be lying about. One simply had to start somewhere and see where it led – up or down, centre or periphery. The end of this initial stage came when there seemed sufficient reason to alert local environmental organisations and the local paper, hoping to stimulate them to pursue vigorously from the issues uncovered so far. The way chosen to alert them was to write and circulate a private caution about Attwoods. The result of this was not encouraging.

Working on the Puzzle: Florida

The first documents looked at were concerned with IWS and the nation's largest waste disposal company, Waste Management Inc., headquartered in Illinois with subsidiaries all over the country and much of the rest of world. Several years earlier the government had accused both firms and certain key officers in two distinct but overlapping cases of antitrust violations in their garbage operations in South Florida.[7] Although Waste Management and IWS were the centre pieces of this probe, the government named numerous co-conspirators among the region's rubbish firms, many of which seemed familiar and were in a sense laid aside by me as potential jigsaw pieces. In the first case co-conspirator IWS was also known as World Sanitation and its officers were Jack R. Casagrande, Ralph Velocci and John Lawson.[8] One of the other conspirators was Certified Waste Systems whose head was John Lawson's brother, Edward. The Lawsons were duly noted as potentially interesting individuals.

The primary case for review was USA *v.* Industrial Waste Service, Inc., in which Lewis R. Goodman of Waste Management and John E. Lawson from IWS were defendants.[9] Other conspirators included Jack R. Casagrande and Ralph Velocci from IWS as well as another Casagrande named Al. The government charged that the conspiracy was an illegal agreement among the carters not to solicit each other's customers, and that 'All established customers of the co-conspirators companies were subject to the allocation agreement.'[10] The scheme's structure has been called for many years the 'property rights system'. The government also charged Goodman with obstruction of justice. Specifically he was accused of removing subpoenaed documents from the files of Waste Management's subsidiary United Sanitation Services and then producing altered and counterfeit ones which were handed over to the Grand Jury. I suspected that Waste Management and IWS were either convicted or pleaded 'no contest' to the charges and that Goodman and at least one other official were convicted. In any case, the first review revealed Attwood's American subsidiary had quite recently been successfully charged with a 15-year conspiracy to violate the Sherman Antitrust Act.[11]

In the course of past work an important special report on the garbage and recycling industry in Florida compiled in 1973 had fallen my way. It was the confidential product of the Florida Department of Law Enforcement (FDLE) and had been compiled because various sources 'indicated the possibility of organized crime infiltration' into the industry. One of the report's sections dealt with 'Independent Operations in Florida', i.e. companies not associated (at least in 1973) with national solid waste firms. These independent operations were of interest because they had financial backing from New York State and/or were associated with 'questionable individuals in Dade County'. Under this category 'of interest to law enforcement' was Industrial Waste Services then at 3840 NW 37th

Court, Miami. President in 1973 was Albert Casagrande (no doubt the Al noted in the 1985 indictment), Vice-President was Jack R. Casagrande and Lawson was Secretary/Treasurer. The Florida investigators remarked that Lawson was Casagrande's brother-in-law (although which Casagrande was being referred to was not clear) and that IWS appeared to be backed by New York figures. Furthermore, Lawson stated in an interview that 'we are World Sanitation', while the investigators added they may also be the Great Eastern Hauling Corporation from New York.[12]

In the same section other independents were discussed including Naranja Sanitation Service. This firm was strongly believed to be controlled by organised crime. It was run by the brothers Laratro who were the sons of Joseph 'Joey Narrows' Laratro, a member of the Lucchese organised crime syndicate. The Laratros, it was reported, had bought Naranja from Salvatore Rizzo, an exceptionally notorious New Jersey racketeer who had become a real-estate developer in South Florida. While his sons managed Naranja, 'Joey Narrows' retained a substantial interest in the business which, in the years to come, was bought by IWS. The potential relevance of this purchase, what it mean about the character of IWS and its close associates, wasn't addressed until 1989.[13]

Florida investigators in 1973 also detailed a number of the national waste companies at work in their site. One that commanded attention was Sanitas Services among whose subsidiaries was United Sanitation, president Lewis R. Goodman. There were no allegations about organised crime and Sanitas in the 1973 Florida report. Four years later the situation changed dramatically. In 1977 a scandal emerged in Indiana with Sanitas accused of organised-crime influence and political corruption. In a series of articles for the Indianapolis *Star*, reporters found that the Department of Justice had mysteriously dropped a criminal investigation of bribes, kickbacks and laundered political contributions by Sanitas despite sworn testimony on violations in six US cities and Puerto Rico. The *Star* had obtained secret testimony from a Securities and Exchange Commission (SEC) inquiry revealing wrongdoing in Indianapolis, Boston, Detroit, Phoenix, Houston, an unidentified city in Connecticut, and Puerto Rico. Boston was the main focus. SEC testimony included statements of cash payments to Boston Mayor Kevin White who naturally denied the charges. Nevertheless the SEC believed the testimony of the company's vice-president that they had paid to secure lucrative Boston dumping contracts. Sanitas also paid $18,000 a month in cash to landfill operators to get lower rates. In some instances, these payments allowed Sanitas to dump prohibited hazardous wastes. There were also highly 'questionable cash payments for an illegal dump near Wayland, Massachusetts, and even an alleged cash payment to obtain a contract at Harvard University'. Sources said SEC investigators gave their information to the Justice Department following a 1973–4 probe of securities violations that had centred on officers of Sanitas and turned up this incriminating material. However, it was reported that the US Attorney from Boston, James Gabriel, determined that a full-scale investigation would have required far too much time and manpower.

Among the SEC's findings were that the Vice-President, Chief Financial Officer, and the Chairman of the Board conspired to conceal more than $1.2 million in political payoffs, contributions and kickbacks. Sanitas falsely labelled the money as fees paid for consulting, subcontracting and dumping services. Sanitas worked out a consent agreement with the SEC acknowledging it wouldn't do these things but without specifically admitting or denying the charges. The news of the SEC investigation coupled with revelations about Sanitas's practices in Indiana, which reportedly included threats of violence against several independent Indianapolis companies finally taken over by Sanitas and claims that organised crime figures operated on behalf of the firm in Arizona as well as Indiana, led to the company's demise. It broke apart, transforming some of what was left into another corporation which eventually ended up in the hands of Waste Management. Given this background, the charges levelled against Goodman and his new employer were not surprising.

In 1984 a reporter from Orlando, Florida, writing on illicit toxic-waste hauling, had told me that her police sources revealed that active racketeers in Florida's garbage industry included Anthony Carione, Carmine Persico and his cousin Andrew Russo, Rocco Velocci, Jack R. Casagrande, and Morton Robson (a former US Attorney in New York) then with Casagrande in some capacity or another. The reporter made a special point about Casagrande's and Robson's activities in respect to IWS and another firm called Urban Waste Disposal which was active in Ocala, Florida. Needing additional scrutiny were also two 'mother' corporations in New York.[14]

The Puzzle in New York

There had been federal, state and local investigations of the private

carting industry in the New York metropolitan region since the
1950s. What first came to mind, though, were records generated in
the late 1960s concerning mob activities in two Long Island counties,
Nassau and Suffolk. The issue of criminal influence in the private
sanitation industry was the subject of a law enforcement report
composed of material from several police investigations. The police
concluded that an association of carting firms in Nassau County had
employed as its representative Annielo Mancuso, an important
member of the Gambino crime syndicate. Additionally, this association's postal box was listed to Anthony Carione (mentioned above
as one of the organised-crime figures active in Florida). His brother
Frank Carione, the police then believed, was the association's
president.

Appended to the police documents was a synopsis of a New York
Daily News article published on 22 December 1967 which contained
what seems to be contradictory information. It said that the Nassau
County District Attorney was conducting Grand Jury proceedings,
and that John Casagrande of Five Counties Carting, headquartered
in Jamaica, Queens, and Umberto Velocci from a town on Long
Island were called to testify. Neither had anything to say to the
Grand Jury, it was reported, beyond invoking the Fifth Amendment.
The police documents added that both men were officers in a carters'
association which also availed itself of Mancuso's help and direction. The police stated, for instance, that Mancuso and another
notorious gangster represented this association at a meeting with
Suffolk County cartmen. At the time this material was put together,
Casagrande was thought to be the president and Velocci the vice-
president of the Nassau Waste Removal Institute. The synopsis ended
by noting that the US Attorney in New York's Southern District had
obtained the Waste Removal Institute's books for investigative
purposes.[15]

The history of trade waste associations on Long Island is baffling
at first glance and often unclear in police reports. One of the reasons
for the difficulty in tracing these organisations lies with their own
officers who are either confused about the organisation's past or
wish to be obscure in statements given to police interrogators. This
is not uncommon particularly in mob-dominated organisations where
officers are frequently 'fronts', sometimes totally unaware of their
positions, or else are mobsters themselves and prefer to give ellipt-
ical statements.

In any case, the waste association history as later recounted by the
New York State Commission of Investigation starts in the 1950s with

the Inter-County Cartmen's Association run by Gennaro Mancuso (Annielo's brother), described as 'a soldier in the Gambino organized crime family'. After US Senate hearings disclosed organised crime's control of the Association, Long Island carters formed two smaller ones. The first group was known as the Nassau–Suffolk Trade Waste Association (NSTWA) and John Casagrande was its original president. The second was the Nassau Waste Removal Institute which was headed by Nicholas Ferrante. John Casagrande left the NSTWA at some point and became an officer of the Waste Removal Institute. The dual association arrangement on Long Island did not last very long as subsequently a new entry, the Suffolk County Cartmen's Association, was formed. However, the gaoling of its leading organised-crime figure produced an anarchic situation finally resolved in the late 1970s with the formation of a new association.[16]

Other records dealt with this overall enquiry. One from the Suffolk County Police had the caption 'Intelligence Squad Case 114–67' and was dated 28 February 1968. It contained two lists, the first headed 'Members or Associates of Organized Crime'. Featured on this roll were Mancuso, Andrew Russo (referred to earlier), Vincent Angelo Garofalo, and John 'Joe' Morea. Concerning the latter, it was pointed out that Morea was suspected of being a silent partner in two carting firms – Long Island Rubbish and Jamaica Ash & Rubbish. The second list was composed of what the police thought were key associations in the carting industry by marriage and so on. Under this heading John Casagrande was prominently listed, as were several of his supposed in-laws. These included reported brothers-in-law Mario Reali of Republic Carting, Emedio 'Mimi' Fazzini of Jamaica Ash & Rubbish (see Morea above), Frank Grillo and Andrew Coniglio of Peninsula Carting.[17]

Fazzini was identified in hearings held by President Reagan's Commission on Organized Crime in 1985 as a member of the Lucchese crime syndicate. He and three other prominent organised-crime figures dominated the private carting industry on Long Island through control of the carting association called the Private Sanitation Industry, or PSI, formed in 1978–9 after the 'internal struggle among syndicate bosses for control of the industry'.[18]

The President's Commission confirmed the substance of numerous other documents gathered from police sources on Long Island which contended long-standing mob control of garbage carting through all the trade associations. In 1974 organised crime's prime controller in Suffolk County, Salvatore Spatarella, was sentenced to prison for three years. Although Spatarella tried to maintain control from prison, his incarceration provided other mobsters with an opportunity to muscle in. The winner in this conflict was Sal Avellino, owner of Salem Carting, and a leading member of the Lucchese syndicate.[19]

Naturally enough, the turmoil on Long Island came to the attention of the Organized-Crime Strike Force operating in New York's Eastern District which covers all of Long Island including Brooklyn and Queens. In March 1976 William J. Quinn from the Strike Force questioned Nicholas Ferrante, the president of the Waste Removal Institute. Ferrante identified the officers of his association: Fiori 'Perry' Persichilli, vice-president; John Casagrande, treasurer; and Sidney Fenster, secretary. In identifying Persichilli, Ferrante commented that he was a partner with Joe Morea in Long Island Rubbish. Ferrante thus added considerable weight to the suspicion that racketeer Joe Morea had an interest in that firm.[20] The role of Long Island Rubbish in the affairs of the Casagrandes and Veloccis was not yet apparent. But as this research progressed and more information was gathered, an intriguing relationship surfaced. Even at this point, though, it was obvious that many members of the mobster-dominated PSI had been officers and members of the Waste Removal Institute. The 1983 PSI Board of Directors included Ferrante, Persichilli, Fenster and John Casagrande. Sal Avellino, Frank Carione and 'Mimi' Fazzini were also directors.[21]

The Five Counties/John Casagrande 'milieu' was becoming more distinct, but there still was a distance to travel before the relationships between Five Counties and IWS, and John and Jack R. Casagrande (not to mention the Veloccis) were as sharp. Fortunately, there was a way to start plotting some of the connections. Among the papers from the DA's office one identified the stockholders of World Sanitation of Nassau Inc. which had 'consolidated with Five Counties Carting Corporation'.[22] Recalling John Lawson's remark to the Florida investigators of IWS in 1973 that 'We are World Sanitation', this enumeration of stockholders from 1971 through 1978 had to be helpful.

Rocco Velocci	president, director
John Lawson	vice-president, director
Ralph Velocci	secretary, director
Jack R. Casagrande	treasurer, director

Jack Casagrande   vice-president, director
Carl Casagrande   vice-president, director
Albert Casagrande   vice-president, director
Rocco Casagrande   vice-president, director
Vito Tropiano   vice-president, director
Romano Celli   vice-president, director

Of course, the roll was both enlightening and confusing. There was no doubt the officers of IWS were also stockholders and officers of World and presumably Five Counties. But where was John Casagrande, he of the organised-crime controlled NSTWA, Nassau Waste Removal Institute, and PSI?[23] The answer was soon found. The above list was reportedly complete for World and World had indeed 'consolidated' with Five Counties, but their officers were not similar. Five Counties' official structure was different as could plainly be seen when a comparison was made using the World stockholder/ officer list with a 1979 register of private carting companies which had permits to operate in the Long Island towns of Hempstead, North Hempstead and Oyster Bay. Five Counties, located at 172–33 Douglas Avenue, Jamaica, New York, reported as officers: John Casagrande, president; Frank Grillo, vice-president; Thomas Antonacci, secretary; and Vito Leone, treasurer.[24]

With material identifying the carters permitted to work in the three Long Island towns the examination continued for other firms such as Long Island Rubbish which already seemed important because of the strong allegations of organised-crime control.[25] The Long Island Rubbish Removal Corporation, headquartered in West Babylon, Long Island, was found. Its officers were Martin Masci, Michael Morea, 'Perry' Persichilli and Michael A. Perna.[26] One wondered what relationship, if any, Michael Morea might have had with racketeer Joe Morea.[27] It was also interesting to find this same group had another firm, the Michael A. Perna Company, situated at the identical address.

Among the other businesses on this list were several Casagrande and Velocci ones. The primary Velocci company was Southside Carting in New Hyde Park, Long Island. Its officers were Umberto Velocci, president; Orlando Velocci, vice-president; and Vincent Del-Broccolo, treasurer.[28] To make matters increasingly complex there were two more Casagrandes found in two other carting firms: Enrico Casagrande, head of Green Bay Sanitation, and James A. Casagrande, president of V & J Rubbish Removal.[29]

A corporate relationship, therefore, was established between IWS, convicted of anti-trust violations in Florida, and Five Counties in New York headed by John Casagrande, an officer of long standing in several organised-crime controlled trade waste associations.[30] World Sanitation could be viewed as a bridging organisation which brought together many of the important family players. It was also certain that IWS had expanded in Florida by buying at least one known organised-crime firm.[31]

In the New York State prosecutions which followed in the wake of the US Senate hearings into organised crime and rubbish collection held in 1957, dozens of New York carting firms were accused of restraint of trade. The State's object was to secure a permanent injunction against each of the defendants pursuant to Article 22 of the General Business Law of the State of New York, commonly known as the Donnelly Act. The named defendants were required to agree to the injunction and not to conspire to restrain trade any more. This was surely one of the least effective examples of state regulation of an industry rife with criminality. In trooped company officers to sign an agreement of no discernible consequence.

Despite the tepid nature of the case it did provide the earliest listing of the region's private carting firms caught in multiple instances of criminality. By scrutinising the firms for those with Casagrandes, Veloccis and those already known to be partners and associates, the following were located:

(1) World Ash and Rubbish Removal – Angelo Casagrande, Daniel Casagrande;
(2) Four Counties Carting (predecessor to Five Counties) – John Casagrande, Anthony Casagrande, Assunta Casagrande, Louis Cinelli;
(3) RocMar Carting – Vito Rocco Leone, Rocco Christina;
(4) Roman Carting – Frank Casagrande, Lorenzo Taglienti (it is unfortunately unclear from the court documents whether Frank Casagrande really existed or was the name used by 'Mastrantanti');
(5) Southside Carting – Umberto Velocci, Benedetto Velocci, Vincent DelBroccolo;
(6) Star Carting – Rocco Velocci, Peter Dibiase.[32]

The Crimes of Mel Cooper

One of the many ways in which organised crime operates in the private carting industry is through loansharking. The FBI had investigated a company known as Cooper Funding which had several subsidiaries such as Cooper Equities and 'Clean Taner' [correctly spelled Kleentainer] Corporation. The significance of these Cooper companies, according to an FBI document dated 30 March 1977, was that they engaged in arranging fraudulent leases for several organised-crime-affiliated companies particularly in the rubbish industry.[33] The Eastern District Strike Force issued subpoenas to Banker's Trust, Chemical Bank and the National Bank of North America for all records of leases arranged by Cooper Funding from January 1974 to June 1976.

In June of 1977 the FBI reported that Mort Robson, an attorney representing Cooper Funding Ltd, 'provided xerox copies of leases arranged by Cooper Funding pursuant to subpoena'. Robson was the former US Attorney identified by Florida authorities to the Orlando reporter as involved in criminal activities with Jack R. Casagrande in IWS and particularly in the Ocala firm named Urban Waste Disposal.[34] It was the Cooper/IWS leases, described by the FBI, which established without doubt a connection between IWS and organised crime as commonly understood.

There were two Cooper/IWS leases produced for the FBI and appended along with all the others to the field agents report. The first, no. 74 134, was supposedly for 'wide mouth compactors' and the vendor was an outfit called Florida Municipal Sales Company in Opa Locka, Florida; the second, lease no. 75–281, was for 99 alleged containers in various sizes. The vendor in this case was Anrose Steel Containers of Miami. A close look at the leases turned up another potentially significant lead. Cooper lease no. 75–332 was with an organised-crime carting firm from New Jersey. The vendor for this lease was something called the Cartman's Container Corporation which had the same New York address as Five Counties.[35]

Cooper Funding was a family business with its major office in Brooklyn, New York. The president was Mel Cooper while the other officers were his father Sam, his uncle Jack and a cousin Joel. The Cooper activities involved several financial crimes tied in with organised crime. For example, an FBI report filed by two Special Agents on 13 October 1976 noted a scheme involving fraudulent leases secured by Cooper Funding for use by a notorious organised-crime figure in the carting business. The object of this exercise was to bankrupt a third party.

In the course of the FBI's investigation it was determined that the Coopers had offices in Southern California and South Florida. Working in California as salesmen for Cooper Funding was Edward Vanasco (formerly resident in Valley Stream, New York) and Phil Gentile, whose speciality appears to have been phoney leases for California garbage firms.[36] Cooper operations included many complex financial scams such as 'advance fee' and 'add-on fee' schemes, false billing, theft of services and so on. There were also some rather straightforward ones signifying Coopers' criminal services. In one example, a carter out of Babylon, Long Island, who had purchased containers from a Cooper company in 1974 found he needed $10,000 in cash the following year. Cooper Funding 'loansharked' the money by arranging a phoney lease for the same containers at inflated 1975 prices.

Mel Cooper was involved in government funded work too. Through a number of corrupt associates in Congress, government agencies and private religious organisations, he was able to have the federal government pay a large portion of his salesmen's salaries. But only a part of the government payments was given out by Cooper. The rest he pocketed and probably split with his corrupt associates. The organised-crime people Cooper worked with at the time of this FBI probe were members of the Colombo, Gambino and Genovese crime syndicates, several of whom held official positions with the New York and Brooklyn Trade Waste Associations.[37]

Nothing came of this FBI action despite recommendations for prosecution on wire and mail fraud, and the Coopers proceeded with their activities for several years to come. It wasn't until the mid-1980s that federal action finally took place and Mel Cooper was tried for racketeering enterprises, convicted and sentenced to 30 years in prison. By then his organised-crime associates were the very top echelon of New York's most infamous crime syndicates. In the *Sentencing Memorandum* the US Attorney stated that Cooper Funding was

> alleged to be influenced by several LCN figures, including Joseph Schipani, . . . Capo in the Genovese LCN Family, Victor Arena, soldier in the Colombo LCN Family, John Franzese, . . . capo in the Colombo LCN Family, Michael Franzese, soldier in the Colombo

LCN Family, Alphonse Persico, Consigliere of the Colombo LCN Family, Sam Galasso, Sr., soldier in the Colombo LCN Family and vice-president of the Brooklyn Waste Trades [*sic*] Association, Jerry Zimmerman, associate of the Colombo LCN Family, Patsy D'Avanso, an associate of the Colombo LCN Family, . . . Joe Gentile, a soldier in the Colombo LCN Family, . . . and several other members and associates of the LCN.[38]

It was emphasised that the Brooklyn Trade Waste Association's vice-president and Colombo 'soldier', Galasso Sr and his son, were both salesmen for Cooper Funding. Cooper dealt with far more organised-crime figures than enumerated above, including the head of the Gambino syndicate, the boss of a major New Jersey racket group, a member of a Cleveland syndicate and, finally, Antonio Corallo the leader of the Lucchese crime syndicate. It was Corallo's man Avellino who controlled carting on Long Island through the PSI.[39]

Other police information possibly linked the Casagrandes and Cooper or Five Counties to mob activities. Mel Cooper had used the Chemical Bank, particularly its Small Business Loan Department, to provide loanshark funds for many of his phoney leases. In 1976 the Suffolk Police reported in a memo dated 17 November 1976, concerned with the movement of certain Long Island carters to the Albuquerque, New Mexico area, that 'informant information' held that Frank Antonacci was a 'mob contact man to get loans' from the Chemical Bank. If the informant was correct, this suggests Frank Antonacci was working either hand in glove with Cooper or on his own in Cooper-type operations.[40] The significance of this allegation for the Casagrande clan was derived from a Florida Department of Law Enforcement report which maintained that 'a Dun & Bradstreet report dated 6/18/76 indicated that Frank and Thomas Antonacci brothers both born 1924, were officers along with John Casagrande in Five Counties Carting Corp'.[41] The fact of Thomas's status was clear from the 1979 listing of permitted carters in North Hempstead and so on; this was the first indication about Frank.[42]

Environmental Politics

In May 1988 I wrote a short paper entitled 'Thoughts on Waste Disposal in Centre County Pennsylvania'. In it I reviewed very briefly the proposed new Attwoods' landfill and commented on support for it by both the Executive Director of the Centre County Solid Waste Authority and the Centre County Planning Director. The latter had stated the big picture which he derived from Snow Shoe's marvellously strategic location. He was quoted as saying 'if you draw a big circle around the New York – New Jersey – Philadelphia area, the Mountaintop [the name often used for Snow Show and adjacent area] offers private waste disposal firms some of the closest landfill space available to the Eastern Seaboard Cities.' Perhaps without meaning to, the Planning Director's vision was itself one of the major concerns local residents had about the Attwoods' deal. They were utterly, and it seemed to us quite rightly, opposed to Snow Shoe becoming a garbage pit for Philadelphia, New Jersey and New York.

In the last pages of the paper I turned to the recent federal case against IWS, commenting that it was during this time of trouble that Attwoods Environmental was born and that Attwoods PLC bought IWS, making Jack R. Casagrande an officer.[43] Not deterred by the firm's proven criminality, Attwoods welcomed Ralph Velocci as an officer just three weeks before IWS was fined.[44] I ended the caution by stating that a careful reading of IWS's history made it, and thus Attwoods, an unacceptable business for Centre County. That history, I added, should act as a 'red flag' to Pennsylvania's DER, as it now does to the county's residents.[45]

BOX PRODUCTIONS, LTD

Sometime in the autumn or winter I was contacted by a London television company called Box Productions which developed documentaries funded by and shown on Britain's Channel 4. Box was seeking information about an American and British scheme to dump toxic wastes abroad. The waste apparently moved from the US to northern Europe under false bills of lading, then was transhipped to the impoverished West African nation of Benin. There the military unloaded and trucked the waste north, dumping it near Benin's border with Niger. Box asked for my assistance in researching the Americans and eventually I signed on as a consultant for the project. I suggested to them the Attwoods' story, pointing out that because the then Prime Minister's husband, Denis Thatcher, was an Attwoods' director and shareholder, there should be considerable interest in Great Britain.[46] The Box group's first hurdle was research and development funding which had to be squeezed out of Channel 4. By the late winter and early spring the project had a budget.

In England, the Box people tackled Attwoods' formation, investigating the background of the British firm and its principals, determined when Thatcher came on board, and collected documents on the merger or buyout of IWS by Attwoods. In addition, they contacted American law enforcement agents in Florida and New York seeking information on any past or on-going investigations of IWS or its subsidiaries.

In central Pennsylvania the news that a British television firm was considering a documentary was passed to the protestors who were mildly encouraged but suspicious and sceptical of what impact it could have on stopping the Attwoods landfill. In order to accomplish this, local residents were working on their own ideas. One concerned changing township zoning regulations to keep out the landfill, another was a demand that DER investigate the effects of toxic-waste dumping at the Carlin landfill which was still running, not yet closed. A number of Mountaintop residents either witnessed or took part in toxic dumping in the area in the years before the creation of federal legislation outlawing it. Many drove tankers for local chemical companies and were directed, so they stated at public meetings and later before DER investigators, to dump toxic-laden tankers in different parts of Carlin's landfill.[47]

These admissions touched a number of quite sensitive local nerves – Carlin's, the chemical firms, the DER's regional office and developers anxious to have the new landfill which was potentially important for real-estate expansion in Centre County. These admissions of toxic-waste dumping meant the DER would have to investigate. Though none of the ex-drivers and none of the local protestors believed DER would actually ever find anything, they felt the time gained by this manoeuvre was itself important. The opinion of DER's obtuseness or collusion with R. S. Carlin in the matter of toxic-dumping was a standard of faith on the Mountaintop.

Box sent a reporter to the American side. His name was Adam Kemp and he already knew IWS was involved in some sort of imbroglio over a landfill in Ocala, and IWS officers Jack R. Casagrande and Ralph Velocci had probably bribed the mayor of Opa Locka, Florida, in order to secure the town's municipal garbage contract.[48] Florida looked very promising.

In New York attention was centred on Five Counties and especially on the recent federal investigation of private carting on Long

Island. Material from that probe, particularly those taped conversations between Avellino, his boss Corallo, 'Mimi' Fazzini, and other organised-crime figures active in private carting on Long Island which had been presented to the President's Commission on Organized Crime, was available.[49]

The Miami Police Department's Organized Crime Bureau along with the State Attorney's Office, having reason to believe that Opa Locka's Mayor John Riley was corrupt and involved in several illicit activities, successfully petitioned the Circuit Judge of the Eleventh Judicial District of Florida in 1985 for permission to wiretap two of Riley's phones. Calls from Jack R. Casagrande were monitored on 6, 7 and 8 November. The point of the calls, the police reported, was for IWS to secure Opa Locka's residential garbage business with special help from Riley.[50] IWS already enjoyed an exclusive license to haul Opa Locka's commercial trash. On 4 December Casagrande phoned Riley. That evening the City Commission met and 'voted to issue only Industrial Waste Services a license for commercial trash hauling'. The only dissenting voice was that of a Commissioner named George Lipkins.

The police and investigators from the State Attorney's Office then checked Riley's bank account and established that he was paid $6000 by Casagrande and Ralph Velocci back in September. The money was funnelled through their attorney's account.[51] Casagrande and Riley had other deals overhead on the phones, one of which involved a $3000 payment from Casagrande to the Mayor on 20 November.[52] Although this matter has yet to go to court, the evidence for bribery appears strong.

Resource Recovery – From Garbage to Gold

Opa Locka, however, was only a sideshow to what was taking place in Ocala. West of Daytona Beach and south of Gainesville, Ocala is a rapidly growing north-central Florida city situated in Marion County. Kemp discovered that IWS principals had been charged by the Statewide Prosecutor with several counts of racketeering, criminal conspiracy, grand theft and fraud.[53] Those accused include Jack R. Casagrande, Rocco Velocci, Morton Robson, Leslie Erber, Pericles Constantinou, IWS of Marion County (wholly owned by IWS), Urban Waste Disposal, and Waste Technology Corporation which was first known as BW Energy Systems. Marion County was incensed, believing it was the victim of a waste-to-energy scam which began in Florida in the summer of 1981.[54]

The Marion County affair, it would turn out, proved beyond a shadow of a doubt that the deepest fears of Snow Shoe residents were correct. When all the fancy talk was over, the promises made to run an environmentally-sound operation with so-called 'state-of-the-art' technology were hollow. Instead, it would be people associated with organised crime running the landfill and their major past experience in 'advanced' landfill management was the outrage in Marion County.[55]

At the heart of the matter was a fairy-tale machine called a pyrolytic converter certified to be able to convert garbage into a form of usable energy. Of course it couldn't. In fact, the particular machine promised by Casagrande and associates to Marion County represented a swindle of long standing. It was also one in which racketeer Mel Cooper played a central part; and he wasn't the only mobster involved.[56] That Cooper was wrapped up in some way with the dream machine was clear as soon as Kemp received the first documents from Ocala. One of the firms charged was Waste Technology which had begun corporate life as BW Energy Systems. A 1978 Dun & Bradstreet report on Cooper Funding noted that Cooper officials appear as principals in BW Energy Systems, Lexington Avenue, New York. This firm, the report went on to say, had the 'marketing rights to a pyrolysis system'.

The conspiracy began in approximately 1975 when a couple of shady entrepreneurs, Les Erber and Perry Constantinou, joined with Mel Cooper and two of his salesmen, Phil Gentile and Edward Vanasco, to establish BW Energy and market a pyrolytic converter.[57] Theoretical development had been undertaken by the Duke Engineering Company of Santa Ana, California. Duke Engineering's backing came from actor John Wayne, hence its title. They pyrolytic system was called the DECO process. Orval Gould, an engineer with his own company called Enterprise, came on the scene sometime in 1974 to actually build a pilot DECO system and then to handle future DECO manufacturing. Patent rights, for whatever they were worth, remained with Duke Wayne's firm; most importantly, though, marketing rights went to BW Energy.

In December 1975 a test of DECO in a modified version was held in Santa Ana for the benefit of Los Angeles County Sanitation Districts. A report was issued by John D. Parkhurst, Chief Engineer and General Manager for the county districts. Parkhurst described the system and stated the following: 'During the demonstration, approximately 100 lbs. of shredded household refuse was introduced into the unit over an approximate 2-hour period. . . . Approximately

41 pounds of oil was produced.'[58] Gould, Parkhurst remarked, also claimed that Enterprise had recently 'received a signed contract from a New York City-based refuse collector for design, furnishing and construction of a completed DECO system plant capable of processing 150 tons-per-day of household refuse'. This contract was reportedly with Five Counties, and demonstrated how early its pyrolytic involvement started.[59] Gould, trying to influence the guests, added that the system bound for New York at a cost of about $5 million was guaranteed to be operational in six months.

Parkhurst may have been impressed, but his conclusions were guarded. The test, he noted, was of a small prototype and thus the system needed to be demonstrated on a large-scale basis; certain technical details were not disclosed; and there was no data on air emissions. His last words were unintentionally prophetic as no system was ever successfully built and deployed; 'Completion and operational review of the proposed New York installation will provide a great deal of information to assist in future evaluation of the DECO system.'

The outline of the scam that would proceed for over a decade was set. Gould would supposedly try but constantly fail to build the machine while Cooper and the other 'fast-money boys' turned to fund-raising and marketing. Within a year BW raised $610,000 from the Casagrandes and their associates. One of the sellers was Mort Robson and he claimed in a 1987 Deposition in the Ocala case, that he was concerned, hoping the prototype actually worked. He seems to have been especially anxious that it wasn't a fraud because these were Italians in the garbage industry who might strongly (the implication was extra-legally) object. His apprehension concerned whether the oil was actually produced through pyrolysis or had been placed at the end of a phoney process of conversion: like salting a gold mine, he put it.[60]

The 'Italian garbage men' now on board as investors soon formed a company to handle pyrolysis. According to Robson, Rocco Velocci assumed the leadership of F & W Energy Resources which itself owned about 44 per cent of Urban Waste Disposal. Robson re-collected F & W's share of Urban's stock was held in Rocco's name but he was only acting as a nominee for the F & W group.[61]

Among the new documents Kemp accumulated in this second phase of research was the State of Delaware's Certificate of Incorporation of F & W. It was formed on 25 November 1975, the same year as BW. Indeed, its date of incorporation preceded by almost a

month the first pyrolysis test in Santa Ana. This surely points to a
mature plan already at work among the Casagrande/Velocci group
in league with Cooper and his associates including Robson, despite
Robson's misty recollections. Rocco Velocci was F & W's president,
Carl Casagrande its vice-president, and John Casagrande (the head
of Five Counties) the firm's secretary. Among the shareholders were
the other officers of Five Counties and World Sanitation, the officers
of IWS including Albert Casagrande, Jack R. Casagrande, Ralph
Velocci and John Lawson. The Long Island Rubbish crowd was
represented in F & W by 'Perry' Persichilli and Michael Perna. There
were still more New York area carters with shaky backgrounds in
F & W.[62]

Whether it was F & W Energy or BW Energy, the point was to flog
this failed pyrolytic converter somewhere using here and there the
always-unfulfilled (although never so stated) Five Counties' contract as proof that big-time waste entrepreneurs had signed on.
Erber, Constantinou and Rocco Velocci seem to have been the most
energetic salesmen. Velocci's efforts are of compelling interest.

Avellino's Role

In the spring of 1980 reporter Mark McIntyre of Long Island's most
comprehensive newspaper, *Newsday*, wrote about a proposal by a
group of Long Island carters led by Rocco Velocci to 'erect small
resource-recovery plants that would extract oil from garbage in
Smithtown and Freeport'. Another outspoken partisan of pyrolysis,
McIntyre commented, was Sal Avellino.[63]

Opposing the plan was David Sussman of the Environmental
Protection Agency who held that pyrolysis didn't work. Sussman
added, 'there are no pyrolysis plants heating garbage to produce oil
in commercial operation in existence anywhere'. That negative opinion didn't deter either Avellino or his associate Velocci who had
both presented to Smithtown Supervisor, the Honorable Patrick R.
Vecchio, their plan which was accompanied by supposedly positive
pyrolytic test data developed by the firm of Burns & Roe of Paramus,
New Jersey. A further meeting was scheduled between the Supervisor and the pyrolytic enthusiasts.[64]

Adam Kemp and I called Smithtown and found that Vecchio was
still its Supervisor. He clearly remembered the incident and kindly
agreed to meet us. Before moving to Smithtown he had been a New
York police officer whose speciality was liaising with the US Secret

Service. Vecchio guarded Presidents and Prime Ministers; nothing
fazed him. He told us the decisive meeting he had had with Velocci
and Avellino. By then he knew the pyrolytic converter was nothing
but junk. None the less, Avellino pushed its potential, citing the need
Smithtown had to get on the right side of the issue, 'to play ball'.
Vecchio flared at the implied threat and kicked both Avellino and
Velocci out of his office.[65]

Vecchio gave us copies of an 'Analysis of DECO Process' done by
the Town Engineer, Donal A. Devine, and submitted on 28 April
1980. Devine 'reviewed the material submitted by Mr Rocco Velocci
and Mr Sal Avellino' and concluded that the Burns & Roe report was
'incomplete, often vague, contains no economic data and certainly
is not comprehensive enough to permit an in-depth engineering
judgement as to the reliability of the system.' Interestingly, Devine
noted the system under discussion was examined in Los Angeles
County and owned by BW Energy. There was no mention of F & W.[66]

The Avellino/Velocci team representing either or both BW Energy (Velocci held over 68,000 shares of it) and F & W (Velocci was
its president, Carl Casagrande its vice-president and John Casagrande
its secretary) had more success in getting a pyrolytic converter
contract from the town of Freeport on Long Island. But, as it was
explained to us, some Freeport officials had been financially encouraged.[67] The necessary analysis of pyrolysis was conducted by the son
of an important town official. He had studied chemistry in high
school, and had, in fact, graduated and was judged more than adequate to review the material. Reportedly, he thought it looked
pretty good. Though Freeport was apparently ready, the machine
wasn't; Gould had yet to build it.

Obviously there wasn't much money coming in for those on the
marketing end. Thus BW Energy decided to offer the public a chance
to purchase stock in a successor company – Waste Technology. A
public offering was prepared and various so-called experts in new
waste-disposal technologies were made members of an Advisory
Committee purely for the purpose of the promotion and offer. In
addition, the underwriter insisted on selecting one company director. The individual chosen was the founder of SCA Services Inc.,
once the third largest waste-disposal company in the US. Left
unmentioned, for obvious reasons, was SCA's history of fraud by
its top officers and benumbing associations with organised crime.
Waste Technology's officers were Erber and Robson (there from the
beginning), the underwriter's man and two other new ones. They

were Bert Greenglass, formerly with the Department of Energy where he was Director of the Office of Energy from Municipal Waste, and Howard E. Morse, a public-relations man. It was pointed out that Morse had been a communications consultant for BW since its founding in 1975. He, therefore, may have been responsible for such nonsense as found in a booklet Kemp located called *The Garbage into Oil Book*. It contained such ludicrous statements as:

> With our system, the end of garbage is only the beginning. The Enterprise Pyrolytic Conversion System. It destroys garbage. And it creates fuels.
>
> Now is when the Enterprise Pyrolytic Conversion System is available.
>
> You won't have to make any explanations about why the system you're interested in needs 'further development'.
>
> You won't have to sit through a 2-year, or 3-year, or 4-year delivery lag.
>
> One of our 150-ton-per-day systems will be converting solid waste for Nassau County in early 1982. . . .
>
> Just call Perry Constantinou or Les Erber at (212) 697–4760;
> Or write:
>
> BW Energy Systems, Inc.
> 420 Lexington Avenue
> New York, New York 10017

In 1982, the F & W/BW Energy/Waste Technology/World Sanitation/IWS/IWS Marion County/Urban Waste Disposal/Five Counties entrepreneurs were busy trying to sell their machine in the midwest, to the city of Franklin, Ohio. On 21 October 1982 William Leone as Five Counties' treasurer wrote to Franklin's City Manager asking him to confirm 'our [Five Counties] Franklin bid deposit for F & W Energy Resources'. About six months later, the waste-to-energy game in Franklin appeared over. As an officer now of F & W Energy, Leone was informed by the environmental scientist for the Southwestern Ohio Air Pollution Control Agency: 'Unless we receive the required detailed process data information and calculations to support your application within the next thirty (30) days, your application will be processed for denial.'[68] The Ohio venture came to naught although there may yet be pending the disposition of fraud charges against one or more of the scam's principals.[69]

To more easily understand the interlocking corporate ties see Figure 4.1 below.

For years the marketing of the converter was clearly hampered by the unalterable fact of its non-existence. It was Ocala which finally bit hard, believing no doubt that the machine was real, soon on its way, lacking only a nut here and bolt there. When Marion County finally determined it was the victim of a massive fraud, Florida officials charged that Les Erber along with Rocco Velocci and Jack R. Casagrande false told the Marion County Commission that 'ten million dollars had been invested in research and development of the Enterprise Company pyrolytic converter; that fifty-ton-per-day horizonal pyrolytic converters would be delivered; that IWS handles fourteen hundred tons of garbage per day in Florida and New York'.[70] Moreover, they 'misrepresented' that the system 'would produce one barrel of marketable oil per ton of solid waste' and that the gas would be 'pipeline grade'. Florida officials also noted the conspirators didn't report their failure to secure environmental permits in Ohio, and that the principals of the several companies involved including Urban Waste Disposal (the primary actor in Ocala) were also the principals in BW Energy, and so on.

Among the score of listed lies and misrepresentations, perhaps none was more telling than those gleaned from 'the private placement memorandum for Urban Waste Disposal Associates of Marion County'. This document 'failed to report the environmental problems that plagued the Enterprise Company pyrolytic conversion system', and that whatever oil this system produced was of such inferior quality that it could not be marketed 'and, as such, it was toxic waste'.[71] This certainly was the bottom line – the machine that turned garbage into gold couldn't be built beyond the prototype stage and even then its product wasn't gold but toxic waste.

Back to London

We summarised what we had found. IWS and its major officers were convicted of 'restraining trade' in Dade County; very likely bribed the Mayor of Opa Locka; and in Ocala were charged in this complex fraud which revealed long-standing ties to major organised-crime figures such as Mel Cooper and Sal Avellino. IWS and its officers were part of a garbage 'racketeering milieu' which stretched from New York to California and Florida.[72] Back Kemp went to London laden with documents, eager to begin filming. The sleuthing paid off

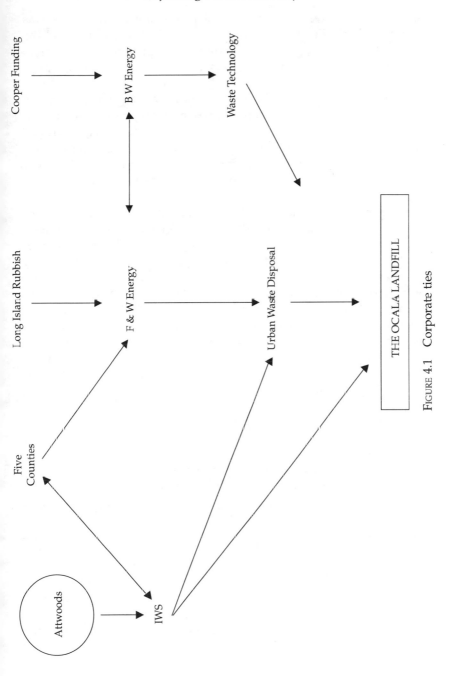

FIGURE 4.1   Corporate ties

and Channel 4 agreed to move the project forward. Money was allocated and a shooting schedule was worked out. Kemp and the rest of Box Productions hoped the film would prove disconcerting to Prime Minister Thatcher. There was an initial eagerness to confront Denis Thatcher.

The film schedule called for Kemp, Sean McPhilemy, the head of Box, a presenter (commentator we would call him) named John Plender who doubled as a reporter for the London *Financial Times*, and a crew of three to film in Florida, New York and Pennsylvania. In Pennsylvania the Box team was to interview several of the Snow Shoe protestors and me as an 'expert' on organised crime and the garbage industry. After some evasive action to get rid of Carlin security people the interviews went smoothly. Phase one was over.

The next day's schedule called for an on-camera interview with me. I said IWS seemed to me mobster-connected. They had a record as garbage racketeers and spent over a decade in a very shady business with Mel Cooper among others. I thought it was also quite vital and meaningful that Sal Avellino of the Lucchese crime syndicate worked with them or rather with Rocco Velocci on behalf of them. Soon the crew was putting the equipment away and I was explaining how best to drive to New York. My part was finished. There was still quite a lot of work for Box – filming in New York, writing a proper script, editing the film, voice-overs, publicity and scheduling the show.

Changes in Tone: Continuing Developments

My agenda called for a long trip to Holland during which time the programme was supposed to be transmitted. I kept in touch with Box but in these conversations there now appeared an increasing uneasiness. I was in fact discouraged from travelling to London in order to see the show. The scheduling wasn't clear and lawyers for Attwoods were meeting with lawyers for Channel 4. There were objections to many things, although it was still to go ahead. I was told that many script revisions were demanded. Eventually, it became clear that my on-camera contribution had been dropped.

I couldn't see the show and would simply have to wait until returning to the States for a copy. The film entitled 'A Special Relationship' was transmitted the first week in July and a story by John Plender followed in the *Financial Times*.[73] I avidly read the short report which was briefly touched on some of the main points discovered so laboriously. Plender wrote: 'A Downing Street spokes-woman said the Prime Minister's office never discussed the affairs of the Prime Minister's husband.'

At the end of July I finally watched the film at home on video tape. There was no doubt that Box had done a competent job. None the less it seemed tame, to lacked bite, and the Thatcher/Attwoods' people came through better than we expected. It was not the film I thought it would be and I doubted that it affected the Thatchers or Attwoods much at all. In one post-film conversation I heard that Attwood's stock took a mild beating on the London market follow-ing the show. Not very impressive after all that work, I thought, and the film and accompanying story appeared to have had no discern-ible impact in Centre County.

There were, however, local developments which had the capacity to change materially the situation for the better. Over the course of the year since the paper was written and distributed, the attitude in Centre County towards landfill problems and particularly oppor-tunities changed. For several months at least, the local paper re-ported on negotiations between solid-waste officials in Centre County and those from neighbouring Clinton County. They were discussing a new venture which would mean that Centre County rubbish would go to an expanded Clinton County landfill. There was no mention of Attwoods in these talks.[74] In mid-August a formal agreement was reached between the two counties which seemed to preclude Attwoods from the regional market.

Meanwhile, though, Attwoods continued to pursue its DER per mit for the Snow Shoe property. This naturally raised in my mind ever more strongly that Attwood's intention was to secure their landfill for 'out-of-state' garbage even though their State College area representative, Hal Johnson, had categorically promised at sev-eral public meetings that this just wasn't so. This landfill, he had said, was strictly for Centre County trash. But if this was truly so, and Centre County had decided to move in another direction, then what would Attwoods do when and if DER approved their permit? Several interviews with Bob Donaldson of Centre County's Solid-Waste Authority and Mike Reeder from the DER's regional office in Williamsport, which reviews and passes on landfill permits, indicate that both believe Attwoods will probably have a difficult time ob-taining its permit. Donaldson seems most strongly opposed, won-dering also where the trash for an 800-ton-per-day landfill will come from, given Attwood's mandatory enumeration of potential customers on its application. Without State College and a few of the other larger towns in the area, there is not enough waste generated in the region to come close to the 800-ton figure. Donaldson did point out, however, that Attwoods had listed one transfer station which was located some distance from the region and which com-pacted New York area waste as a potential customer. But, as he further noted, this certainly would violate Attwood's year-long pres-entation to local residents and the various county authorities and might prove an insurmountable hurdle for the firm's application.[75]

Reeder also seems sceptical of Attwoods' chances for a permit for much the same reasons Donaldson mentioned, at least one based on their original unmodified application.[76] None the less, there is no sign that Attwoods (which has never had an office in Centre County and is thus extremely hard to find in Pennsylvania) is pulling out of the process. In fact, they have recently submitted phase 2 of their application despite their lack of success so far in having phase 1 approved. This is not, I've been told, the usual procedure. The pro-cess continues, although undoubtedly most important changes have occurred during the year.

These weren't the summer's only interesting modifications. For instance, Marion County, which had been offered $15 million by the defendants to settle the landfill, fraud and racketeering problems, turned it down.[77] And in New York a series of innovative law-enforcement moves as well as the settlement of a federal civil suit filed in the winter of 1985 were perhaps more significant for my purposes. The 1985 case was partially resolved when 'seventeen Long Island carters charged with conspiracy to carve up Long Is-land's garbage collection business' agreed to refund several million dollars to municipalities they were charged with defrauding. It was the 'property rights' system, which New York's Attorney General argued, in this case began in 1977. Among those admitting no wrong-doing but promising not to do it again and to pay restitution was Five Counties.[78]

This was small beer when compared with the government's next move announced on 7 June 1989. The US Attorney for the Eastern District of New York filed a civil racketeering complaint against the Lucchese and Gambino crime syndicates, the PSI, Teamster Local 813 and several score carting companies and individuals.[79] This first federal suit against an entire industry was designed to rid 'the rack-eteering influence of organised crime' over the Long Island rubbish trade. It aims to eliminate the Teamsters Union and PSI from the industry as well as to finally force individual defendants out of garbage carting. In this most dramatic manoeuvre, several firms of particular interest were charged, including the Velocci stronghold South Side Carting, another Casagrande company called Hillside Carting, operated and controlled by Pasquale (Patsy) Casagrande and Peter Reali, and Long Island Rubbish. Hillside's business address was only doors from Five Counties, I should add.[80]

Also in the summer of 1989 New York authorities chared Rocco Velocci with falsifying business records. In particular, New York officials claimed that he failed to list his 1986 Florida indictment as required by New York law when he, as an officer of Five Counties , bid for a rubbish contract with the Long Island Rail Road (LIRR) in 1987.[81] The LIRR is owned by the Metropolitan Transit Authority, 'a government instrumentality of the State of New York'. According to the terms of the contract, failure to answer correctly several questions, including 'Does your firm, or any principal, director, officer, or shareholder owning 10 per cent or more of the stock of the corporation, or managerial employee thereof in connection with the business of the firm or any other firm which is related by common ownership, control or otherwise, have pending an indictment in the state of New York or any other jurisdiction for the commission of a crime which has not been terminated in favour of the firm's principal, director, officer, shareholder or managerial employee', places one under 'penalty of perjury'.[82]

There is certainly no doubt about the 'milieu' within which the firms bought by Attwoods operate. It is also obvious that studying them gives us a rare insight into a range of rubbish-related crimes. But nothing is ultimately quite so significant, in my estimation, as the light their activities shed on an aspect of resource recovery. The realisation that certain resource-recovery operations have been spawned if not captured early on by organised crime must give all pause for thought when considering so-called 'new advanced technological' solutions to pressing environmental problems.[83]

Notes

1. This was originally submitted as testimony to the Pennsylvania State Senate, Committee on Environmental Resources and Energy, *Hearing: Waste Industry Disclosure Law*, Harrisburg, PA., 13 February 1990.
2. 'Atwoods [sic] Takes 1st Step to Get Landfill Permit', *Centre Daily*

Times: 'Atwoods [*sic*] Inc. of Miami is taking . . . samples in Snowshoe Township for a landfill application . . . many residents of the Mountaintop area have said they oppose the Atwoods [*sic*] landfill. . . . Atwoods [*sic*] is the U.S. branch of Atwoods [*sic*] PLC, an English company involved in waste management and quarries. If the project in Snow Shoe is approved, it would be the company's first in America' (3 September 1988); '2 Mountaintop Residents Ask for Landfill Hearing', *Centre Daily Times*: 'Two Mountaintop residents asked Centre County commissioners yesterday to hold a public hearing on proposed landfill developments and on reports of chemical dumping in the Mountaintop area' (17 August 1988); 'New Landfill Proposed, Snow Shoe Site Targeted, But It Won't Take Philly Trash', *Centre Daily Times*: 'A Miami-based solid waste management firm . . . Snow Shoe Township Supervisor Paul Veneziano . . . emphasized, however, that Johnson [Hal Johnson] a State college-based representative of Attwoods, Inc., told the board that the proposed landfill would be receiving trash from Centre County and surrounding counties – "and definitely would not be taking any Philadelphia trash."'. Attwoods Files Paperwork to Develop Waste Landfill in Snow Shoe', *Centre Daily Times*, 11 April 1989; 'Mountaintop Moves to Block Landfills', *Centre Daily Times*, 8 April 1989; 'Snow Shoe Area Landfill promoted', *Centre Daily Times*: 'Hal Johnson, regional vice president for Attwoods Inc. of Miami . . . said . . . All of the waste would come from Centre and surrounding counties. None of it would be hauled in from Philadelphia or another large metropolitan areas . . .'; 'Trash Problem Acts as Call to Arms on Mountaintop', *Centre Daily Times*, 8 April 1989.

3.   Video-taped public meeting in which discussion is held about 'DER and Chemical Dumping', 11 May 1989. The meeting was held at the Snow Shoe skating rink. In a taped interview with Mountaintop residents conducted on 18 March 1989 the following statements were made about the DER: 'And what they've done over the years is they have compromised; they've compromised their butts into a real sling. And part of the problem has come out, especially in our own regional office . . . a lot of the individuals . . . have had so many dealings with industry, and have backed down, and have actually covered up different things that have occurred, and that they've known about that now they're scared to death to even be open or honest because they're afraid their own butt is going to end up in front of a judge somewhere. . . . A citizen's group to them doesn't know anything, doesn't count for anything. It's just a burr under their saddle. . . . But DER, because of their relationship with industry, has now found itself in a position that if any of the individuals step up to stop industry, the industry could blow the whistle on them. . . . I worked for the company in State College when some of this [toxic waste dumping] was going on. I was driving tractor trailer for them. . . . Nease Chemical Company. . . . The situation there was DER told them the regs are heavy, you better get this out of here. And they allowed them to get it out of here. And they brought it to the mountaintop area. . . . Hauled it in tankers. . . . The head of the regional office even followed the tankers from Nease Chemical up here to the mountain and watched them dump.'

Also see document received from Snow Shoe residents in May 1988 with information about 'extensive dumping . . . on the Snow Shoe, Pa. quadrangle, . . . on land of the Carlin Coal Company'. The document is compiled by individuals who worked for the American Color and Chemical Company, Lock Haven, PA. Appended to this is a long list of individuals that 'took part in, . . . chemical dumping in the Mountaintop area'.

'New Chemical Dumping Charge Leveled', *Centre Daily Times*: 'A 4,000-gallon tank of industrial waste was hauled from the former Nease Chemical Co. in College Township and buried in a trench in an abandoned R. S. Carlin strip-mine in Snow Shoe Township about 14 years ago, a former supervisor of the Carlin landfill [Andy Seprish] says. . . . Seprish's story is backed by Athol Burfield of Snow Shoe, who said he was the Carlin bulldozer operator who excavated the hole for the tank. . . . The state Department of Environmental Resources earlier this week began interviewing former Carlin workers. The workers said they frequently hauled industrial waste, both from Nease Chemical and from the former American Aniline Co. of Lock Haven, and disposed of the material in a half dozen different Carlin strip-mines in the neighbouring Mountaintop-area municipalities of Snow Shoe and Burnside townships' (6 April 1988).

4.   'Atwoods [*sic*] Takes 1st Step to Get Landfill Permit', *Centre Daily Times*, 3 September 1988.

5.   'ARTICLE OF AGREEMENT FOR SALE OF LAND, made 8 January 1988 by and between R. S. Carlin, a Pennsylvania corporation, of Snow Shoe, Centre County, . . . and ATTWOODS INC., a Delaware corporation with its office and principal place of business at 3225 Aviation Avenue, Coconut Grove, Florida, . . . D. Buyer is in the business of solid waste disposal and is desirous of purchasing the property from Seller . . . for the purpose of securing a permit for the disposal on the premises of solid waste consisting of municipal and industrial waste. . . '. (p. 14), '*Successors and Assigns.* Buyer may assign this agreement to any corporation that is a wholly-owned subsidiary of buyer or of buyer's sold stockholder, provided however, that Buyer shall remain liable for payment of any and all royalties pursuant to paragraph 5 hereof. . . .' (signing for Attwoods Inc. was M. Kenneth Foreman, President, and Ralph Velocci, Vice-President).

6.   Rowe & Pitman, 1 Finsbury Avenue, London, EC2M 2PA, 'R & P Miscellaneous, Attwoods', in which it is reported that 'Because the opportunities for major expansion in the U.K. were limited, Attwoods turned its attractions to the U.S. . . . Industrial Waste Services Inc. (IWS) was thus acquired . . . in November [1984]' (14 February 1985) p. 5; SECURITIES AND EXCHANGE COMMISSION, Form 20-F, ANNUAL REPORT for the fiscal year ended 31 July 1988, Commission File number 015350, ATTWOODS PLC, 'United States Operations, *Industrial Waste Service Inc., (IWSI)*. Acquired in November 1984, . . .' (p. 5).

7.   United States District Court, Southern District of Florida, United States of America *v.* Industrial Waste Service Inc.; Lewis R. Goodman; and John E. Lawson, *Indictment* No. 85–61940–CR–Gonzalez, 7 November 1985; United States District Court, Southern District of Florida, Fort

Lauderdale Division, United States of America *v.* David Hoopen-gardner, *Indictment* No. 84–6107–CR–JLK, 26 July 1984.

8.   USA *v.* David Hoopengardner, Voluntary Statement of Particulars, 1 November 1984, p. 4.

9.   USA *v.* Industrial Waste Services, Inc., No. 85–61940–CR–Gonzalez.

10.   USA *v.* Industrial Waste Services, Voluntary Statement of Particulars, 10 January 1986, p. 10.

11.   United States District Court, Southern District of Florida, *Finding & Judgement*: Lewis R. Goodman, **Guilty**; John E. Lawson, **Guilty**, 6 February 1987; David Hoopengardner, **Guilty**, 25 April 1986; Indus-trial Waste Service, Inc., **Guilty**, 24 October 1986; Waste Management Inc. of Florida d/b/a United Sanitation Service, **Guilty**, 15 January 1988.

12.   Florida Department of Law Enforcement, 'Special Report – Garbage & Recycling Industry in Florida: Independent Operations, Dade County' (August 1973) np.

13.   Nassau County Police Department, Organized Crime Unit, 'Thomas Lucchese Family – Laratro, Joseph', FBI No. 263439D, n.d.; Investiga-tors, Inc. to Mr William R. Fusselman, Senior Vice-President, First Equity of Florida, 'Report of Investigation – Inquiry Concerning Pos-sible Mafia Associations on the Part of the Principals of Industrial Waste Service (Miami, Florida) and Five Counties Carting Company (Jamaica, New York)', 3 November 1983, p. 4.

14.   Interview with *Orlando Sentinel* reporter Victoria Churchville.

15.   County of Nassau Police Department, 'Organized Crime in the Rub-bish Carting Industry' (24 November 1967); City of New York Police Department, Organized-Crime Control Bureau, 'The Long Island Arena' (25 August 1975); New York *Newsday*, 'Cahn Probes Reports of Garbage-Mob Link' (22 December 1967); US Department of Justice, Federal Bureau of Investigation, 'Criminal Influence in Nassau County Private Sanitation Industry –NY 92 5026,' (April 1968, pp. 1–3; US Department of Justice, Federal Bureau of Investigation, 'Criminal In-fluence in the Suffolk County Private Sanitation Industry – NY 92 5025,' (April 1968, p. 1).

16.   New York State Commission of Investigation, 'The Multi-Town Solid Waste Management Authority and the Crisis of Solid Waste Manage-ment' (October 1984) pp. 76–7.

17.   Suffolk County Police Department, 'Intelligence Squad Case 114–67', 28 February 1968.

18.   President's Commission on Organized Crime, *Organized Crime and Labor-Management Racketeering in the United States: Record of Hearing VI*, 22–4 April 1985, Chicago, Illinois (Government Printing Office, April 1985) pp. 545, 547–560.

19.   Ibid.

20.   United States, Department of Justice, Federal Bureau of Investigation, 'Criminal Influence in Private Sanitation – Suffolk County', Bureau File 92–10750: 'Interviews of the following three persons: Nicholas Ferrante, John Pagano, Salvatore 'Bud' Maggio'; 'Interview of Nicholas Ferrante' by SAS John K. Egan and William J. Quinn, 15 December 1975, pp. 3–7.

21. Private Sanitation Industry, Roster of Regular Members, 4th Anniversary Edition 1983, James J. Corrigan, Jr Executive Director, One Huntington Quadrangle, Suite 1609, Melville, LI. 11747; Private Sanitation Industry Association Nassau/Suffolk, Inc. 1983 Board of Directors', p.1; Waste Removal Institute of Nassau, 50 Eads Street, West Babylon, New York 11704, 'Firm Membership', Five Counties Carting (John Casagrande); Jamaica Ash (Mimi Fazzini); Long Island Rubbish ([Fiore] Perry Persichilli).

22. Kings County District Attorney's Office, *Papers*, 'Stockholders of World Sanitation of Nassau Inc. with their Present Addresses from 1971 Through September 1978 – Consolidated with 5 Counties Carting Corp.: John-Lawson, Rocco Velocci, Ralph Velocci, Jack R. Casagrande, Jack Casagrande, Carl Casagrande, Albert Casagrande, Rocco Casagrande, Vito Tropiano, Romano Celli (retired Feb 26/74)'.

23. President's Commission on Organized Crime, op. cit.; County of Nassau Police Department, op. cit.; FBI NY 92 5025, op. cit., and NY 92 5026, op. cit.

24. '1979 List of Private Carting Companies which have Permits in the Town of Hempstead, North Hempstead and Oyster Bay', p. 2 (list kept in the Kings County District Attorney's office, Rackets Squad File Room).

25. Suffolk County Police Department, 'Intelligence Squad Case 114–67' (28 February 1968), under the heading 'Members or Associates of Organized Crime' it lists 'John "Joe" Morea B/13823 – "may be part owner of Long Island Rubbish and Jamaica Ash and Rubbish which handles large portions of Nassau supermarkets"'. Supreme Court of the State of New York, County of Suffolk, The People of the State of New York *v.* Arthur Romsera and Vito Biondo, *Indictment* No. 1476–84, *Count One*: 'Throughout the period of the conspiracy, Fiore Persichilli was a principal of Long Island Rubbish Removal, Inc., and a member of the Board of Directors of PSI [Private Sanitation Industry], with specific authority to authorize expenditures out of its funds. . . . The aforesaid Grand Jury, by this indictment, accuses the defendants of the crime of Bribe Receiving in the Second Degree. . . . From on or about August 18, 1982 through in or about December 1983, the defendants, both public servants, . . . accepted . . . $12,000 in monetary contributions . . . from the Private Sanitation Industry Association of Nassau/Suffolk Inc., . . . Fiore Persichilli, Salvatore Avellino, Jr., and others' (pp. 1–7). Indictment brought by New York State Organised Crime Task Force, 1984.

26. '1979 List of Private Carting Companies', op. cit., p. 4.

27. Suffolk County Police Dept., 'Intelligence Squad Case', op. cit.

28. '1979 List of Private Carting Companies', op. cit., p. 5.

29. Ibid., pp. 3, 6.

30. Investigators, Inc., op. cit.; 'Private Sanitation Industry Association 1983 Board of Directors', op. cit., p. 1; President's Commission, op. cit.; County of Nassau Police Department, op. cit.; FBI, NY 92–5025, op. cit., and NY 92–5026, op. cit.; US District Court, Southern District of Florida, **Finding & Judgement**, Industrial Waste Service, Inc., **Guilty**, 24 October 1986.

31.   Florida Department of Law Enforcement, 'Special Report – Garbage &
       Recycling Industry in Florida', Independent operations, Dade County;
       Naranja Sanitation Service Corporation': 'the Laratro's purchased
       Naranja Sanitation from Salvatore (Sam) Rizzo, . . . financed by the
       Teamsters Union. David and Thomas Laratro are the sons of Joseph
       Laratro, an identified lieutenant in the New York Lucchese LCN "fam-
       ily" now headed by Carmine Tramunti' (August 1973, np); Investiga-
       tors, Inc., op. cit., 3 November 1983, p. 4.
32.   Supreme Court of the State of New York held in and for the County of
       New York 'The People of the State of New York: *Plaintiffs, against*:
       Vincent J. Squillante *et al., Defendants*, 'Ordered, Adjudged and De-
       creed that the defendants in Schedule "A", are hereby perpetually
       enjoined, restrained and prohibited from: (A) Agreeing, combining
       and/or conspiring together with another to restrain competition . . .
       (C) Agreeing, combining and/or conspiring together with another to
       persuade, coerce or intimidate by means of threats or otherwise, . . .
       with, . . . any person, firm, . . . in the service or business of private
       collection, removal, or disposal of garbage, refuse, rubbish . . . *Schedule
       "A" – Schedule of Consenting Defendants*, pp. 1–8, filed 8 July 1959; and
       People of the State of New York, *Plaintiffs, against*: Vincent J. Squillante
       et al., Defendants, Verified Complaint, Index no. 41871/1957.
33.   US Department of Justice, Federal Bureau of Investigation, 'Cooper
       Funding/Limited – Racketeer Influenced and Corrupt Organizations;
       Mail Fraud; Fraud by Wire', Bureau File no. 1833–905, Field Office File
       no. 183–362 (30 March 1977).
34.   Ibid. Robson interviewed 1 June 1977 by SA L. M. Grob; author's
       interview with Churchville, op. cit.; 'Certificate of Incorporation of
       Urban Waste Disposal, Inc.' under Section 402 of the Business Cor-
       poration Law, New York, 28 April 1977; State of Florida, Department
       of State, 'Application by Foreign Corporation for Authorization to
       Transact Business in Florida, Urban Waste Disposal, Inc.', filed 12
       April 1982; 'Attachment to Urban Waste Disposal, Inc., Application by
       Foreign Corporation for Authorization to Transact Business in Florida':
       Names of Officers – Les Erba, John Jennings, Perry Constantinou, Mort
       Robson, Rocco P. Velocci, C. Ray Greene; *Names of Directors* – Les Erba
       [*sic*], Perry Constantinou, Rocco P. Velocci, Jack R. Casagrande, 12
       April 1982.
            Dan Guido, 'Commission OKs Waste Contract', *Ocala Star-Banner*,
       17 April 1982, p. 1A; Dan Guido, 'Grand Jury Inquiry Sought to Clear
       Air', *Ocala Star-Banner*, 20 April 1982, p. 1A; Dan Guido, 'Three Com-
       missioners Say Federal Waste Probe Best', *Ocala Star-Banner*, 5 May
       1982.
35.   FBI, File no. NY 183–362, op. cit.; List of Lessee; Type of Equipment;
       Vendor; Lease Number in Cooper Funding Limited, 'Racketeering
       Influenced and Corrupt Organizations', . . . Lease no. 75–332; *Vendor*
       Cartmen's Container Corporation, 172–33 Douglas Avenue, Jamaica,
       New York. State of New York, City of New York, County of New
       York, State of New York, *Plaintiff, v.* Salem Sanitary Carting Corp., *et
       al., Defendants*, Affidavit of Service of Summons and Complaint, Index

no. CV 85–0208; '. . . on the 23rd day of January, 1985 at No. 172–33 Douglas Avenue, City of Jamaica, Queens, City of New York, . . . he served the foregoing Summons and Complaint on Five Counties Carting Corp' (11 February 1985).

36. FBI, File no. NY 183–362, op. cit.: interview of Edward Vanasco by SA L. M. Grob, 12 January 1977; 'Vanasco stated that a lease was arranged by Phil Gentile, Cooper Funding, between George Briggerman, Briggerman Sanitation, Los Alamitos, California (Seal Beach Section), and an unknown bank for 10 garbage trucks on November 1975. Vanasco advised that the above package amounted to a total of 10 leases (1 truck per lease). . . . Vanasco stated that the banks had actually turned down the leases and the Cooper Funding refused to refund Briggerman's advanced payments.'

37. Ibid., p. 54a: interview with Edward Vanasco by SA L. M. Grob, 26 April 1977; Vanasco stated Cooper worked with organised crime figures 'Joe Lombardo', 'Sal Sindone' (officer of the Brooklyn Trade Waste Association) – 'Vanasco stated that according to Joel Cooper a meeting occurred approximately 8 months ago between Tony (LNU) of the Brooklyn Trade Waste Association, Sindone and Mel Cooper'. New York State Senate Select Committee on Crime, 'Papers on Cooper Funding' (from Suffolk County Police, identified by Committee Counsel); 'GJ-1 reported in July (see July 7 memo re: Petrizzo–Mancuso) Mancuso and Petrizzo were incensed over Cooper Funding with its lending of money to the late Sal Spatarella [organized crime figure]. . . . Both men were particularly incensed because they discovered that a hidden owner of Cooper Funding was a Sam Galasso, former president of the Brooklyn Trade Waste Association' (nd).

38. United States District Court, Southern District of New York, United States of America *v.* Jesse David Hyman, a/k/a/ 'Doc', Melvin Cooper, Joseph M Biasucci, Chaim Gerlitz, Oscar Louis Albenga, a/k/a 'Al', Stanley Gramovot, and Anthony Charles Capo Jr; *Defendants, Sentencing Memorandum*: 'B. *Cooper* – Cooper Funding was a company established to provide lease financing of equipment, primarily in the garbage collection industry. It was owned originally by Melvin Cooper, his father, **Sam Cooper** [*my emphasis*], and his uncle, **Jack Cooper** [*my emphasis*]. The company was incorporated in New York State on January 1, 1973. Etna Leasing Services Limited and Cooper Equities were allied companies. They were consolidated into Resource Capital Group in the spring of 1982 with the retirement of Jack Cooper and the paper purchase of Sam Cooper's interest in the companies by Jesse Hyman through Penvest, Inc. Melvin Cooper retained interests of varying degrees in M. Cooper Motor Leasing, Kleentainer, Inc., Cooper Tank and Welding, and **BW Energy systems** [*my emphasis*], and other companies after the formation of Resource Capital Group.
Cooper Funding had a large number of leading accounts in the garbage industry. It was alleged to be influenced by several LCN figures, including Joseph Schipani, . . . capo in the Genovese LCN Family, Victor Arena, soldier in the Colombo LCN family, John Franzese, . . . capo in the Colombo LCN family, Michael Franzese,

soldier in the Colombo LCN Family, Alphonse Persico, . . . Consigliere in the Colombo LCN Family, Sam Galasso, Sr, soldier in the Colombo LCN Family and vice-president of the Brooklyn Waste Trades Association, Jerry Zimmerman, associate of the Colombo LCN Family, Patsy D'Avanso, an associate of the Colombo LCN Family . . . Galasso and his son, Sam Galasso, Jr, were both salesmen for Cooper Funding. Zimmerman had a relationship with the Cooper Funding branch in California in the late 1970s.

'One Cooper Funding employee, Richard Slomowitz, a/k/a 'Richard Stone', was murdered on 28 November 1982. . . . Prior to the death of Stone, Stone met with Arena, Ralph Lombardo, and Cooper on one occasion. Cooper told Stone at one point that Allie Boy Persico had told Cooper and Arena to be careful around Stone. Arena told Cooper to have only legitimate deals with Stone and that Arena was "investigating" Stone.

'Interceptions in the instant case demonstrate Cooper's continuing involvement in a wide range of criminal activities including narcotics, counterfeit videotapes, loansharking, ERISA embezzlements, advance-fee schemes, grand larceny, petty larceny, bank frauds, SBA frauds, and money laundering. Cooper engaged in conversations concerning the following LCN figures: Vincent Rotondo (capo, DeCalvacante LCN family); . . . Antonio Corallo (boss, Lucchese LCN family); Paul Castellano (boss, Gambino LCN family); John Montana (soldier, Cleveland LCN family); Jimmy Napoli (capo, Genovese LCN family); . . . Victor Arena (soldier, Colombo LCN family).'

Of particular importance is the tape in evidence in the instant case as GX 124. In a part of this conversation between Oscar Albenga and Frank Castagnaro, these two criminals agree that it is Mel Cooper who has taught organised crime in New York City the sophisticated brand of loansharking, characterised by fake documents and security interests, that the Government proved before this Court. S 84 Cr. 479 (LBS), 24 May 1985, p.16–22. The City of New York Police Department, Commanding Officer, Brooklyn Burglary Coordinating Command to Chief of Detectives, '*Subject*: Business Alleged to be Operated by Organized Crime . . . 2. a. Brooklyn Trade Waste Company, Granada Hotel, Brooklyn, is controlled by organised crime. . . . 4. Investigation reveals . . . President, Pat Davanzo . . . Vice-President, Sam Galasso . . . 5. Check of records of this Department reveals that Sam Galasso, is known to this Department under B#480359 with one arrest for 974 P.L. (Policy). Pat Davanzo, is known to this Department under B#264804 with one arrest for Possession of a Dangerous Weapon and Felonious Assault'. (4 May 1972, pp. 1–2).

39.   *Sentencing Memorandum*, op. cit.; President's Commission on Organized Crime, op. cit.

40.   Suffolk County Police Department, Detectives to Commanding Officer, Command 1200, C. I. B. Folder no. 110A: 'It is also relevant that *Michael Antonacci's* brother, *Frank Antonacci*, also a partner in *South Bay Sanitation*, is a frequent visitor to *John Del Mastro*. Informant information . . . indicates that Frank Antonacci was the man to contact for

financing in the carting industry, as well as in the recycling business. This source stated that Frank Antonacci was the mob contact man to get loans out of the former Security National Bank (. . . the Chemical Bank) Small Business Loan Department' (17 November 1976, pp. 1, 3).

41. Florida Department of Law Enforcement, Assistance Report, FDLE Case no. 350–75 0011: 'A Dun and Bradstreet report dated 6/18/76 indicated that Frank and Thomas Antonacci brothers both born 1924, were officers along with John Casagrande in Five Counties Carting Corp., 172–23 Douglas Avenue, Jamaica, New York providing service to Queens, Brooklyn, Nassau and Suffolk counties' (30 July 1980 p. 3).

42. '1979 List of Private Carting Companies', op. cit.

43. State of Delaware, 'Certificate of Incorporation of Attwoods Environmental Inc.', 8 August 1984.

44. Attwoods PLC, 'Annual Report and Accounts 1987, Report of the Directors': 'Directors – R. Velocci (appointed 1 October 1986)', p. 17.; State of Delaware, Secretary of State, 1986 Annual Franchise Tax Report: '11 Directors – . . . Jack R. Casagrande . . . Ralph Velocci . . . 12. Officers – . . . Vice-President Jack R. Casagrande . . . Other Officers Ralph Velocci Vice Pres.' (1 March 1987); Securities and Exchange Commission, Form 20-F, 'Annual Report Pursuant to Section 13 or 15 (d) of the Securities and Exchange Act of 1934, for the fiscal year ended 31 July 1988', Commission file no. 015350, Attwoods plc, '*United States Operations Industrial Waste Services Inc.* ("IWSI"), acquired in November 1984, IWSI was founded in Florida in 1970 and provides a range of waste management services' (p. 5).

45. State of Florida, 'In the Circuit Court of the Fifth Judicial District, in and for Marion County, Florida', a political subdivision of the State of Florida, *Plaintiff, v.* Urban Waste Disposal, Inc., a corporation, *et al., Defendants*: '*Amended Complaint for Fraud, Breach of Contract, Civil Conspiracy, Piercing of the Corporate Veil, Violations of the Florida Racketeering Influenced Corrupt Organizations, Acts, the Federal Racketeering Influenced Corrupt Organizations Act, 8 U.S.C., 1981, et seq., Negligence, Injunctive Relief and Damages*'; 'The Plaintiff, . . . sues the defendants . . . I.W.S. of Marion County, Inc., a/k/a I.W.S. of Ocala, Inc., a/k/a Industrial Waste Services of Marion County, Inc., a Florida corporation (hereafter called "I.W.S. Marion"), Industrial Waste Service, Inc., a/k/a I.W.S., Inc., a Florida corporation (hereafter called "I.W.S."), . . . and says: . . .
Count 1 – Fraud. . . .
'**14.** (b) that Hermes was properly supervising the operation of the Landfill operations and had been employed by IWS Marion to run the landfill in accordance with all governmental regulations; (c) that the equipment of the County used in the operation of the Landfill was being properly used and maintained; (d) that proper records concerning tonnage of garbage being dumped in the Landfill were being kept; . . . (g) that Urban, IWS and Hermes were installing proper wells around the Landfill to monitor ground water pollution and were, in fact, monitoring ground water pollution; . . . (o) that a system for the recovery of methane gas from the Landfill had been and was being

installed which would produce $60,000 per year in revenue for the County; . . .

'15. . . . Velocci, Erber, Robson, Casagrande, IWS, IWS Marion, . . . each knew that the statements specified in Paragraph 14 (a)–(r) were material, false and misleading, or were false and misleading. . . .

'18. After May 22, 1984, and prior to May 13, 1986, Velocci, . . . on their own behalf and with the knowledge and consent, and on behalf of IWS, IWS Marion, Urban, . . . continued to make the misstatements and omissions of material fact . . . and made the additional misstatements of material fact as follows: . . . (b) that accurate accounts for tonnage of garbage being placed in the Landfill were being kept and were available to the County; (c) that only solid waste authorised by law was being placed in the Landfill; . . .

'22. . . . the following additional misrepresentations of material facts: (a) that there was a smoldering fire at the Landfill which was delaying the completion of the Pyrolytic Converter; . . . (c) that because of smoldering fire at the Landfill, modifications to the Pyrolytic converter would be necessary, and they would take six months; (d) that infrared photos of the smoldering fire in the Landfill had been taken by a special process; . . .

'34. As a result of the above alleged misstatement and omissions of material fact . . . which the County believed and upon which it reasonably relied, . . . As a result, the following matters occurred and, in the future, will continue to occur: . . . (b) the Landfill life was drastically reduced; (c) the Landfill was operated in such a manner that the structures and environment in and around the Landfill were rendered unsafe and polluted, and currently constitute a danger and threat to the health, safety and welfare of the people of Marion County; . . .

'35. As a result of the matters hereinafter alleged: (a) the County will be required to spend millions of dollars to correct the damage done to the Landfill, to construct environmentally safe structures in conjunction with the Landfill to project the health and welfare of people of Marion County, and to purchase and repair equipment damaged in the operation of the Landfill;

'**Count IV – Piercing the** *Corporate Veil of IWS Marion.* . . .

'48. In truth and in fact, IWS Marion was a mere shell. All of its stock was owned by IWS and the officers, directors and agents of IWS were its only agents. IWS Marion was formed and perpetuated by IWS to shield IWS from liability for its fradulent acts, . . . (a) all of the money purportedly collected by it in the operation of the Landfill was transferred to Velocci in the State of New York and then to IWS in Miami, Florida, so that it effectively never had any cash as its own, . . . (c) Hundreds of thousands of dollars were skimmed by IWS from the operation of the Landfill by the device of having IWS Marion collect the funds and simply pay them to IWS; . . . *Wherefore*, the County prays that it be adjudicated that IWS Marion is the alter ego of IWS and that IWS is legally responsible for each and every act of IWS Marion' (Case no. 87–719–CA–A, pp. 1–5, 9–14, 22–4).

Commonwealth of Pennsylvania, Department of Environmental
Resources, Bureau of Waste Management, *Form C – Compliance History*
(formerly module no. 10):

'1. Name of Permit or License Applicant/Permittee/Licensee:
Attwoods Environmental of Pennsylvania, Inc., Instructions for Form
C – Compliance History, . . . **Instructions:** 1. Information shall be
submitted for the 10-year period prior to the date on which the form
is completed. . . . 4. For the purposes of completing "Form C", the term
"**related party**" shall mean a person or municipality that is a partner,
associate, officer, parent corporation, subsidiary corporation, . . . 6.
The term "**violation**" includes . . . any court actions whether pending
or settled. . . . *Attachment* Form C – Compliance History – B. *General
Information Regarding "Related Parties"'* B.1 Attwoods Environmental,
Inc. – parent and sole stockholder of Applicant – Stockley Road, Inc. –
parent and sole stockholder of Attwoods Environmental, Inc. –
Attwoods American Holdings Ltd. – parent and sole stockholder of
Stockley Road, Inc. – Attwoods plc – ultimate parent and sole share-
holder of Attwoods American Holdings Ltd. . . . B.4 (ii) US subsidiar-
ies of Attwoods plc are: . . . Attwoods, Inc., 3225 Aviation Avenue,
Coconut Grove, Miami, Fl. 33132. . . . (iv) The US subsidiaries of
Attwoods, Inc., are: Industrial Waste Services, Inc. – IWS of Marion
County, Inc. c/o Industrial Waste Services, Inc. – Sub. of Industrial
Waste Services. . . . Mountaintop Municipal Waste Landfill, Phase 1
Application, Form C – Compliance History, Dade County Department
of Environmental Resources Management, *Complainant, v.* **Industrial
Waste Services, Inc.** [*my emphasis*], 'Consent Agreement; . . . Metro-
politan Dade County, Florida, Environmental Resources Management,
Miami, Florida, to Mr John Casagrande, Jr, **Industrial Waste Services,
Inc.** [*my emphasis*], *Final Notice Prior to Court* and *Notice of Permit
Revocation'.* Index, 1. Form C – Compliance History '2. Response Nar
rative to Form C Questions. C. *Specific information regarding the Applicant and its Related Parties.* . . . D. *Compliance Background.* . . . D.2.
Neither Applicant nor a related party as defined by the Department's
regulations and as requested in 25 Pa. Code | | 271.125(8) and (9) has
any violation outside of Pennsylvania. **In the interest of providing all
information available, even if not required by the Department's
regulations, the following information is provided, for members of
the Attwoods plc corporate family which are not "related parties."**
[*my emphasis*] . . . D.2 (b) Attwoods, Inc.: out-of-state "violations" of
Attwoods, Inc. and/or its subsidiaries: (i) Industrial Waste Services,
Inc., received a final notice prior to court and notice of permit revocation dated August 30, 1988 from the Dade County Department of
Environmental Resources Management (DERM) for disposing of un-
authorised sludge and failure to file monthly transportation reports.'
  Despite the disclaimers in Attwoods Form C, a brief check of
Attwoods plc Annual Report to the Securities and Exchange Commis-
sion, 31 January 1990, reveals, under the heading 'United States Op-
erations', the following companies: Industrial Waste Services Inc.
('IWSI'); County Sanitation Inc.; Peterson Companies; MedX Inc.; Vesta

Technology, Ltd.; Eastern Waste Industries, Inc.; and Pending Acquisitions . . . National Waste Disposal; Atlantic Disposal [but nothing about Attwoods of Pennsylvania, Inc.], and the following under the heading Mineral Extraction and Landfill Sites': 'Until March 6, 1987, the Company managed a landfill site in Central Florida under a ten-year agreement with a third person which commenced in 1982. The site was owned by Marion County, and the Company received from the third person a management fee equal to the operating costs incurred by the Company plus a percentage on a sliding scale of operating expenses.' And, under 'Item 10 – Directors and Officers of Registrant' the following is noted: *Attwoods plc – Officer and Directors –* J. R. Casagrande – Director and Chief Executive Officer of US Operations; *Date of Appointment as Director* – January 1, 1985; R. Velocci – Director and Senior Vice-President of US Operations; *Date of Appointment as Director* – October 1, 1986'; on the following page is found this list of 'Senior Officers in Attwoods's subsidiary companies, . . . *US Subsidiaries – IWSI* – R. Velocci, Chief Executive Officer, since 1987', and no listing of Attwoods of Pennsylvania.

The failure to list all charges against IWSI on the Mountaintop Application, particularly those in the civil suit alleging serious environmental charges, as well as the failure to list the civil and, at the time of the Application, criminal charges against IWSI and Attwood's Director Jack R. Casagrande appears to be a violation of the Commonwealth's rules and regulations. Moreover, by Attwoods of Pennsylvania bringing in IWSI on its Application, although in a disingenuous manner, it opened the door that requires full disclosure.

46.   Michael Gillard, 'New Threat to Denis's Firm', *Observer*, 14 June 1987: 'A new legal threat is looming for Attwoods, the British waste disposal group of which Mr Denis Thatcher, the Prime Minister's husband, is deputy chairman. . . . Mr Thatcher has declined to comment on the disclosures in *The Observer* last Sunday about the links between two of his Attwoods co-directors and a New York company, Five Counties Carting, which is a defendant in a civil case alleging Mafia control of the waste disposal business in New York. Attwoods director Jack R. Casagrande is a Five Counties shareholder. Other members of his family and a brother of fellow Attwoods director Ralph Velocci are also directors and shareholders. At the time Attwoods bought IWS in late 1984, the Florida company provided a $1.5 million bank guarantee for Five Counties. And Five Counties founder John Casagrande, a cousin of the Attwoods director, was a member of the board of the Private Sanitation Industry Association through which the Lucchese crime family controlled the waste disposal business on Long Island.'

Michael Gillard, *Observer*, 5 June 1988: 'The main American subsidiary of Attwoods, the British company of which Denis Thatcher is the deputy chairman, has paid damages and penalties totalling $145,000 (more than £80,000) to settle a price-fixing case. Industrial Waste Services, Florida's second largest refuse disposal company, was sued on behalf of eight public bodies, including schools and government offices. . . .'

Michael Gillard, 'Attwoods buys Firm with "Mafia link"', *Observer*, 9 July 1989: 'An American waste disposal company due to be acquired by Attwoods, whose deputy chairman is Denis Thatcher, has been linked by the FBI to an alleged Mafia associate. Two months ago Attwoods agreed to pay at least $20 million for National Waste Disposal, a New Jersey company run by the two sons of John Zuccarelli, employed as a consultant by the company. In August 1981, the then FBI director, William Webster, in a letter to a United States Congressional committee investigating Mafia involvement in the New Jersey garbage business, identified Zuccarelli as a "reputed associate of organised crime".'

47. See notes 2 and 3.
48. State of Florida, *Plaintiff, v.* Leslie Erber *et al.*, Defendant, Case no. 86–2954–DF–AZ, op. cit., and State of Florida, Plaintiff, *v.* Urban Waste Disposal, Inc., op. cit.:
State of Florida, 'In the Circuit Court of the Eleventh Judicial Circuit of Florida in and for Dade County, in Re: application of the State of Florida for an Order Authorizing the Interception of Wire or Oral Communications of John Riley, Brian Hooten, Stuart Susaneck, Joseph Lazar, Ezra Tissona, Larry Tritsch, and Other Persons at this Time Unknown Occurring on Telephone Number (305) 688–0159, Said Number Being Registered to Mayor John Riley and Located at 2963 Northwest 135 Street, Opa Locka, Dade County, Florida, *Order Authorizing an Extension of Time for the Interception of Wire or Oral Communications*, in the Name of the State of Florida': '. . . the Court, on the basis of the facts submitted in the Application, Affidavit and Authorization, specifically finds: 1. There is probable cause to believe that John Riley, . . . Jack Casagrande, . . . and other persons . . . are committing, have committed, or about to commit particular offenses . . . to wit: Bribery, . . . and Conspiracy to Commit Bribery' (3 December 1985, p. 1).
49. President's Commission, op. cit (see note 18).
50. State of Florida, 'In the Circuit Court of the Eleventh Judicial Circuit of Florida, in and for Dade County, in Re: Application . . . Affidavit by Sergeant Harold M. Hasenbank and Detective Chris A. Dangler, "sworn Deputy Sheriffs, in and for Dade County, Florida . . . currently assigned to the Organized Crime Bureau, Tactical Investigations Unit' (pp. 11–12); Metro–Dade Police Organized Crime Bureau, 'Re: Report on the Interception of Wire Communications on Telephone Numbers (305) 687-5145, and (305) 688-0159' (12 November 1985, p. 3).
51. Metro–Dade Police Organized Crime Bureau, 'Re: Report on the Interception of Wire Communications on Telephone Number (305) 688–0159' (13 December 1985, p. 3).
52. Metro–Dade Police Organized Crime Bureau, Re: Report on the Interception of Wire Communications on Telephone Numbers (305) 687–5145 & (305) 688–0159' (22 November 1985, pp. 3–4).
53. State of Florida, 'In the Circuit Court of the Fifth Judicial Circuit, in and for Marion County, Florida', State of Florida *v.* Leslie Erber *et al.*, Case no. 86–2954–CF–AZ, Criminal Division, 'Amended Information', 27 May 1987.

54.   State of Florida *v.* Leslie Erber *et al.*, Case no. 86–2954–CF–AZ, op. cit.;
       State of Florida *v.* Urban Waste Disposal, Inc., *Amended Complaint for
       Fraud*, Case no. 87–719–CA–A, op. cit., '**COUNT I – FRAUD**': '**3**. On or
       about September 1, 1981, Velocci, Erber, [Jack R.] Casagrande, and
       IWS, acting on their own behalf, on behalf and with knowledge and
       consent of Robson, Gould, Constantinou, and Enterprise made to the
       County the following misrepresentations of material fact: (a) That
       there was then in existence an operable machine called a Pyrolytic
       Converter capable of processing solid waste, . . . (b) That the pyrolytic
       converter would reduce the bulk of each of the 150 tons of solid waste
       by approximately ninety per cent, the result of which reduction would
       be a burnable char consisting of pure carbon, 150 gallons of commer-
       cial grade heating oil and carbon dioxide or other environmentally
       acceptable gases; . . . (e) That [Rocco P.] Velocci, [Jack R.] Casagrande
       and IWS would operate the Landfill in connection with the operation
       of the Pyrolytic Converter; (f) That Velocci, Casagrande and IWS were
       experienced Landfill operators with many years experience in the
       Landfill business; (g) That IWS, Casagrande, Velocci, Erber and others
       were all part of a joint enterprise which could successfully operate the
       Landfill and the Pyrolitic Converter as an integrated operation. **4.**
       Each of the above misrepresentations specified in Paragraph 3(a)–(g),
       were material, false and misleading, or were false or misleading.
       Velocci, Casagrande, IWS, Erber, Robson, Constantinou, Gould and
       Enterprise each knew that the representations were material, false and
       misleading' (pp. 3–4).
           An important part of the conspiracy was the contract to operate the
       county landfill obtained, the charge read, 'through false pretenses,
       fraud, deception, [and] willful misrepresentation'.
55.   Ibid., 'Count I – Fraud': '12. After September, 1981, and prior to April
       15, 1982, Velocci, Green, Erber, Constantinou, Casagrande, IWS,
       Robson, Urban Associates, Waste, Enterprise and Gould, concealed
       and omitted to inform, or concealed, or omitted to inform, the County
       of material facts of which they were aware, which material facts, if
       known by the County, would have resulted in the County refusing to
       enter SWMA [Solid Waste Management Agreement] or SWMA, as
       modified, or having business dealings with the Defendants, . . . The
       said omitted material facts were: (a) Constantinou, who was vice-
       president of Urban, and signed SWMA, was a convicted securities
       swindler and perpetrator of numerous securities frauds; (b) Erber had
       pleaded no contest to securities frauds and had mismanaged secur-
       ities trust accounts so that receivers had to be appointed to protect
       investors whom he had induced into fraudulent schemes; . . . (d)
       Robson had been disciplined by a United States District Court in Ohio
       for unethical conduct and removed as an attorney in a bankruptcy
       case for conflict of interest; (e) IWS had been under continuing Federal
       Grand Jury Investigation in Dade County, Florida, for violations of
       the Anti-Trust laws; . . . (g) Neither Velocci, Casagrande, IWS, nor IWS
       Marion County had previously been the manager of a landfill opera-
       tion' (pp. 8–9).

In the same case the Defendants included 'Waste Technology Corp., a/k/a B. W. Energy Systems, Inc., a/k/a B. W. Energy Corporation' (p. 1).

A look at the following was also instructive. Waste Technology Corp., 'prospectus', 1,500,000 Shares Common Stock, 12 November 1985 (received Securities and Exchange Commission, 13 November 1985), 'Notes to Financial Statements – Note 1 – Organization and Business – The company was incorporated on September 19, 1975 under the laws of the State of Delaware originally under the corporate name B. W. Energy Systems Inc. The name was changed to Waste Technology Corp. in August 1983' (p. F-6).

Also, New York State Senate Select Committee on Crime, 'Commercial Leasing/Loan History of Cooper Funding, Ltd., . . . Corporations – G. Cooper and Sons Realty Corp. Cooper Funding Corp. Cooper Funding Ltd., Inc. Cooper Tank and Welding Corp. Kleentainers Corp. Cooper Equities Inc. Cooper Motor Leasing Inc. B. W. Energy Systems Inc. [*my emphasis*]. M. Cooper Motor Leasing, Ltd. Cooper Muffler, Ltd. – Executive Officers – Mel Cooper, President; Sam Cooper, Vice-President; Jack Cooper, Secretary/Treasurer'. And see Dun & Bradstreet, 'Cooper Funding Ltd Inc., Date – Printed, July 21 1978' – Mel Cooper, Pres . . . . History – 02/18/78 Mel Cooper, Pres., Samuel Cooper, Sec. & Treas. . . . – Affiliates: Officers appear as principals in the following concerns: . . . B. W. Energy Systems, Lexington Ave, . . . Has marketing rights to a pyrolysis system. . . . '

And, State of Florida, *v.* Leslie Erber, op. cit., FL BAR ID 27 9250, Deposition of Morton S. Robson:

A. . . . One of the things I wanted to make clear is that I have never been a principle [*sic*], in the true sense of the word of Urban Waste Disposal, Inc. I was retained by Les Erber and Perry Constantinou back in about 1975, at which time the predecessor of Waste Technology, Incorporated, was formed, and it was B. W. Energy Systems, and I am not sure, but I think I formed Urban Waste Disposal, Inc., at some point as attorney.

I represented them, both B. W. Energy Systems and Urban Waste, for years . . . but at some point in time before Gould got to the point where he had built this up to a 50-ton-per-day unit, Erber and Constantinou brought to him a group of garbage carters from the metropolitan New York area which included Rocco Velocci, and I think Jack Casagrande was in that group, but all told, I think there were 16 people. . . . B. W. Energy, which was the entity that was trying to market this product, never had any money. The initial principals put in a few bucks apiece, . . . and then from time to time they loaned it money. Initially there were five principals, . . .

Q. Well, when did it become Waste Technology?

A. In 1985 they negotiated a public offering and they changed the name to Waste Technology at that time. . . .

Q. Do you know for a fact that there has been no money generated by the operation of the land fill?

A. . . . I've been advised by Constantinou and I've been advised by [Rocco] Velocci that there has never been enough cash-flow from the landfill to cover the operating expenses. The operating expenses all go to IWS. I have no idea whether IWS's expenses are puffed or not. . . . There was a family named Cooper that had been involved initially in putting this company together. . . .

Q. Well, were you aware that Less [*sic*] Erber told the County Commission, the Marion County Commission, that $10,000,000 was spent by his company on research and development of that pyrolytic reactor?

A. I've never heard that to this moment. . . .

Q. So, if he said it, it's not true?

A. Waste Technology never spent any money on research and development on this project.

Q. How about B. W.?

A. B. W. was Waste Technology.

Q. Well, how did Marion County get selected, do you know, to be the location of this –

A. It's my understanding – again, this is secondhand, but it's my understanding that, through Rocco Velocci and somebody that he knew down here, that they had a company that was doing carting work in Florida, and they learned that Marion County was looking for something to dispose of waste and prolong the land fill, . . . and were thinking in terms of getting somebody in to operate the landfill, and so, whoever that was – and I think Velocci is the guy who brought it to Urban, because Velocci has an interest in Urban, and I think he spoke to Erber and Constantinou about it, and I think it came to him through somebody he was in partnership with in one of these carting companies. . . .

Q. . . . You indicated that you negotiated the agreement between B. W. Energy Systems and Enterprise which gave B. W. the exclusive marketing rights for the pyrolytic reactor.

A. East of the Mississippi.

Q. Who is F & W Energy Resources?

A. That's a company through which Rocco Velocci and his group have an interest, and they owned 44 and-a-half per cent of Urban Waste Disposal, Inc.
I think I was held in Velocci's name, but he was holding it as a nominee for this group. I don't know who the principals are. . . .

Q. Then the system that F & W apparently marketed same pyrolytic system in a town – or in an Ohio town, specifically in Franklin, Ohio. What was B. W.'s involvement in that situation?

A. I never heard anything about what you're talking about. F & W didn't market anything that I know of. They didn't have the rights to market anything. . . .

Q. What about Mr. Velocci, was he authorised to market the system for B. W. Energy Systems?

A. When you say 'was he authorised', there was an informal relationship and he was cooperating with them.

Q. Okay. So his contacts, then, with the town officials in the Town of Smithtown would have been at the behest of or on the behalf of B. W., or do you have any idea what I'm talking about?

A. Well, I remember – yeah, Smithtown is something I've heard about. . . . somebody told Velocci that the Town of Smithtown might be interested and somebody set up a meeting, . . . it never went any further, but, as I say, I'm sure that Velocci was authorised on some informal basis to go and represent – I shouldn't say represent himself as being part of Waste Technology – but as being an agent for them.'   (10 April 1987)

And see also State of Delaware, 'Certificate of Incorporation of F & W Energy Resources, Ltd, 25 November 1975'; State of Delaware, '1979 Annual Franchise Tax Report, F & W Energy Resources Ltd': *Officers* – *President* Rocco P. Velocci; *Vice-President* Carl Casagrande; *Secretary* John Casagrande. – *Shareholders*: John Casagrande, Rocco Cristina, Frank Antonacci, Estate of Vito Leone, Rocco P. Velocci, Vito Tropiano, Rocco Casagrande Jr, Jack Casagrande, Peter Lomagistro, Albert Casagrande, Jack R. Casagrande, Ralph Velocci, Carl Casagrande, John F. Casagrande, John Lawson, Michael Perna, Anthony Masci, Fiori L. Persichilli [*sic*], Marjorie Battioti, Frank Lomangino, John Battisti, Leo Lomangino, Steve Florio, Guy Antonacci, Theresa Antonacci, Peter J. Lomagistro, Angela Antonacci, Vito Leone, Thomas Antonacci, Frank Grillo, Michael Perna Jr., A. Lomagistro.

Next consider The City of New York Police Department, 'Re: Queens Trade Waste Association – 1'. The following is a 1970 list of officers of the Queens Trade Waste Association, located at 39–01 Queens Boulevard, Queens, New York: *President* – Frank Grillo; *Treasurer* – Mario Reali; *Secretary* – Anthony Casagrande; *Sergeant at Arms* – Thomas Antonacci; *Chairman of Board* – Vito Leone; *Business Agent* – Nicola Mellilo. **Nicola Mellilo is a Soldier in the Gambino Crime family** [*my emphasis*]' (30 August 1977).

See also Kings County District Attorney's Office, 'Stockholders of World Sanitation . . . Consolidated with 5 Counties Carting' (see note 22): 'John Lawson, Rocco Velocci, Ralph Velocci, Jack R. Casagrande, Jack Casagrande, Carl Casagrande, Albert Casagrande, Vito Tropiano, Romano Celli'; and '1979 List of Private Carting Companies' (see note 24): 'Five Counties, *President*, John Casagrande; *Vice-President*, Frank Grillo; *Secretary*, Thomas Antonacci; *Treasurer*, Vito Leone.'

And Federal Bureau of Investigation, 'Criminal Influence in Private Sanitation – Suffolk County', Bureau File 92-10750 (see note 20): 'Interviews of the following three persons: . . .'.

See Supreme Court of the State of New York, County of Suffolk,

'The People of the State of New York *v.* Arthur Romsera and Vito Biondo' (see note 25), for discussion of Fiore Persichilli, Salvatore Avellino, Jr.

See also United State District Court Southern District of New York, United States of America *v*. . . . Melvin Cooper (see note 38); President's Commission on Organized Crime (see note 18); United States District Court, Eastern District of New York, United States of America, Plaintiff, *v.* The Lucchese Organized Crime Family of La Cosa Nostra; The Gambino Organized Crime Family of La Cosa Nostra; Private Sanitation Industry Association of Nassau/Suffolk Inc; '. . . Hillside Carting Company [Mike Reali part owner, Peter Reali and Pasaquale Casagrande named in indictment as operators and controllers, p. 25], Inc.; Long Island Rubbish Removal Service Corp. [Fiore Persichilli]; Investigators, Inc. (see note 13), 'Principals of Industrial Waste Services and Five Counties Carting Company': 'Albert Casagrande, Jack Casagrande, Ralph Velocci, Jack R. Casagrande, Rocco Casagrande, John Casagrande, John F. Casagrande, Carl Casagrande, Peter Lomagistro, Frank Antonacci, Rocco Cristina, William F. Leone, Rocco P. Velocci, Vito Tropiano' (pp. 9–10); 'The evolution of World Sanitation of Jamaica, Five Counties Carting of Jamaica, Industrial Waste Services of Florida, World Sanitation of Florida and Jamaica Paper Stock Company of Jamaica. With the exception of World Sanitation of Jamaica, all of the above companies are operational today and all have the same fourteen principals. . . . In 1973, due to cash needs, IWS sold 45% of IWS to Five Counties Carting for $300,000. Subsequently, on September 1, 1978, World Sanitation merged with Five Counties Carting. In October 1979, World Sanitation of Florida was founded. This company is co-located with IWS in Miami, Florida' (p. 11). However on the following page the deal seems to have been just slightly different: 'December 1972 Industrial Waste Services, officially acquired by World Sanitation 1973 – World sold 45% interest in IWS to Five Counties for $300,000' (p. 12). 'Industrial Waste Service – *Interview Jack Casagrande* . . . He stated that his oldest brother, Patsy, presently resides in Jamaica, New York, and is in partnership with his [Patsy's] brothers-in-law, Pete and Mike Reali, in the firm of Hillside Carting Company, Jamaica, New York' (p. 31). '*Interview: Rocco Velocci.* . . . Mr. Velocci advised he is secretary of Five Counties Carting Company and, as such, oversees all operations, paying specific interest to the Mechanical Shop. . . . In addition, he runs the IWS operation in Ocala, Florida, where IWS has a large landfill contract. Additionally, he is presently involved with other associates in an operation called 'Urban Waste', which is a $10-million project involving a resource recovery machine. . . . It is expected to open in one year. In addition to IWS interest, other persons having an interest are: Les Erber, Mort Robeson [*sic*] and Perry Constantinou, who are all associates of B & W Energy in New York City. . . . Once the recovery machine operation becomes functional, IWS will no longer be engaged in the landfill project in Ocala. . . . In regard to the partnership arrangement, he advised that all partners have an equal share of IWS; however, in Five Counties Carting Company, the partners own various amounts' (p. 36). '*Interview: William Leone* . . . Mr. Leone informed that he is the Treasurer of Five Counties Carting Company and as such **monitors all matters relative to finances for Five Counties Carting Company and IWS** [*my emphasis*]' (p. 37).

And United States District Court, Eastern District of New York, State of New York, Plaintiff, *v.* Salem Sanitary Carting Corp., **Five Counties Carting Corp.** [*my emphasis*], Private Sanitation Industry Association of Nassau/Suffolk County, . . . Salvatore Avellino, Jr, . . . Antonio Corallo, . . . (CV 85–0208).

I should add that John Casagrande, Sr, of 5 Counties Carting, the PSI, Nassau Trade Waste Removal, etc., is acknowledged by Jack R. Casagrande CEO of US operation of Attwoods plc, etc., to be currently an employee of an Attwoods subsidiary in Florida in a letter to New Jersey State Police, 27 June 1990.

56. State of Florida *v.* Leslie Erber (see note 48); State of Florida *v.* Urban Waste Disposal (see note 45); United States District Court, Southern District of New York, United States of America *v.* . . . Melvin Cooper, (see note 38); and United States District Court, Eastern District of New York, United States of America, Plaintiff, *v.* The Lucchese Organized Crime Family of La Cosa Nostra (see note 55); and ' . . . Long Island Rubbish Removal Service Corp.' (see note 25).

57. State of Florida, 'Deposition of Morton S. Robson', op. cit.; Dun & Bradstreet, 'Cooper Funding', op. cit.; Waste Technology Corp., 'Prospectus', op. cit.; State of Florida *v.* Urban Waste Disposal, op. cit.

58. County Sanitation Districts of Los Angeles County, California, John D. Parkhurst, Chief Engineer & General Manager, 'Report on Status of Technology in the Recovery of Resources from Solid Waste' (nd) p. 144.

59. Ibid., p 145; and Waste Technology Corp., 'Prospectus' (received Securities and Exchange Commission, 13 November 1985), op. cit.: ' . . . Urban has entered into a contract with Five Counties Carting Corp., a consortium of private haulers covering parts of Nassau and Queens Counties, New York, to build a system which Urban has agreed that it will purchase from the Company and pursuant to which Five Counties has agreed to supply at least 300 tons of garbage per day for twenty years' (p. 5).

Securities and Exchange Commission, Waste Technology Corp., Amendment No. 1 to Form S-18, Registration Statement under the Securities Act of 1933, received by SEC 13 August 1985, Exhibit 10.m.: '1. Urban has entered into an agreement dated November 18, 1981 and amended May 1, 1983 and April 29, 1985 with Five Counties Carting Corp. ('Five Counties'), by which Urban has agreed to construct a system ("the system") which will dispose of 46,800 tons of solid waste per year in Nassau and Queens Counties, New York. Urban represents to Waste that said agreement with Five Counties is in full force and effect, and that to Urban's knowledge said agreement is intended by both parties thereto to continue in full force and effect throughout the construction and operation of the System' (pp. 384–5). Morton Robson signed for Urban Waste as Secretary-Treasurer.

I should add that whatever was told to Parkhurst in 1975 about a Five Counties contract appears to have been untrue.

60. Robson Deposition, 10 April 1987, op. cit., pp. 4–5, 11.
61. Ibid., p. 64.
62. State of Delaware, Certificate of Incorporation of F & W Energy Resources Ltd, op. cit.; United States District Court, Eastern District of New York, State of New York, Plaintiff *v.* Salem Sanitary Carting Corp., . . . Five Counties Carting Corp, op. cit. (see note 35).
63. Mark McIntyre, 'Carters Offer Plan for Smaller Plants', *Newsday*, 11 April 1980: A group of Long Island carters has proposed to erect small resource-recover plants that would extract oil from garbage in Smithtown and Freeport . . . Rocco Velocci, a Dix Hills carter, touted the scheme . . . Sal Avellino, an influential Long Island carter . . . who set up last Friday's meeting with Smithtown officials, said, ". . . This is not something that we invented last night, I feel we can do a better job." Avellino said the $15 million plant would be built with private funds on 2.5 acres of leased town land and could begin operation within 18 months.'
64. Interview with Patrick R. Vecchio, Smithtown, New York, 23 March 1989.
65. Ibid.
66. Donal A. Devine, Town Engineer to Hon. Patrick R. Vecchio, Supervisor, 'Analysis of DECO Process (Enterprise Pyrolysis Unit)', 28 April 1980.
67. Certificate of Incorporation of F & W Energy Resources, Ltd., op. cit.; State of Delaware, 1979 Annual Franchise Tax Report, No. 710122, filed 2 January 1980, op. cit., which lists the company's officers and was signed on 8 December 1979 by President Rocco P. Velocci.

The information on Freeport was gained by Kemp in an interview with a Freeport official in the spring of 1989.

68. Five Counties Carting Corp., 172–33 Douglas Avenue, Jamaica, **William Leone, Treasurer Five Counties Carting Corp.** [*my emphasis*], 'letter' to Mr. Phil Herrick, City Manager, City of Franklin Ohio, 35 East Fourth Street, Franklin, Ohio: 'Our auditors, Thomas J. Merlo and Company, Certified Public Accountants, 99 North West 183 Street Suite 230 Miami, Florida 33169, are making an examination of our financial statements. Please confirm to them our Franklin bid deposit for F & W Energy Resources Ltd. held by you in the amount of $50,000 as of August 31, 1982' (21 October 1982).

Southwestern Ohio Air Pollution Control Agency, Ray Silbernagel, Environmental Scientist, 'letter' to **Mr. William Leone, F & W Energy Resources, 172–33 Douglas Avenue, Jamaica** [*my emphasis*]: ' . . . In short, none of the items in the past submittals have been addressed properly by providing detailed engineering background data and calculation documentation for the specific processes to be used at this proposed facility. Unless we receive the required detailed process data information and calculations to support your application within the next thirty (30) days, your application will be processed for denial' (12 April 1983).

69. Adam Kemp's interviews with Florida and Ohio officials.
70. State of Florida *v.* Leslie Erber, 'Amended Statement of Particulars', op. cit.
71. State of Florida, *v.* Urban Waste Disposal, op. cit., 'Count 1 – Fraud – 22. (A), (C), (D); 34. (B), (C); 35. (A)'; and the Amended Complaint for Fraud; 'Count 1 – Fraud – 3. (a), (c), (f), (g); 4.' (op. cit.).
72. Review citations on IWS convictions, Metro–Dade Organized Crime Bureau wiretaps, BW Energy, Cooper Funding, Robson Deposition, etc.
73. John Plender, 'Thatcher Link with US Waste Company Scrutinized', *Financial Times*, 4 July 1989, p. 6: ' . . . Court documents assert that Mr [Jack R.] Casagrande was a director of Urban Waste Disposal from 1982 to 1987 and a shareholder. Mr Casagrande's lawyers claim that he was registered as a director through a clerical error and resigned in 1987. Also involved is Mr Rocco Velocci, a director of the Attwoods subsidiary at the time it managed the Ocala landfill site. . . . Mr Velocci had been involved in marketing the controversial waste-to-energy machine in Florida and in Long Island, New York, where he did so in the company of Mr Salvatore Avellino Jr, an identified member of organised crime . . .'
74. Nick Hays, 'Centre County Commissioners Back Clinton Garbage Deal', *Centre Daily Times*, 7 January 1990: 'The commissioners unanimously reaffirmed their belief that working with Clinton would be better for the county than dumping at a private company's landfill' (p. B1).
75. Interview with Bob Donaldson (nd). Donaldson said, among other things, that a 'memo of understanding [between Centre and Clinton Counties] approved last night, Attwoods has no office; . . . [Attwoods] white elephant unless trash comes from somewhere else; . . . don't know their real intent; counties listed are not realistic; plan becomes illogical; . . . can't figure out what Attwoods is doing'.
76. Interview with Dick Reeder from DER Williamsport office (nd). About Attwoods, Reeder commented that a 'serious hurdle needs to be jumped by these people; . . . Centre County Planning Commission, [has] strong objection to Attwoods; . . . appears to me it's going to be hard for them to site the Snow Shoe landfill now.'
77. Statement by Attwoods plc attorney made in the film 'A Special Relationship'.
78. Andrew J. Maloney, US Attorney for the Eastern District of New York, 'Press Release, 7 June 1989: 'Andrew J. Maloney, . . . today announced the filing of a civil racketeering (RICO) complaint against the Lucchese and Gambino Crime Families of La Cosa Nostra, the Private Sanitation Industry Association of Nassau/Suffolk, Inc. (PSIA), Teamster Local 813, 44 Long Island carting companies and 64 individuals including organised crime figures, Long Island carters, and former public officials and employees. Mr. Maloney stated that "this lawsuit

seeks to eliminate the racketeering influence of organised crime over the Long Island garbage disposal industry . . . The solid-waste carting industry on Long Island has been infiltrated by organised crime since the 1950s." . . . This industry, according to Mr. Maloney, "is run as a cartel, under which individual carting companies are allocated specific residential and commercial waste collection stops which become the 'property' of the carter. . . . According to the complaint, the garbage cartel's **property rights system is enforced by organised crime elements in the industry** [*my emphasis*]. . . . The present action also **complements a pending anti-trust suit brought by the New York State Attorney General against various Long Island carters by seeking the broader and more expansive remedies available to the United States under the RICO statute** [*my emphasis*]'" (pp. 1–4).

'Abrams Settles Suit Against 17 Long Island Garbage Carters, Obtains more than $3 Million in Restitution' (nd): 'Mr. Abrams alleged the garbage carter treated customers and routes as "property", to be bought and sold by companies engaged in a conspiracy to frustrate competition. . . . The 15 settlement agreements, if approved by the court, would dispose of claims against the following defendants: . . . Five Counties Carting Corp. 172–33 Douglas Avenue, Jamaica' (pp. 1–2).

79. United States District Court, Eastern District of New York, United States of America, Plaintiff *v.* The Lucchese Organized Crime Family, et al., defendants, Civil Aviation no. CV 89 1848, op. cit.

80. Ibid.

81. Supreme Court of the State of New York, County of Queens, People of the State of New York, Plaintiff, *v.* Rocco P. Velocci, *Indictment* no. 3067/89.

82. Long Island Rail Road, Contract Administration, Contracts and Materials Department, 'Contract Documents for Contract No. 1487: Pickup 7 Disposal of Rubbish and Debris in Containers & Compactors', Schedule III, Contractor Responsibility Information, CB-11, 13.

83. Review citations concerning the pyrolytic converter.
     See also State of New York, Commission of Investigation, op. cit.: 'There is a third technology, known as pyrolysis, a method of breaking down burnable waste by combustion in the absence of air. During a conference entitled "Waste Disposal on Long Island" (sponsored by the New York Chapter of the National Solid-Wastes Management Association and Long Island Sanitation Officials Association on **June 3, 1983** [*my emphasis*], Dr. Ronald J. Alvarez, Ph.D., Professor of Engineering at Hofstra University, stated that pyrolysis has received some experimental treatment, but has largely been discarded by the engineering community because it requires consistent fuel sources which are not produced by municipal solid waste and is **thus not considered a viable technology** [*my emphasis*]' (p. 22).
     See also State of Florida, Department of Legal Affairs, Office of Statewide Prosecution, Statewide Grand Jury, Deposition of Rocco Velocci (8 July 1986):

Q. All right. Let's see if I can understand a little bit better. B. W. Energy was what? . . .

A. [Mort Robson] That's a corporation which is now a public corporation which name has been changed to Waste Technology.

Q. And you are saying they have not sold any stock?

A. [Robson] Oh, yeah. They have sold stock.

Q. How much?

A. [Robson] Four and a half million dollars worth.

Q. Where is that money going?

A. [Robson] Where is it going?

Q. Where has it gone?

A. [Robson] It's in the bank.

Q. It's sitting in a bank?

A. [Robson] Yes. . . .

Q. And what relationship do you have to Urban Waste Disposal, if any?

A. Urban Waste Disposal, I am an officer in –

Q. What type of officer?

A. I am – I think I am listed as Secretary. . . .

Q. Who is the Vice President?

A. I don't know. . . .

Q. What are you and your associates incorporated under or what partnership agreement do you have?

A. We – we – we run a – I run – I run a garbage company in New York called Five Counties Carting and we have a small division of that company called the Douglas Associates, . . .

Q. You actually run Five Counties Carting?

A. Yes; me and my partners. Yes, sir.

Q. And who is your partner?

A. I have a handful of partners up there. . . . Casagrande is my partner there. Frankie Antinocci is my partner there. What is the other partner, now? Bill Leonie is a partner there with me.

Q. How about Aviliena [*sic*. Avellino]? . . .

A. No. I know of him. . . .

Q. You sold out?

A. IWS. . . .

Q. You sold that out?

A. Sold my share out, yes.

Q. Did your brother [Ralph Velocci] sell his share out?

A. Yes, sir.

Q. You all no longer have an interest in International [*sic*] Waste at all –

A. Well – . . . We hold a lot of stock – we hold a lot of stock in the company and **they** [*my emphasis*, 'they' is Attwoods] bought it for the company. . . .

Q. Industrial Waste of Marion County, is that any subsidiary of Industrial Waste?

A. Well . . . It was a separate corporation formed to run the landfill. . . . It's really separate. It is not really a subsidiary, what I mean by that; but yet **everything is done in the office in Miami on those books and they pay all the bills down there** [*my emphasis*]. . . .

Q. You were just out in Los Angeles? . . . Did you visit with Mr Gould while you were out there?

A. I went out there because of all the rumours that were going around that possibly Orville was not building the machine. . . .

Q. And?

A. I am convinced he is doing something. I seen machinery. . . .

Q. What is your connection with the Baseline Landfill contract?

A. . . . I was involved with it from the beginning. I am operating the landfill. I am overseeing the landfill. . . .

Q. Who is Industrial Waste Services of Marion County? . . .

A. They – me. . . . I am a corporate officer in that corporation and so is **Jack Casagrande, a corporate officer in that corporation . . . Jack is President** [*my emphasis*].

Q. Okay. You told us that you had not been out to Santa Ana, California to view the property for years?

A. Oh, yes. Maybe more. . . .

Q. Was the . . . pyrolytic converter in operation or was it being constructed at that time, do you know?

A. I presume it was under construction. A portion of it was done. . . .

Q. Who told you what the reason for the delays have been for the last four years?

A. Well, first of all, in the beginning we had some trouble with the permitting. We didn't get the permitting. . . .

Q. **By the way, did he show you the old horizontal pyrolytic converter? . . . It is in the junkyard there?**

A. **Yeah.**

Q. **It is in the junkyard there?**

A. **Yeah. I didn't go over there; but Les [Erber] did.**

Q. **Did he show it to you?**

A. **Yes. It's laying there. . . .**

Q. **All right. Have you yourself attempted to market this pyrolytic converter anyplace else?**

A. **Oh, yeah. . . . 'A lot of places. . . . You might say that I have been around trying to get the machine on the line.**

Q. **Which one?**

A. **The old one. . . . the one that is laying out in the junkyard** [*my emphasis*] **(pp. 25–53).**

5

The *Camorra*
'Clean' Capital and Organised Crime
VINCENZO RUGGIERO*

INTRODUCTION

It is recognised that definitions of 'organised crime' are still very much a matter of controversy. Some authors define it along specifically quantitative lines: the number of people engaged in illegal activities would thus determine the degree of organisation.[1] Others align the organisational dimension with a variable that is, in the main, temporal – that is to say, the length of time that the illicit activity has been going on.[2] In turn, one must not neglect certain structural characteristics when attempting such a definition: one may speak of criminal organisation when diverse structures and practices come into play, capable of engaging themselves in a range of activities. Furthermore, such a form of organisation must be able to respond to the peculiar demands associated with its condition of illegality. First among all these demands, although it remains covert, is that of making its powers of dissuasion and coercion publicly felt. An even balance is thus required between openness and secrecy, which only a complex structure could be in a position to supply. Secondly, there is the need to neutralise the intervention of the law in matters of the oath of secrecy, corruption, reprisals. And finally, the organisation must reconcile its own internal order, conducted through specific forms of control and conflict-solving, with its legitimacy in external terms, mediated through the distribution of social, albeit illicit, opportunity.[3]

Other authors base their definition of organised crime on the professionalism of its participants, who acquire skills and career-advancement as a result of the full-time illegal practices in which they are involved.[4] Such a writer, for example, is John Mack, who seems to be approaching some helpful definition when he traces a preliminary parallel between the criminal and the industrial world.

This author concludes, however, by concerning himself exclusively with white-collar crime, exactly as though industry deployed only the white-collar sector and had no need of live labour.[5]

For his part, a classic authority like Herman Mannheim devotes a mere ten pages out of the 882 of his hefty treatise to the subject of organised crime. The reason can perhaps be found in the introduction to his study, where the author examines criminal behaviour as behaviour that *in any case* requires a certain level of organisation, or at least a mode of association between individuals. In his view, the term 'organised crime' can thus be applied to the majority of illicit activities that are economically motivated.[6]

The point of view recently emphasised in the definition of organised crime concerns the collective customer of its activities. Organised crime exists, it has been said, when the public or a client is offered a series of goods or services that can officially be defined as illegal.[7] In this case, the structure of organised crime would just fill a gap left by the lack of institutional agencies which are not in a position to distribute those goods and services or that, morally, do not hold with such things. On this issue, it remains a matter of controversy whether it is the criminal structure that creates the need for illicit goods and services or whether, on the contrary, it is a widespread demand for these things that stimulates and nourishes the illegal activities of the organised groups.

The definitions proposed by Mary McIntosh constitute a further elaboration of these points.[8] This author categorises modes of criminal organisation according to a kind of historical and structural evolution from the picturesque to the craft organisations, from project groups right up to the business organisations. In her view, and in that of other authors, the business organisations are to be distinguished in so far as they are permanent, and in so far as they have sustained a continuity of operation. McIntosh then adds that the extortion and the distribution of goods and services lend themselves ideally to implementation in an organised criminal structure and, at the same time, allow a covert relation to take shape between the offenders and the victims. These latter 'know what is going on and for some reason accept it . . . whether because they desire the goods and services supplied or because they see the extortionist as having more power in their parish than the agents of the state, they are not willing to co-operate in the prevention of crime'.[9]

We are thus approaching more complex definitions, where the offender–victim relation loses a large part of its criminological significance and loses some centrality in the context of relationships whose significance is in the first place of an economic nature. Indeed, in Pino Arlacchi's argument, organised crime is principally a business undertaking; it presents innovative developments from the point of view of production; it acts according to principles of rationality and capitalist risk–benefit calculation and, at the same time, it preserves an irrational aspect, that is to say, those 'animal spirits' that Keynes held to be essential in facing the risks of any entrepreneurial venture.[10] It would take a separate essay to rehearse all the definitions of organised crime so far put forward. I have therefore sought to select those that are more accessible and that must lend themselves to consideration. Two constants must now be underlined, inasmuch as they are almost necessarily present in every definition of organised crime. The first concerns so-called corruption. There is a more or less universal notion that a form of organised crime exists where criminal groups have the power to corrupt institutional bodies which, closing one eye to illicit goings-on, promote their well-being. Linked to this idea is a notion according to which criminal forces assert themselves in circumstances where the power of the state is weak, or simply absent, or, if one prefers, in the *adolescent* stages of the state apparatus and regulation. A modern democratic state, on the other hand, would exclude corruption and as a result remove the cultural base from the structure of organised crime.[11]

A second interpretative constant lapses on more strictly economic grounds. The presence of organised criminal groups is most often associated with backward socioeconomic systems. Poor productivity comes to be seen as the source of all social breakdown and of disruption, and particularly so in the southern regions of the world. A trenchant politics of development and modernisation would solve the problem. Administrative irregularities, illegality of all kinds, will, in short, remain as 'surviving traces' of the old modes of production that only industrialisation and the market, with the resultant forms of democratic representation, will be capable of removing.[12]

In the following pages I shall outline a brief history of the Neapolitan *Camorra*, a typical organised criminal structure of the Italian Campania region. At the same time, and especially in the conclusion to the chapter, I shall seek to evaluate the extent to which the case of the *Camorra* conforms to the above-mentioned features by which organised crime is commonly identified. I wish to acknowledge that some of the definitions listed above will be loudly challenged, and that a lot of work is still necessary to formulate new definitions, truly capable of placing the features of organised crime, without moralism or false consciousness, in the contemporary context.[13]

THE OLD *CAMORRA*

These initial remarks are of a linguistic nature. *Guapparia* and *Camorra* are very common expressions in the Neapolitan dialect, and the two words do not always evoke sinister images. *Guapparia* comes from *guappo* and is derived from the Spanish word meaning 'beautiful', 'impressive'. *Guappo* is even applied to children, to signify their cleverness or courage, even the kind that expresses itself in a subtle sort of bullying.

Among the *guappi* many people live in an illegal manner, but nevertheless an indulgent popular tradition would have them resolute and ruthless but also honourable, fair and generous. The last of these traditional *guappi* died in Naples recently, after having acted for years as an informal 'justice of the peace' in one of the most crowded areas of the city. He settled disputes and, it is said, helped the poor. He had recently given an interview in which he mourned the end of an era – that of the men of honour who succoured the people – and condemned the present, dominated by cruel, greedy and unscrupulous individuals. Thousands attended his funeral.[14]

The *guappi* of the old era came together in a secret society called *Camorra*. The original use of this word seems to derive from Miguel Cervantes, who introduces it in a short story centred on a naïve young robber.[15] Cervantes' character believes it possible to practice 'freely' the art of theft without paying taxes or toll-money. There exists instead an organisation that vests itself with the task of collecting percentages on the profits of all illegal activity; Cervantes presents this organisation as a 'Brotherhood of honour'. This is a matter of a group, organised to the last detail, which keeps precise accounts of income and of wages paid to its members. This Spanish Brotherhood is believed to be the ancestor of a similar organisation that will be found in Naples at the start of the nineteenth century, calling itself *Camorra*.

There is historical evidence that in 1820 the *guappi* of Naples met in a small church in the city to formalise their existence and their collective identity as the 'Bella Società Riformata'.[16] Their ceremonies of affiliation borrowed something from the bloody terms typical of aristocratic rituals and of political sects of a Masonic type. And it is not a paradox that an association of outlaws, from its very beginning, should emulate the rituals and affect the pride of aristocrats; indeed, its acolytes came from the aristocracy of the outcasts, they were the plebeian élite. During the nineteenth century the *Camorra* recruited the non-mendicant poor, and gave them work and respectability. However, this neutralised the potential for rebellion among the poor and directed the energies of the people toward commercial activity and well-structured business.

In drawing a profile of the *Camorra* type of organisation one must not overlook the use of violence. Certainly, the *guappi* or *camorristi* used violence, but at the same time they managed to contain it, and for this reason, perhaps, their great social utility became acknowledged.

Violence became disciplined and ritualised by *professionals*, who tempered the excesses and the random conflicts with which society was (and is?) saturated. The *Camorristi*, in short, made violence recognisable, planned and predictable, so that it would not break out suddenly. Increasingly, they demonstrated their capacity and their right to exercise it, and increasingly they formulated it in specific rules, in negotiating procedures which were paradoxical perhaps, but socially cohesive. In point of fact, in the patois of the *Camorra*, the punitive gesture became known as the *freno* (brakes), to signify that a group had the right, precisely, *to put the brakes on* possible escalations of brutality and unproductive, pointless vendettas. 'Violence is a benefit which must not be wasted unnecessarily and the Camorra of the 19th century was very conscious of this.'[17]

The activities of the old *Camorra* were principally made up of the protection it exercised over the economy, whether legal or illegal, and this activity called for firm military resources and precise internal hierarchical structures into which new members could be drawn by career prospects.

Two historical episodes may complete the profile of *Camorra* as it looked in the last century. At the time of the unification of the Italian peninsula (1860–1), the local authorities in Naples entrusted the task of maintaining public order to the *Camorra*, as the regular police had been sent to back up Garibaldi's army. The authority of the *guappi* in fact became accepted by everyone as the only power likely to guarantee order in a situation of war, when internal conflict breaching every rule could easily break out.[18] The *Camorra* was here playing (*avant la lettre*) the role of broker – acting as a mediator between a turbulent society and the official authorities – a role destined to evolve and to adapt in the years to come. In their capacity as police within the working classes, efficient and respected, they achieved results that the official police would have found it hard to bring off. One interesting detail: a group of *Camorristi* were taken on specifically as a Customs squad. This is a crucial precedent in the understanding of the later development of the *Camorra* in foreign trade and contraband.

This identification with a law-and-order role informed an incident of the same period in the penitentiary on the island of San Stefano. The battery of the army that was occupying the island was posted to another military zone, where Garibaldi was getting ready to move north in order to complete the unification. In the penitentiary, of course, an uprising broke out, led by imprisoned *Camorristi* who founded a mock 'independent republic'. The entire island fell under their control and laws were enacted, with fines for offenders. The provisional government could not have asked for more: the prisoners had not mutinied but had remained neutral, acquiescent as they certainly were to the *Camorra*'s rule, however severe this was in spirit and brutal in execution.[19]

IRREGULAR WORKERS AND IRREGULAR DELINQUENTS

The two examples outlined above were not chosen at random. On one hand, the role of *law* maintained by the *Camorra* would be destined in modern times to assume more complex characteristics. On the other hand, the experience acquired in trade and in the control of the foreign movement of goods permitted the organisation to refine its techniques and its expertise in precisely what would become its principal fields of economic interest. Among the most remunerative economic activities, in fact – and not only in the last century – would be agricultural contraband, along with forms of protection on the legal activities of the agriculture market itself. And the modes of extortion would become more and more complex and varied with the growing complexity of relations in the market. In short, legal economic forms will, out of themselves, create corresponding illegal ones.[20]

The incident concerning the San Stefano prison would also have its aftermath. The *Camorra* would soon become a real power in Italian prisons, from which it continued to organise its operations and from which it would continuously recruit new followers. In addition, it would take care of imprisoned colleagues to the extent that one element of its membership still constitutes a ready financial source guaranteeing help for those arrested and for all of their families.

As can be seen, some of these traditional elements point towards a certain modernity, and one cannot omit a final feature which has survived in the organised crime of Naples in our own time. This is a strictly political matter: the *Camorra* was indeed a state within the state, which it deprived of a monopoly in the use of violence; but this did not prevent it from maintaining a role, albeit that of a junior partner, in the organisation of local affairs. Those of its members who enjoyed the greatest following and popular respect were, after compensation, charged with the task of delivering votes through grass-roots propaganda, which was made more than easy by their continual contact with the people. Here we encounter an embryonic example of patronage, of political graft, even if at this stage the *Camorristi* were limited to the role of a type of mercenary, not yet having developed organisational relations with the political arena. These relations, very much modernised, would take shape later, in the contemporary period.[21]

The particular social composition of the *Camorra* may be demonstrated by the two major judicial actions brought against the organisation. The first took place in 1863 with more than 1200 people indicted. Half the accused were under 30 years of age; 75 per cent turned out officially not to own any property nor to have a steady income at their disposal; 60 per cent claimed to work occasionally at manual occupations: in the docks, at the railway station, in the fruit and vegetable market. The greater part was made up of porters, employed, as has already been suggested, in places where large quantities of goods were traded. The majority of the accused, in short, comprised *irregular workers* who, every now and then, became *irregular delinquents*, paid by the day or 'on commission'. It is significant that none of those arrested came from the craft or even the manufacturing classes: all of them were thus alienated from the official modes of production, which have never been in a dominant position in Naples.[22]

The second *Camorra* trial began in 1907 and ended in 1912. The behaviour of the forces of law had clear, even if brutal, characteristics that in its procedures took on the same features as the *Camorra*. If the *Camorra* were illegal, the means of combating it were equally so. Five hundred were indicted, to the outrage of the enlightened who denounced the abrogation of all proper processes of law and who were not disposed to believe that there could really be 500 leaders of the organisation. Naples was held in inexorable suspense for eight months, 'but it seemed that it would never end'. Everyone sensed the danger of ending up in prison. 'Everybody tried to re- member whether he could have had some contact, even merely occasional, with the accused. The entire city fell under suspicion.'[23] On this occasion, the social composition of the suspects was more varied – either a sign of an excessive criminalisation or of greater flexibility in the *Camorra*'s structure, which was by now in a position to form alliances in different classes and to set up its own real professional management sector.

It is now necessary to jump forward in this historical reconstruction of the *Camorra* to examine at this stage the postwar period. The reasons for this may become clear in what follows. For several decades the designation *Camorra* used to signal a criminal phenom- enon which came and went, and had nothing to do with the old centralised and clearly identifiable structure. In fact, until the middle of this century, there emerged from time to time various groups who exhibited none of the odd rituals and habits of secrecy that distin- guished the *Camorra*. From a criminological point of view it is important to underline, then, that in relation to the period of Italian Fascism, it is impossible to reconstruct the reality of crime, whose very existence was officially 'uprooted'.

DEVELOPERS AND SMUGGLERS

To identify the major destructive forces at work in Naples after the war we must leave organised crime to one side for a while, and spend a moment examining the building trade. The Naples that Goethe had given up trying to describe, incapable, as he said, of finding adjectives equal to its beauty, would become gutted in little more than ten years. Undisciplined urban growth altered the fea- tures of the city and brought into prominence a class of developers closely tied to local political organisation.[24] For about twenty years building went on everywhere, at minimum cost in terms of both material used and payment for human labour. Only in the early 1970s did a few magistrates bring to light the wholesale irregularities and even the open falsifications in the urban development plan: falsifications that could only have been carried out with the connivance of local government, and that had virtually wiped the 'protected area' status off the city's map.[25] And only in 1981 would this reality become apparent, with the earthquake in Naples when whole quarters of the city crumbled, revealing the quality of the materials and the technical competence with which they had been constructed.[26]

This group of developers is not usually ranked among the participants of organised crime. But soon they would be obliged to resort to it, just as they would to an ordinary financial institution. Now, not all of these developers could approach a mutual banker, being unable to offer official guarantees of credit. Organised crime therefore practised a modern form of usury, sometimes even offering interest rates that were competitive with those of the official banks.

In economic terms, the meeting between legal business and organised crime took place in the gaps within competitive capital, where adventurous behaviour and frenzied law-breaking are everywhere taken for granted. The organised criminal groups had enormous sums at their disposal, thanks to the early accumulations principally brought about by two specific activities: those which had the control of wholesale food markets as their legacy and those, more modern, involved in contraband. Every day about 300 goods wagons, full of fruit and vegetables, leave the general markets of Naples for Germany, the Benelux countries and Scandinavia. Every one of this sector's operations was marked by the intervention of what came to be called the *Nuova Camorra: camorristi* taking money from the peasants for the supposed protection of their land; from the makers of the crates used in packaging; similarly, from the transport-firms; from exporters; from wholesalers. In a short time *camorristi* themselves became tradesmen and exporters: not a crate of tomatoes could move without their agreement.[27]

But the most lucrative activities were those tied up with contraband, sustained and enlarged by the huge black market which had prospered during the war years. Contraband was the principal trade of a substantial part of the population of Naples: first in food, then in textiles and clothes, and then in domestic appliances and cigarettes. 'From being a job for necessity and survival, it will become a normal job, daily work for thousands and thousands of people. For decades it will be one of the city's economic activities.'[28]

We shall now look in more detail at the illicit tobacco trade. In the period between 1950 and 1970 the demand for non-Italian tobacco grew considerably: sales of foreign cigarettes rose from 397 to 14,555 tonnes. According to statistics furnished by government sources, 10,000 tonnes of tobacco were sold on the black market. A glance at the structure of the supply of goods reveals that the financiers of the contraband trade in cigarettes were not residents of Naples but formed part of a French-organised network. The *Nuova Camorra* acted as wholesale distributors, at least throughout the 1950s.[29] Distribution at a day-to-day level was carried on by thousands of people on every street-corner, with plenty of stalls and attractive posters, in broad daylight. In this case, one cannot speak of a criminal subculture: 'the greater part of illegal economic activity before the 1970s . . . took place in the open, subsumed more or less completely by the everyday life of the working-class areas'.[30] We shall see how significant this feature becomes when we go on to examine the labour-market in the distribution of drugs.

Let us now turn back to the 'pirate-entrepreneurs'. The point has already been made that developers often had recourse to the credit offered by organised criminal groups. It must be noted that re-investment of their profits could not be directed, in a circular pro-cess, toward further construction projects, as a provisional *ceiling* would quickly be reached. Nor could their profits find a way into the so-called intermediate economy or into the infrastructure of indus-try which was already about to fall into the hands of northern Italian monopoly capital. Competitive money, most forcefully represented in Naples by the builders, will often move towards illegal dealings, as a logical consequence of the good relations that existed there between big business and criminal enterprise. This situation becomes evident when organised crime in Naples begins to free itself from the economic and organisational predominance of foreign partner-competitors and opportunities are thus opened up for investment on a larger scale in the contraband cigarette trade. In short, the *Nuova Camorra* will not limit itself to medium-scale and wholesale dis-tributors but will control the whole circuit of buying and selling operations.

The *Nuova Camorra* harvested the first fruits of its victory in the competition with the French network, and its achievement is not only to be understood in terms of superior military power.[31] In support of its activities, from the beginning of the 1970s, it could count, on the one hand, upon its own capital, and on the other, upon capital 'legally' acquired from small and medium-sized business in Naples. This was by now more than a simple commercial partner, becoming an integrated structural branch of the *Camorra*.[32] We are face-to-face here with an initial example of symbiosis, a bilateral relationship between legal and criminal money, which the judiciary managed to uncover only on rare occasions. According to the Anti-Mafia Commission, the financiers of the contraband cigarette trade were to be sought among businessmen, sometimes above suspicion, who were drawn by big and very fast profits. 'These people range from large scale developers who got rich on real estate speculation to the owners of large transport businesses.'[33]

One must add that the decline of French domination made it necessary for the *Camorra* to ally itself with Sicilian and Calabrian groups, and it should be pointed out that to this alliance can be traced the union of the contraband cigarette network and the distribution network of morphine and heroin, which the Sicilian Mafia had already started to sell in the early 1960s. The Neapolitan *Camorra*, in short, grew beyond its provincial base and was compelled to establish economically significant relations whether at a national or at an international level. We shall see how the organisations of Naples responded to these demands.

THE NEW ORGANISED *CAMORRA* AND THE *NUOVA FAMIGLIA*

In the last fifteen years, no single organised group has had the monopoly of illegal activity in Naples. There are two principal organisations which, taking up the old rituals, have called themselves respectively the *Nuova Camorra Organizzata* and the *Nuova Famiglia*. Let us look briefly at their characteristics.

The former is mainly influential in the suburbs: it is the heir of the rural *Camorra* and its undisputed leader is Raffaele Cutolo. The old features of the *Nuova Camorra Organizzata* may be suggested not simply by its rituals and the publicly self-important language, but in the conviction of its members that they are 'men of respect' and benefactors of the people. Following the tradition of the *Camorra*, the NCO recruits in prisons, where it is a powerful force and whence it directs its economic operations. It should be noted that Raffaele Cutolo, who has now been in prison for more than ten years, has many times been prosecuted for murder in the role of originator and mastermind during his time behind bars.

The *Nuova Camorra Organizzata* has also been defined as the *Mass Camorra*: an organisation which involves every form of illegal activity, from the humblest level to the highest. In short, an organisation that recruits every kind of talent, is open to the full range of criminal experience and draws in an indiscriminate way on the *criminal reserve army*.[34] The NCO offers rapid career advancement after a very brief apprenticeship: it is a short step from skilful use of the knife to the high echelons of the hierarchy. Raffaele Cutolo himself dedicated a feverish poem to the magic of the knife in a collection he published a few years ago.[35]

The *NCO* is thus distinguished by its mass character, by its virtual monopoly of small-scale illegality, by the strength of its recruitment among the young. To these last it has furnished real, proper work and has encouraged a sense of pride: if you're tough, you can have dignity, you can escape your poor background, you can be a *camorrista*: you can be somebody. This traditional characteristic, drawn from popular culture, this feeling of organised religion among its followers and the much vaunted popularity of its leaders, comprise the strength of the *NCO* but in time will also constitute its weakness. Very much locally rooted, even in its politics, Cutolo's *Camorra* is not in a position to make the leap to the national and international role made inevitable by the entrance of heroin. The recent (apparent?) defeat of the *NCO*, after hundred of arrests in its ranks, is not attributable, as has been suggested, to its *openness*, its uncompartmentalised nature, or to its mass character, which may have facilitated infiltration or repentance among its members. Nor, perhaps, is it owing to those features of self-advertising populism that led the organisation, aping political groups, to claim (in telephone calls and by leaflets) responsibility for military action.[36] A more economically based reading will show that the *NCO* remains linked to the least innovative forms of local business, with the kind of capital that had favoured its expansion. Ancient and modern do not combine very well, and this seems to have been the case with the *Nuova Famiglia*. Cutolo's scarcely practical ambition was, in brief, the reconciliation of a power, provincial in nature and in its mode of operation, with economic enterprises of a far bigger scale.

It now seems that the *Nuova Famiglia* has so far realised this aim. Its appearance is of a mass character, its organisation has an urban origin, with popular and adaptable features. There is evidence of this in the extreme variety of the individuals who make up its workforce. To work for the *Nuova Famiglia* it is not essential to belong to a particular subculture nor to exhibit characteristic elements of gangsterism in the use of violence. Students, the unemployed, but also those in work and professional people, can find a role: for some it is a principal employment, for others a second job.[37] This modern profile became emphatically clear a few years ago when the *Nuova Famiglia* rapidly moved from contraband cigarettes into drug-trafficking. An unofficial committee was formed among its employees, of workers who suddenly found themselves without wages; the committee publicly expressed its 'concern' at the crisis in the cigarette sector and some of its protesting manifestoes were much in evidence on the streets of Naples.[38]

The *Nuova Famiglia* still maintains excellent business relations with national criminal organisations and has considerable knowledge and experience of the dynamics of transnational economics. In the field of public finance, for example, its influence is not limited to local government, which is, none the less, an important economic force in Southern Italy. The *Nuova Famiglia* has access to international financial bodies – among them the EEC – and consequently can launch operations of a similarly international nature.[39]

The successful *Camorra*, in the final analysis, is the one which has grasped the necessity of getting out of the competitive-productive network and of looking for its real partners among the representatives of monopoly-production. Its power in the world of finance derives from its status of privileged customer with the banks. Its money-laundering operations paradoxically lend it a great bargaining power and constitute a kind of 'guarantee of seriousness' when unexpected needs arise for credit and easy access to money. This privileged position in the field of finance allows the *Camorra* of Naples to deal as equals with representatives of monopoly capital, with results that are not so different from those of normal joint ventures. The meeting of legal and illegal capital is especially encouraged by two particular economies: those of drugs and arms. The most recent development in the shape of the organised criminal network has been brought about by these two commodities. Let us briefly examine them both.

DRUGS AND ARMS

It is by now acknowledged that the workings of the Italian drug market stand as a clear refutation of several criminological theories.

My own work in the field suggests that many of those involved in
the distribution of drugs are a long way from fitting the image either
of the junkie, always desperate and jobless, or of the callous criminal, skilled and unscrupulous.[40] It is not necessary to have served
a criminal apprenticeship to gain entry to the drug market. At the
level of the labour force many small-time dealers have a background
of legal or semi-legal work, of commercial activity of every kind.
Many are already employed; others participate in drug-dealing on
an occasional basis. Some make up a single operation: they get into
the drug economy and make money out of it, in order then to set up
small- or medium-scale businesses of a different kind. In short,
many do not fit the stereotype according to which drugs are seen as
a stage in a career of crime; for these, on the contrary, the 'drug' stage
is one step in a lawful career. Even at the highest levels of the trade
the subcultural character is neither the dominant one, nor, as many
studies suggest, one which is urgent and inescapable. In the medium
traffic, the purchase of drugs isn't always carried on by 'dirty' money
and professional criminal outfits, but often handled by clean capital
and legitimate financiers. These latter benefited in the past from
money of illicit origins, above all when starting out in business, at
which time they went for loans to the financial groups that controlled organised crime. As debtors, many small entrepreneurs invest in
illicit dealings, often in drugs, in order to clear their debts or to
maximise their early, hard-won profits, or else to rebuild and modify
production in future lawful activities. In a city like Naples a full
range of small- and medium-scale firms were able to establish themselves on the strength of criminal money, just as a lot of criminal
activity can prosper thanks to entrepreneurial capital.

Thus, criminal money becomes 'socialised' in enterprises which,
deploying both casual and conspicuous income, can frequently move
into sophisticated production, even into high technology. The result
of this situation is the introduction of these types of business into
wider markets and, consequently, into the territory of monopoly
capital. It is not, as is often alleged, a question of firms being directly
set up by criminal groups who are investing their profits in legitimate
business. Exactly the opposite is the case. A simple example: it turns
out that many firms, once hit by extortion, ask to be exempted from
the payment of protection-money, and to invest that money in illegal
activities of whose nature they claim, officially, to be ignorant. Often,
these investments are made in the drug economy, which functions

pretty much as a stock market, a pool of financial bonds open to occasional lurches or steady operation.[41]

We are approaching a high synthesis between forms of capital, where 'legitimate' and 'illegitimate' lose a large part of their distinguishing features, and where, indeed, such distinctions sound a little censorious, anachronistic. This synthesis culminates in the terrain of the illicit traffic of money and arms.

It is well known that, nowadays, the export of weapons is controlled by inter-governmental treaties. But it is also the case that, if it has to obey international regulations, most of this kind of production has little chance of coming on to the market. The greater part of the trade in arms is thus forced into illegality. According to some writers, this illegal market comprises three levels or constellations.[42] On the first one finds, naturally enough, the producers, who have close connections with the members of the Department of Defence who exercise control either over the goods produced, or over their destination. The same producers are thus obliged to maintain continuous relations with their respective governments, upon whose decisions they depend for the quality and quantity of the arms exported. The first illicit deals go on at this level: here, incidents of governmental corruption are the order of the day. On the second level are the traders, who are usually nothing more than a reliable, official extension of the producers themselves. The third level is made up of groups of middlemen who take on the risk of the sales operation and who more than anyone know the ins-and-outs of secret international trade. In this category one finds representatives of organised crime who are expert in trade involving all kinds of goods: from heroin to oil products, from cigarettes to provisions. The Mafia and *Camorra* limit themselves, in this case, to offers of help to the big arms-producers, some of whom are connected, in Italy, to the monopoly giant Fiat. A similar service is provided in the traffic of money by the undercover export of clean finance. The circle closes: modern money and monopoly businesses which, in the arms sector, employ about 750,000 workers throughout Europe, need criminal distribution structures, and survive thanks to apparently backward, ancient cultures that are kept alive by these modern structures.[43]

In my view, these are the dynamics that have created the background to the competition between the *Nuova Camorra Organizzata* and the *Nuova Famiglia*: dynamics centred entirely in the respective organisations, on entrepreneurial and commercial experience. The case of the *Camorra* of Naples serves as a starting-point for some concluding reflections and allows us to go back to the brief introductory part of this article, which concerns the search for a complete and up-to-date definition of organised crime.

CONCLUSIONS

If we take the Neapolitan *Camorra* as a model, it isn't easy to give a synthesising definition of organised crime. Certainly, 'flexibility' and 'complexity' are the characteristics that immediately spring into view when one looks at any criminal structure. In fact, the *Camorra* is in a position to deploy productive energy and to offer work opportunities, whether in legal or illegal activity. Thus, on one hand, it can socialise its productive activity and increase its profits in a widened, multi-dimensional process of development. Sheer hoarding is alien to it, and it is hard to accuse the *Camorra* of being unproductive, as is the common charge.[44] Its profits are not simply converted into status-symbols for the members of its higher echelons but are more widely distributed, in the form of social opportunity and material wealth. On the other hand, in its relations with the more progressive lawful undertakings, the *Camorra* displays its high degree of flexibility when it offers *non-material benefits*: services of mediation which, as in the case of arms-deals, accelerate the circulation of goods and are a continual stimulus to markets.

Moreover, so complex a structure cannot simply base itself on the professionalism of its members. Certain definitions of organised crime which point to 'professionalism' as one of its peculiar characteristics overlook the fact that every business, even the most technologically sophisticated, has to combine expert and non-expert labour, a high input of money in its own organisation with wide social distribution of its product; and finally must reconcile the making of relative surplus-value with the making of absolute surplus-value. Criminal undertakings seem to fulfil these requirements, in so far as they mobilise both highly trained personnel and a mass labour-force, lacking specific training, who are given work on a sort of illegal assembly-line.

Let us add to this a further consideration, which calls into question other writers and other definitions. When, as in the case of Mannheim, one attributes to any type of criminal activity, *however* economically motivated, a certain degree of organisation, one expresses oneself tautologically and fails to draw a substantial distinction. The professional groups who were dominant in the past bring to mind a model that could be defined as *criminal partnership*, where individual skills combine in collective projects. The *criminal partnership* is horizontal in structure, permitting every member to participate in the planning, in the execution and finally in the distribution of profits.[45] In this case, we have a *technical division* of labour, which, in organised crime, becomes a *social division*. Organised crime, in fact, has a vertical and fragmented structure: its labour-force is not in a position to control the production cycle of which it is a part, and is scarcely capable of controlling the alienating work-sector in which it is employed. In the case of the drug-cycle, then, the dependence of the 'delinquent worker' on the criminal enterprise combines with the dependence on the commodity (drugs) itself, forging as a result an army of perfectly acquiescent and obedient labourers.[46]

This is the legacy of the old *Camorra*: it is precisely in this acquiescence and discipline that the old function of *order* survives, in its modern shape continually informed by the traditional organisations.

Examining the case of the *Camorra*, one cannot assert that organised crime prospers where there is little sense of a state; on the contrary, it prospers where there is too much state, or at least where the state is present in formal bureaucratic details, routine, hypertrophied and predatory. In many circumstances organised crime does not need to corrupt the legal apparatus but is corrupted by it; it prospers, and becomes piratical, thanks to the analogously piratical nature of the public system. In short, one is the faithful reflection of the other. In the last analysis, it is part of the political trade to be crimino-genetic.

The second assumption deserving a similar reversal is that according to which contexts of underdevelopment will favour the growth of organised crime of the Mafia type. It seems, rather, that economic growth itself periodically employs the forms and structures of the Mafia to pursue innovation and further development. From clean money to criminal money and vice versa, the direction seems to be reversible: while the Mafia does business, business *mafiosizes* itself. As I write, a dramatic example of this equation is taking shape. Advanced money, tied up in the construction of pharaonic works for the next World Cup, is subcontracting various pieces of work to small firms. Fifteen workers have already died in accidents brought about precisely by the illegal, cavalier and Mafia-style character of these firms. Ancient and modern, underdeveloped and fully developed, one could not find a more devastating combination. Advanced capital seems, in short, to have at its disposal apparently anomalous *islands* in which it finds means of investing, making money, relaunching. These illegal islands are an integral part of its development and constitute a form of laboratory, necessary for trying out new systems of profit-making and for preparing the ground for further legalisation, in an intermittent but continuous to-and-fro. Organised crime is therefore no obstacle to development; at the most, it is development in an obscene but complementary version. The very distinctions between capital as collective reason (legal capital) and capital as egoistic interest (criminal) lose much of their analytic sense: the two dimensions combine and cross-refer in a process of development that benefits them both. One example: during the rebuilding after the Naples earthquake, the *Camorra*'s habit of cornering the contracts suited perfectly the building firms of Northern Italy who ran to the *Campania* without too much hair-splitting with the partners and middlemen with whom they had to negotiate.[47]

A final consideration takes us back to that characteristic feature of organised crime residing in the use of violence. From where do we derive the bewilderment we feel at every Mafia or *Camorra* act of violence? Not perhaps from the episode in itself, which takes place as just another arbitrary act of death in a scenario where arbitrariness and death are statutory rules. Perhaps what perplexes us stems from the fact that the violence deployed by organised crime, for some reason or other connected with its glamour, lends itself perfectly to widespread social emulation. The legal business, as has been said, *mafiosizes* itself; but, at the same time, certain residual groups, outside organised crime, emulate its behaviour and copy its outlook and its practices. In Naples an already common case is that of small groups, scarcely professional and thus all the more dangerous, who, presenting themselves as part of the *Camorra*, try to impose protection rackets or to exercise other forms of blackmail in the name of an intimidating power that in reality they are in no position to command. However, a more visible and destructive form of emulation occurs in a broader social context. The use of force becomes habitual, becomes a normal form of interaction in daily life, where competition and envy visibly degrade the way we live together. This is one of many 'normal' and legal results of abnormal and illegal dynamics.

Le Goff has written some memorable pages on the relation of the licit and illicit, in the form of a relationship between virtue and sin.

For example, usury was able to move freely in the Christian conscience when the invention of Purgatory made it a venial and redeemable sin. Christians were thus able to 'save their money and their lives' – their eternal lives, it should be understood.[48] The frequent Mafia and *Camorra* trials can be seen in the same way. Legitimate capital, in a symbolitic relationship with criminal capital, reproduces itself periodically, although embodying an illegitimate core as its original sin, recurrent but now and then 'purged'.

Notes

*   The author would like to thank Mike Walters for helping to translate this article.

1.   E. Johnson, 'Organized Crime: Challenge to the American Legal System', *Journal of Criminal Law, Criminology and Political Science*, 54 (1963) pp. 1–29.
2.   F. A. Ianni, *A Family Business: Kinship and Social Control in Organized Crime* (New York: Russell Sage Foundation, 1972).
3.   A. Cohen, 'The Concept of Criminal Organization', *British Journal of Criminology*, 17, 2 (1977) pp. 97–111.
4.   A. Lindesmith, 'Organized Crime', *Annals of the American Academy of Political and Social Science*, 217 (1941) pp. 32–54.
5.   J. Mack and H. Kerner, *The Crime Industry* (Lexington, Va: Saxon House, 1975).
6.   H. Mannheim, *Trattato di criminologia comparata* (Turin: Einaudi, 1975).
7.   Ianni, op. cit.
8.   M. McIntosh, *The Organisation of Crime* (London: Macmillan, 1975).
9.   Ibid., pp. 50–1.
10. P. Arlacchi, *La mafia imprenditrice* (Bologna: Il Mulino, 1983).
11. This, for example, is the opinion of, among others, N. Dalla Chiesa, 'Mafia e potere oggi', *Democrazia e Diritto*, 4 (1983) pp. 34–46.
12. This opinion can be attributed to both P. Arlacchi and N. Dalla Chiesa, *La palude e la citta'* (Milan: Mondadori, 1987).
13. An attempt at a synthesis of the different definitions has been made by F. Ferracuti, *Forme di organizzazione criminali e terrorismo* (Milan: Giuffré, 1988).
14. See the account in the daily newspaper of Naples, *Il Mattino*, 18 September 1989 ('Al funerale di un vecchio guappo').
15. M. Cervantes, 'Rinconete e Cortadillo', in *Opere* (Milan: Rizzoli, 1973).
16. A. De Blasio, *Usi e costumi dei camorristi* (Naples: Esti, 1897), and *La malavita a Napoli* (Naples: Esti, 1905).
17. I. Sales, *La Comorra. Le Camorre* (Rome: Editori Riuniti, 1988).
18. M. Marmo, 'La camorra e lo stato liberale', in F. Barbagallo, *Camorra e criminalita' organizzata in Campania* (Naples: Liguori, 1988) pp. 28–52.

19.   G. Alongi, *La camorra* (Turin: Edizioni MCM, 1890).

20.   H. M. Enzensberger, 'Pupetta o la fine della nuova Camorra', in *Politica e gangsterismo* (Rome: Savelli, 1979).

21.   G. D'agostino, 'Voto e camorra', in Barbagallo, op. cit.

22.   G. Machetti, 'Le leggi eccezionali post-unitarie e la repressione della camorra: un problema di ordine pubblico?', in Barbagallo, op. cit.

23.   G. Garofalo, *La seconda guerra napoletana* (Naples: Tavisano, 1984) pp. 68–9.

24.   A. Belli, *Il labirinto e l'eresia: La politica urbanistica a Napoli tra emergenza e ingovernabilita* (Milan: Frano Angeli, 1986).

25.   P. A. Allum, *Potere e Società a Napoli nel dopoguerra* (Turin: Einaudi, 1975), Italian version of *Politics and Society in Post-War Naples* (Cambridge: Cambridge University Press, 1973).

26.   A. Becchi Collidá, *Napoli miliardaria: Economia e lavoro dopo il terremoto* (Milan: Franco Angeli, 1984).

27.   I have already described these activities in V. Ruggiero, 'La camorra oggi', *Controinformazione*, 21 (1981) pp. 22–36.

28.   Sales, op. cit., pp. 116–20.

29.   A. Pizzorno and P. Arlacchi, *Camorra, contrabbando e mercato della droga in Campania* (Rome: Commissione Parlamentare sul Fenomeno della Mafia, 1985).

30.   Ibid., p. 23.

31.   For a reconstruction of the battle between French and Italian criminal groups, see A. Henman, R. Lewis and T. Malyon, *Big Deal: The Politics of the Illicit Drugs Business* (London: Pluto Press, 1985).

32.   This process has been described well by N. Chieppa, 'Dal contrabbando alla Camorra e dal colera al terremoto', *Osservatorio sulla Camorra*, 4 (1985) pp. 18–31.

33.   Commissione Anti-Mafia, *Documento XXIII*, 2 (Rome: 1976) p. 405.

34.   I. Sales, 'La camorra massa: caratteristiche organizzative e radici sociali', *Osservatorio sulla Camorra*, 5 (1987) pp. 123–42.

35.   R. Cutolo, *Poesie e pensieri* (Naples: Carditi, 1980).

36.   Sales attributes the defeat of the *nuova Camorra Organizzata* to these *open* characteristics, in *La Camorra. Le Camorre*, op. cit.

37.   On social developments in the *Nuova Famiglia* see A. Lamberti, 'Dall'economia criminale all'economia legale: Le linee di tendenza della Camorra imprenditrice', *Osservatorio sulla Camorra*, 5 (1987) 37–51.

38.   In a poster on the walls of the city, furthermore, one could read: 'Hands off contraband trade! Until they give us another means of living. We must organise and unite to defend our right to live. Meeting of all Neapolitan contraband-traders' (see the report 'Giu' le mani dal contrabbando' in the daily national newspaper *Il Manifesto*, 26 June 1983.

39.   Again, on the 'modernity' of the successful Camorra, see A. Lamberti, 'Mercato politico e mercato criminale', *La Citta' Nuova*, 5 (1988) pp. 15–23.

40.   These observations, and what follows on the subject of drugs are part of material collected by me and are in the course of publication.

Similar ideas, advanced as hypotheses, have been expressed in
E. Gallo and V. Ruggiero, 'Il crimine presunto e il delinquente-
lavoratore', *Primo Maggio*, 23/24 (1985) pp. 34–52 and in V.
Ruggiero, 'La droga come merce', *Criminologia*, 5–6 (1986) pp. 34–55.

41. According to information that I have collected, the foremost example
     among these firms is that of the real-estate dealer.
42. On the arms traffic, consult C. Palermo, 'Le forme nuove del crimine
     organizzato', *Democrazia e Diritto*, 4 (1983); and P. Arlacchi *et al.*, *Armi
     e droga. L'atto di accusa del giudice Carlo Palermo* (Rome: Editori Riuniti,
     1988).
43. SIPRI (Stockholm International Peace Research Institute), *World Ar-
     maments and Disarmament* (Stockholm: SIPRI, 1985). On illegal finan-
     cial traffic, see also R. Naylor, *Denaro che scotta* (Milan: Mondadori,
     1989).
44. The productive/unproductive question is broached in V. Ruggiero,
     'The Encounter between Big Business and Organized Crime', *Capital
     & Class*, 26 (1985) 93–104.
45. Some examples of what I define as 'criminal partnership' are outlined
     in the following essays: W. J. Einstadter, 'The Social Organization of
     Armed Robbery', *Social Problems*, 1 (1969) pp. 64–83; M. McIntosh,
     'Changes in the Organization of Thieving', in S. Cohen (ed.), *Images of
     Deviance* (Harmondsworth, Middx: Penguin, 1971); N. Shover, 'The
     Social Organization of Burglary', *Social Problems*, 4 (1973) pp. 499–513.
46. The delinquent/worker is also discussed in E. Gallo and V. Ruggiero,
     Il carcere immateriale (Milan: Sonda, 1989).
47. Sales, *La Camorra. Le Camorre*, op. cit., pp. 198–9.
48. J. Le Goff, *La borsa e la vita. Dall'usuraio al banchiere* (Bari: Laterza, 1987).

6

EEC Fraud
A Suitable Case for Treatment
MICHAEL CLARKE

By the beginning of the 1980s most Europeans probably knew of the existence of EEC fraud. Few, however, had any appreciation of its nature beyond a vague awareness of the exploitation of an ever-expanding budget largely used to sustain various sectors of agriculture, and a proliferating bureaucracy. And no one had a clear measure of its extent. The last part of this chapter will return to the longer-term and political implications of EEC fraud and to likely future developments in attempts to control it, but first it is necessary to identify the nature and extent of the problem. This leads naturally to a consideration of causes, and that in turn to control, which raises wider questions of how and why EEC fraud was discovered, and how and when it is likely to be successfully managed. The final element in the analysis will entail a return to these initial issues by situating the problem in its wider political economic context.

THE NATURE AND EXTENT OF EEC FRAUD

In its most general sense, identifying EEC fraud is straightforward. It is the improper use of EEC funds, which are themselves not only clearly raised and identified as such but subject to detailed regulation as to their expenditure. Further, it is straightforward to identify where the scope for greatest abuse lies, given a simple appraisal of the structure of the funds. In 1987 total revenue was £24.9 billion which was expected to rise to £29 billion in 1989.

Expenditure was as shown in Table 6.1. Of the larger items (those over £1 billion), the largest of all, the European Agricultural Guidance and Guarantee Funds (EAGGF), differs from the rest not only in its preponderance but also in being composed of a myriad of

TABLE 6.1

	£ millions
Administration	1,171
European Agricultural Guidance and Guarantee Funds (EAGGF)	15,975
Agricultural structures	619
Fisheries	110
Regional policy	1,870
Social policy	1,986
Research	626
Reimbursement of member states	1,677
Co-operation with developing countries	553
Total	23,459

SOURCE: House of Lords Paper 27, *Fraud against the Community* (London: HMSO, 1989) p. 9.

much smaller subsidy expenditures on agricultural production, intervention pricing, storage payments and export and other trade subsidies. The other items, by contrast, are almost entirely structural, being concerned with either the maintenance or the initiation of projects evaluated as beneficial to the EEC and its purposes, be this the payment of the salaries of the Commission bureaucracy, the development of projects to aid the economies of the poorer regions of the Community, or to repay those member states, such as Britain, which the system for raising revenue has been hard on. Such expenditure is liable to more detailed scrutiny before it is agreed and is in most cases expected to leave a lasting memorial in its wake whose merits are capable of assessment. It is not that fraud and abuse do not take place but that some awareness of it is reasonably likely at some stage. It is perhaps for this reason that where issues have arisen they have mainly been those of abuse – bending the rules – rather than outright fraud, which involves deliberate deceit and intention of misappropriation.

Such concerns have arisen in respect of most of the structural funds: in respect of the effectiveness of foreign aid;[1] in respect of the numbers of members of the EEC Commission staff receiving early retirement pensions on health grounds;[2] in respect of the habit of the Commission and other EEC institutions of renting its office buildings in Brussels at much greater long-term costs than buying them;[3] in respect of the use of structural funds on agricultural expenditure, such as for the construction of huge silos for grain storage in Ghent and Antwerp which not only will be likely to benefit grain traders rather than farmers, but seem likely to create over-capacity, particularly in the light of trends in the development of the grain trade.[4]

The principal area of concern is hence the EAGGF as the instrument for implementing the Common Agricultural Policy of the EEC. This was established by the original six members in the 1960s to ensure that the Community was more or less self sufficient in food and that farmers had adequate and reliable incomes to induce them to remain in agriculture. The main overt reason for intervening to subsidise prices, agree quotas and promote exports is the tendency of world agricultural prices to wild swings in the wake of harvest failures and surpluses. Perhaps as important, but less overtly stated, was the existence in the three principal countries, France, Germany and Italy, of large numbers of small and, in world market terms, increasingly uncompetitive farmers who traditionally voted for conservative political parties which then held office in these countries – Gaullists in France, Christian Democrats in Italy and Germany.

Abuse against agricultural subsidy funds takes place at three principal points: production; intervention (whether by storage or other means; and export (whether within or outside the Community). Although fraud and abuse have arisen in respect of a wide variety of commodities, including, for example, tobacco, milk and butter, it is fair to say that the main areas of concern have been wine, olive oil, cereals and beef. These will be used as examples of abuse and the difficulties and successes in containing it, and will also illustrate how different commodities lend themselves to abuses at different points in the production, processing and distribution cycle.

WINE

Europe produces far too much wine, or rather, far too much wine of low quality; on this point there is widespread agreement. It ought, hence, to follow that a programme of progressively reducing quotas for production should reduce the surplus, and again this is an agreed point in principle. Implementation, however, is difficult. Other crops of comparable yield are not always easy to substantiate for vines. There is fierce political resistance in wine-growing regions to the impending loss of a livelihood that goes back generations. And the problem has been exacerbated by the arrival in recent years of the additional wine-producing member-states of Greece, Spain and Portugal. Such facts inevitably have meant a delay before supply is brought into line with demand, especially given that *per capita* consumption of wine is falling, and in the meantime pressures have been sustained for support mechanisms for producers. Since low-quality wine does not last well in storage (there is no lack of demand for high-quality wines which do store well), and since bulk storage for more than a few months becomes prohibitively expensive, intervention has mainly taken the form of subsidising storage for a few months to even out seasonal falls in the price of wine and the buying up of quotas of wine for distillation into alcohol. This, albeit a process which costs at least as much as the value of the end-product, does at least result in a much lower-volume product with obvious energy uses.

Distillation has been the principal form of intervention since 1976, but it was rapidly realised by producers that wine sent for distillation required nothing in the way of palatability. The attractive prices offered for wine diverted for distillation have hence stimulated the production of what could pass for wine for distillation purposes, which meant little more than it should have the appropriate appearance and alcohol content. Not only were vineyards stretched to their capacity for conventional production, but grapes were re-processed and a variety of artificial ingredients added by the more unscrupulous. The outcome was that the amount of wine distilled grew from 539 million litres in 1976–7 (4 per cent of the wine sector), peaked at 3399 million litres in 1983–4 (29 per cent of wine produced), before falling back to 1958 million litres in 1986–7 (18 per cent of production) following a series of scandals and enquiries by national governments and the EEC Commission.[5] Even in 1987, by which time producers had been limited to 18 per cent of their output going for subsidised distillation, the Court of Auditors report on the scheme for storage and purchase for distillation noted continuing weaknesses in the management of the scheme, for example:

> With regard to the stock records it was found with all member states visited, with the exception of the Federal Republic of Germany, that although the tanks in which wine or grape must be initially stored were indicated to the controlled bodies, no detailed stock records were available per tank number showing movements between tanks. Neither did the available records make it possible

to clearly identify the wine under a storage contract within the total stocks of the winery at any given moment, thereby inhibiting the transparency of documentary controls. These inadequacies in the stock records can be attributed to weaknesses in community regulations.[6]

[P]articularly in France and Italy . . . the available staff resources were extremely limited and did not allow for on the spot visits to be made with sufficient frequency to ensure that the wine remained in stock during the contracted storage period.[7]

Although the regulations contain a general provision that obliges producers to inform the intervention agency if, during the period of validity of the storage contract, there is any appreciable change in the quality of the product stored, there is no specific provision requiring the control authorities to verify the quality characteristics during or at the end of the contract period. . . .[8]

Given the combination of weaknesses listed above, the only obligation on producers in many instances is to present wine of a similar colour, quality and alcohol strength at the end of the contract period, and in certain instances, not even the respect of these basic requirements is verified. . . . [T]here are not sufficient safeguards to ensure that the long term private storage contracts of table wine achieved the desired objective of keeping specified quantities of table wine off the market.[9]

Community representatives envisaged the authorisation of wine enrichment as an exceptional measure where weather conditions made it necessary. However, . . . in southern wine growing regions of the Community . . . the measure had been authorised on the most widespread basis possible in each year since it was introduced.[10]

A number of weaknesses quite widely characteristic of EEC administration of funds are evident here. First, there may be inadequate precision in the way regulations are written.[11] Secondly, the implementation of controls is frequently left in the hands of those who stand to benefit from the subsidies, and insufficient state staff are available to engage in adequate monitoring. Thirdly, the example of grape must illustrate a not-infrequent tendency for officials of the member-state administering the scheme to interpret regulations in an over-liberal way. Given that for most of the schemes the subsidy monies may be claimed and administered by the member-state in question immediately upon authorisation by its personnel administering the scheme in detail, and that expenditure is only checked some time (often several years) later by the EEC Commission, it is scarcely surprising that abuse and irregularities persist.

Finally and most importantly, the examples indicate the persistence of these practices even when serious and substantial abuses have been established for years. Not only was there a special report of the Court of Auditors in 1987 into the extensive abuse of the wine distillation and storage schemes,[12] but some of the producers who cooked up additional wine to take advantage of the scheme were responsible for over twenty deaths.

The Piedmont region of Italy is the home of some of its most prestigious red wines, Barolo and Barbera. Yet according to the director of the Italian Experimental Wine Research Institute in Asti,[13] the region sells twice as much wine as it produces because the rule that no more than 15 per cent of regionally designated wine may come from outside the region is not adequately policed. Some of the producers in the Puglia region in the south of Italy, where quantities of cheap wine are produced to be used as a supplement to the more expensive and supposedly higher-quality Piedmont wines, were involved in a scheme to produce more or less artificial wine for sale for distillation. To this end they bought 260 tonnes of methyl alcohol to fortify 30 million litres of 'wine'. However, at the end of 1985 they were threatened with denunciation to the authorities and decided instead to sell it for human consumption. Although methyl alcohol is extremely poisonous, it is present in small quantities naturally in wine and the fraudsters probably intended that by the time it had been further blended it should be sufficiently diluted to cause only minimal damage. In practice it was present in sufficient quantities in cheap wine labelled Barbera to kill three people who bought bottles in a Milan supermarket in 1986. This scandal came in the wake of the adulteration of wine with ethylene glycol (antifreeze) in 1985, which, although initially identified in Austria, was shown to be taking place also in Germany and in the Piedmont.

The point about such scandals in the present context is that, as the Auditors Report quoted above shows, monitoring of production is still weak, and adequate resources to improve it have not been forthcoming. Of course, such resources will involve additional expense although, like special investigations by the Inland Revenue, they might markedly reduce abuses and irregular expenditure. More to the point, sufficient political will to deal with the problems clearly has not developed.

OLIVE OIL

In comparison with wine, olive oil is a relative success story. The problem is again one of over-production in the southern agricultural sector of a product for which it is hard to find a substitute crop. Once it was agreed to pay a subsidy to producers to underwrite prices, however, the temptation to exaggerate production was inbuilt. Although there has been, as in the case of wine, some abuse of the alleged quality of the final product, it has been in false claims for volume that abuse has been most substantial. Certain features of olive oil production do, however, lend themselves to effective control. In the first place, overproduction was, until the accession of Spain and Greece, confined to Italy, where efforts at remedy were hence concentrated. Secondly, the mills which slice and press the olives are choke points in the industry. Traditionally this has acted to the disadvantage of growers, who found the prices charged by the millers so high that then profits were all but eliminated. Where mills came under the influence of the mafia, as they regularly did in southern Italy, the chances of diverting a crop to another mill offering better prices were often annihilated by force and exploitation was increased. In the context of production subsidies, the mills became even more exploitable provided the returns to the authorities could be falsified in a convincing way. This did not prove to be a great problem and by the mid-1980s abuses were agreed to be widespread. In addition, it was very difficult to get good data on input because of the problems in undertaking censuses of olive groves, often located in small parcels on hillside terraces with an owner having several small patches of land spread over a wide area. Hence exaggerated claims could not be refuted by reference to the capacities of producers.

The Italian government was finally induced to establish an independent monitoring agency, Agecontrol, which became operational in 1986. It is worth noting in this connection that there were a variety of pressures to do this. It was not just that the scale of abuse was substantial but that under EEC rules member-states are responsible for adequate monitoring of the subsidy schemes. Although, as has already been evident, enforcement of standards in this respect is far from stringent, the Commission does have the ultimate power to refuse to sanction the disbursement of subsidy funds for entire sectors if it believes monitoring is persistently inadequate. In the 1980s as concern at abuse of the EAGGF grew, the prospect increased of this painful sanction being applied. In addition, the involvement of the mafia was not only politically embarrassing internationally but also disadvantageous nationally for a Christian Democrat government which traditionally dominated the south.

In the event, a variety of tactics were combined.[14] A detailed aerial survey was undertaken to provide evidence to reconcile with the growers' returns. Secondly, Agecontrol was established and given substantial powers of access to financial records, including those of the tax authorities and of the state electricity supply corporation, as well as the ability to co-operate with the local police, the carabinieri and the Guardia di Finanza. Checks on electricity consumption at the mills, in combination with checks on the amount of husk left after milling, could then be used to verify production, which could be further checked at local and regional levels with growers' returns and the results of the aerial surcy. A reasonably reliable estimate was finally in prospect on the broad amounts of the crop and the locations at which it was milled. Mills which checks showed were making false claims had their recognition for subsidy withdrawn. In 1986–7 this was the fate of 83 out of 675 mills and 13 out of 107 producers' associations. As Agecontrol increased its expertise and command of data, further inroads into abuse were anticipated. The ECC Commission, in reviewing the control initiative, professed itself satisfied with the progress made and noted that a similar agency had been set up in Greece at the end of 1987, and that subsidy claims in Italy in the first year of operation had fallen by 30 per cent. In its review of arrangements in Spain, the Court of Auditors anticipated that a similar regime would be established there in 1988, but in the meantime noted a series of shortcomings in verifying crop production and processing and in olive tree censuses.[15]

CEREALS

Despite the enormous improvements in technology since 1945, both in crop strains and disease control and in cultivation and harvesting equipment, cereal harvests are still liable to quite sharp variation because of the vagaries of the weather. World prices are subject to much greater changes for the same reasons, notably also because of the persistent weakness of Soviet agriculture. The EEC solution to this problem has been price support, with grain being bought in if prices fall below a certain threshold, accompanied by extensive storage to produce buffer stocks which can sustain supply in times of shortage. Although it is now accepted that this system of inter-vention has produced long-term surpluses beyond what will be needed, the consequences of drought on the North American grain harvest in 1988 indicate the continuing importance of some shortage capacity. As with olive oil, abuses exist over production claims, but the majority of abuses centre around export and storage. As in other sectors, when actual practice in member-states responsible for ad-ministering schemes is investigated, it is evident that, whilst the subsidy monies are EEC funds, the stocks and facilities that they support are by no means governmental or even European but often remain in private hands and for private, and sometimes unscrupu-lous, profit.

In its review of intervention storage of cereals for 1987, the Court of Auditors notes with satisfaction that stocks had fallen 9 per cent by quantity and 18 per cent by value (total stocks including meat and dairy production) over the year. Cereals and rice stocks had fallen from 18.6 million tonnes in 1985 to 10.5 million tonnes in 1987.[16] Given that the quality of stored food products inevitably declines over time to the point at which they are no longer fit for consump-tion, it is clearly important to get stocks down to a level where they function only as the minimum necessary buffer. In the meantime adequate monitoring of the quality of stocks in storage is required, and checks on the volumes claimed in subsidy are essential to the effective operation of the scheme.

The situation revealed in the 1987 review was one which inevit-ably concealed abuse and which was conducive to fraud.[17] Record-keeping at storage facilities was rarely reliable and almost nowhere independent of the owners and storers. Quality-control checks on the stocks were quite inadequate in storage and during and after discharge. Substantial errors were shown to occur in the amount assessed as being in storage and discharged from it month by month. Given that monthly assessments by member-states of amounts in storage are the basis for unquestioned subvention by the EAGGF, there was evidence of a widespread awareness that while the costs of a strict monitoring regime could not be recouped, there was no cost to member-states from tolerating a lax one. How far this laxness concealed outright fraud, whether of a documentary nature or from grossly adulterated stocks, could not be determined. Here as elsewhere, the existence of an intervention and subsidy scheme together with very soft conditions for disbursement are a recipe for trouble. The remedy equally obviously lies in the dismantling of the subsidy or the imposition of stricter conditions for receiving payments.

BEEF

The complexity and variation in the subsidies for beef exports make it ideal for fraudulent abuse, though export-refund abuses are not confined to beef. Of the total EAGGF expenditure, 41 per cent went to export refunds in 1987, or 9375 million ECUs. Beef accounted for 877.9 million ECUs, milk products 2257.9 million ECUs, and cereals 3070.6 million ECUs. The complexity of the refund classifications and the regularity with which they change is such that confusion is likely at busy customs offices. These often have other priorities and may in addition be short of staff with the necessary training in the EEC export-refund schemes. There are 1200 categories of agricultural produce, including nearly 400 for milk products and 80 for beef, and the world is divided into eleven zones for beef exports. There are hence 880 possible rates of subsidy, ranging from zero to nearly 100 per cent of the value of the meat exported. The incentive to cheat and to defraud is hence substantial and the track record of abuse is well established. The Court of Auditors produced a special report on the abuses of export refunds in 1985,[18] and according to Tutt,[19] the largest-ever recorded fraud against the EEC involved the export of beef to Brazil from France which should have attracted no refunds, but which was declared exported to Egypt for which there was a high subsidy and for which 12.3 million ECUs was eventually claimed.

In their 1987 report, the Court of Auditors described a special study of beef exports in Germany, France, Ireland and the UK, which together account for 80 per cent of sectoral expenditure. Their observations are worth quoting at some length:

[O]f 95 export consignments examined by the Court in the member state, only one had been subject to random examination [by the national customs authority of the member state, other than those covered by this audit] at the port of final export from the Community – and the examination revealed an irregular description of the goods concerned.

In another member state examination of cartons being taken into re-financing control at a trader's premises during the Court's audit revealed that trimmings not eligible for refunds had been hidden inside rolled bone beef meat cuts. Extension of the examination . . . revealed an irregularity rate of about 7%.

For two years a trader imported to the EEC prime beefmeat from South America described as offal in order to evade import levies, and exported offal described as prime quality beef in order to obtain export refunds; the irregular transactions involved were in the region of 16 million ECU.

The Commission's investigations into . . . the country of destination for a series of beef meat exports also revealed irregularities in declared weights and descriptions of some of the consignments concerned. The total sum at stake was of the order of 5 million ECU.

Refunds were paid by one member state on exports declared to be beef meat. National controls had failed to detect that the consignments were in fact chicken scraps, and the exporters concerned received regular export refunds totalling about 1.4 million ECU.

From its examination of this procedure the Court acknowledges that control over the weights of live animals attracting export refunds presents practical difficulties. None of the ports visited provided facilities for the weighing of individual animals, which meant that a full check of the weight had to be made by means of the weigh bridge and lairage facilities. The Court notes that certain ports did not have these facilities and had to use facilities located some distance from the area of customs control, with the obvious danger of diversion to home use of animals upon which export refunds were paid.

. . .

Over a period of two years or so, an exporter systematically diverted to home use live animals on which export refunds had been claimed and paid. The total cost of the fraud was about 3 million ECU.

. . .

[I]n one member state the weight taken into account for export refund purposes on all exports of live cattle was not that at the time taking the animals into customs control, but the weight established at the inland collecting centre. The weight loss between the inland centre and the port allowed in the calculation of the export refunds varied between 10% and 15%.

. . .

At one trader's premises other beef meat attracting lower refunds was allowed into the boning and cutting room at the same time as beef meat from adult male animals. The two processing lines merged at the point of packing with the obvious risk of substitution. At the same trader the sealing of cartons with official seals was left at times to the traders' personnel, thereby negating independent controls. At the same trader the identification of the quarters as adult male was supposed to be evidenced by an intervention agency seal. At the time of the Court's audit no evidence was found that these seals were applied. In another member state the labels identifying the individual cuts of meat as of male origin were left in the possession of the trader as were the paper seals, thereby again negating independent control. In the same member state evidence was also found that paper seals were incorrectly applied, not joining the top and bottom of the cartons, allowing easy substitution. . . . The trader referred to above had consistently increased the quantities of meat stated to be from adult males (which attract a higher level of subsidy) by including cuts from other animals at the packing stage.[20]

In addition to this it was noted that there was no established system for notifying other member-states of frauds or suspected frauds, and frequently no targeting of consignments known to be high risk, given the record of the exporter or level of subsidies available. Further, in an evaluation of measures introduced by an EEC Directive in 1977 to require member states to establish effective schemes for later verification that exports had taken place as documents claimed and had arrived at their stated destination, it appeared that, although some improvement had taken place since a special review in 1984, there were still widespread weaknesses in verification, with France and Germany achieving acceptable standards, Greece and Italy still being very poor, and the UK and Ireland intermediate. Indeed, more widely the Court's enquiries showed that:

Paying agencies in the member states had accepted as primary proof of arrival at final destination, and without further enquiry: documents purporting to be the customs entries or annexe to documents without customs signatures and stamps; secondary proofs of dubious authenticity, for example (1) a certificate of importation to Libya with the letter heading 'Foreign Office Bucharest'; (2) certificates of importation dated prior to the arrival of the goods concerned; (3) certificates provided by a commercial superintendent's company with apparently no presence in the country concerned, nor expertise in the commodity traded, and sometimes long after the arrival of the goods concerned; (4) bank certificates showing that the invoices for the goods had been settled, but which gave no evidence of the source of funds.[21]

The success of the export refund scheme depends upon good record-keeping, prompt execution of bureaucratic procedures, rapid response to queries from other member-states and acted upon suspicious cases, well-trained and effective management and the reduction of the over-heavy flow of documentation by the use of computerised record-keeping. All these were demonstrably lacking in most member-states in 1987, and even these remedies, which would not be cheap, would not eliminate fraud in a system so fundamentally conducive to it. The export-refund sector, and beef in particular, illustrates that in some respect a more fundamental reform and simplification of EEC subsidies is essential for securing a grasp upon control. The conditions for achieving this are political rather than administrative or economic.

THE EXTENT AND CAUSES OF FRAUD AND ABUSE

It is evident from the examples above that it is at present impossible to say how much irregularity of all kinds besets the various EAGGF schemes. Time after time it is shown that their administration is too lax for proper figures to emerge. Equally, schemes are often so complex and change so often in their detailed regulations, and the level of documentation is so heavy 4.5 million export receipt copies handled annually at Arnhem, an average of 47,595 daily in Hamm (Germany) and 11,000 daily in Southend – that accurate monitoring and diagnosis of trouble is very difficult.[22]

In the only intensive study of international trade in Europe to date, undertaken in Sweden,[23] which looked at all exports and imports through several customs points over a period of time, half the transactions were found to be irregular to some degree, and even if allowances are made for failings that might be described as purely technical, 30 per cent probably did have a financial impact. The academic researcher who has taken most long-term interest in EEC fraud, Professor Tiedemann, estimates that 10 per cent or ECU 2 billion of the EEC budget is subject to fraud and abuse.[24] This conjecture is based on long experience, especially in Germany, where a uniform reporting system for economic crime was enforced from 1972, and on comparisons with other countries, notably France and Belgium. It is also consistent with what *post factum* checks have been done at various times, which produce rates of irregularity of 10–30 per cent. What is also likely is that levels of abuse will vary over time and place according to the opportunities offered, the extent of the exploitation possible and the stringency of the administrative controls in force.

Even to say this much is to enter the complex realm of causes, which is nevertheless more rewarding to investigate than that of the extent of fraud and abuse. Four broad groups of causes operating at different administrative and political levels in the EEC many be identified as conducive to abuse of funds at present.

The first of these is straightforward and has already been mentioned several times. At a front line administrative level, EAGGF schemes are subject to staffing which is often inadequate in numbers and training and management which is inadequately geared to tackling EEC abuses. At the same time, the documentation involved is becoming overwhelming and the rules to be administered are too many, change too often and are sometimes unclear and conflict with each other. If there is a requirement on the one hand for a shift in priorities and better funding to raise staffing and training levels, there is equally a need for the simplification of the regulations and procedures for administering the schemes, besides the introduction of computerised record-keeping.

The first of these two remedies which involve member-states giving higher priority to EEC fraud is scarcely likely, given the second set of causes which amount to a set of disincentives to detect and report abuses. These take various forms. It has been indicated above (and we shall return to it below) that the Commission is ponderously slow in attempting to put pressure on member-states to limit abuses and to implement effective control systems, and that most schemes are administered in a devolved way by the member-states themselves. Their returns to the Commission are accepted as an adequate basis for the disbursement of funds; *post factum* checks to verify that all has been done according to the book are too weak and too late. Further, each member state is under a formal obligation to detect and report to the Commission instances to fraud and abuse and the outcome of its attempts to recover lost funds. Table 6.2 indicates what has happened in this respect.

Levels of fraud reported are negligible in comparison with esti-mates of actual levels. In one year in Hamburg alone 200 cases of abuse were detected and subsidies revoked, yet West Germany as a whole reported only four cases to the Commission.[25] West Germany, as can be seen from the table and as other evidence confirms, is one of the most, if not *the* most, vigilant and diligent member-states in enforcing EEC regulations to control abuse. A substantial part of the reason for this is that cases identified by member-states are treated by the Commission as funds lost by them, and they are penalised by the deduction of a comparable amount from their subventions. Hence it pays to fail to report cases since those who do report them suffer materially for doing so. This extraordinary situation has to be seen in the context of the schemes themselves and prevailing attitudes to them.

TABLE 6.2   Fraud clear-up rates: recoveries by European governments (£ millions)

	1971–86			1987		
	defrauded	*recovered*	*%*	*defrauded*	*recovered*	*%*
Belgium	8.2	0.3	4	1.8	–	0
Denmark	1.7	1.3	74	0.1	–	57
W. Germany	49.1	21.2	43	0.3	0.1	49
Greece	(no fraud declared)			–	–	0
Spain	(no fraud declared)			(no fraud declared)		
France	6.0	1.6	26	2.6	0.6	23
Ireland	4.5	0.8	18	1.3	–	0
Italy	35.7	1.2	3	52.6	–	0
Luxembourg	(no fraud declared)			(no fraud declared)		
Netherlands	2.9	2.1	70	–	–	–
Portugal	(no fraud declared)			(no fraud declared)		
United Kingdom	6.5	2.3	36	2.4	0.1	5

Source: N. Tutt, *Europe on the Fiddle* (London: Croom Helm, 1989) p. 109.

All the EAGGF schemes have been designed in the light of positive objectives: to support producers and to stimulate trade in certain directions. In many cases, as has been seen from examples above, they are constructed in such a way as to constitute an invitation to abuse. Coupled with the known weaknesses in control systems and the connivance of governments and their officials, they constitute, it may be claimed, an unreasonable temptation for the businessman or farmer trading in the relevant sector.[26] Although attempts are now belatedly being made to achieve it, most of the schemes are not structured to detect and deter abuse but to facilitate payouts. It is only recently (see below) that it has been seriously suggested that schemes with significant inherent vulnerability to abuse should not be proceeded with.

This feature of the subsidy schemes sustains and intensifies a widespread sentiment that, because EEC money comes not from a private person, a corporation or even a nation state, but from an international institution whose impact on the daily lives of citizens very limited, it does not really belong to anyone and hence is there for the taking. Given that it is all tax revenue raised from citizens of the Community, this is, of course, nonsense but none the less it is a widely reported view[27] and one entirely consistent with evidence on attitudes towards money in other contexts. Thieves who steal from the workplace will be reluctant to steal from their workmates; defrauding the tax man or the insurance company is seen as less immoral than defrauding little old ladies of their savings; stealing from a supermarket is seen as less sinful than stealing from your neighbour's house.[28]

These considerations lead naturally to the final group of causes of abuse. It is surely extraordinary that abuse should be tolerated, or rather treated as a non-issue and evidence of it systematically ignored for so long a time, given the obvious dangers of doing so. These include at the very least the practical danger of widespread abuse vitiating the achievement of the objectives of schemes and the potential danger that the institutions of the EEC, and perhaps the entire enterprise, may be brought into disrepute and subject to public cynicism. The House of Lords in their review of the problems cite as the fundamental cause of continued inaction a lack of political will by member-states and the more powerful EEC institutions to take action against abuse.[29] Control of fraud and abuse just has not featured high enough on the political agenda. It is not difficult, given the evidence, to accept this conclusion. What is less obvious is why such inertia has persisted.

To obtain an initial understanding of why political will should be lacking, some appreciation of the nature and structure of the EEC is necessary. Its institutions consist for present purposes (there are others that need not concern us) of the Commission, the Parliament, the Council of Ministers and the Court of Auditors. The Commission is the civil service which, like those of nation-states, advises ministers and implements their policy decisions, but is in this case of course restricted to European, or rather EEC matters. It is staffed by nationals of all member-states, communicating in all the languages of the member-states, though predominantly in French, German and English. It is subject to considerable internal politicisation since, although it has a specific responsibility and a substantial monopoly of expertise in EEC matters, it is not beholden primarily to the European Parliament but to the Council of Ministers. These are ministers not of any European superstate but of member-states, and take their decisions as members of the Council with a constant weather-eye on domestic interests. The Commission staff at senior levels are subject to a quota system that guarantees representation for all member-states.

The Parliament, by contrast, is more genuinely European, especially as it has been directly elected since 1979. Its members represent large Euro-constituencies and work in multinational political alignments, of which the largest is currently the Socialists. A weakness of the Parliament is that it has limited power. It can comment on and review EEC legislation, rules and directives, but it contains no ministers capable of introducing legislation. Legislation is devised by the Commission but is subject to the approval of the Council of Ministers representing member-states. The principal power of the Parliament is approval or rejection of the budget, a power which has been used in recent years but which is a blunt instrument. Power is hence effectively divided between the Commission and the Council of Ministers.

The Court of Auditors was established in 1977 to oversee the implementation of the budget and report annually, besides undertaking special enquiries when necessary. The Court has powers to inspect how member states are administering EEC schemes and funds, but it lacks decisive powers of sanction. It can recommend to the Commission that expenditure wrongly claimed be disallowed and the Commission can impose this sanction on a basis as wide as the entire scheme or sector involved (for example, all claims for wine distillation subsidy in a member-state), subject to challenge in the European Court.

It should be evident from this sketch that the key issue bedevilling fraud control is sovereignty. There is no EEC police force or inspectorate with legal and sanctioning powers; there are extradition problems and difficulties with compatibility of laws in different member-states.[30] The Court of Auditors has powers of enquiry and exposure but not of trial and sanction, and often finds it difficult to gain access to evidence.[31] The Commission and the Parliament are genuinely European institutions, but in the former case especially, greatly restrained by the overriding power of the Council of Ministers. When lack of political will is identified as the root cause this ultimately means lack of will by the Council.

On the subject of fraud and abuse of EEC funds it is easy to see why this persists. It was pointed out above that EAGGF schemes are positive in orientation, designed to stimulate and sustain economic activities of various kinds. It is much easier for representatives of nation-states to agree to this than it is to begin to discuss the implementation of a strict monitoring, evaluation and sanctioning system. The latter inevitably involves the likelihood of embarrassing exposures of one's own nation's failings, as well as the invidious process of finger-pointing in finding fault with the standards and practices of others. Members of the Council of Ministers undoubtedly live in a political glasshouse and are reluctant to throw stones.

Secondly, the ineluctable conclusion of any serious attempt at an effective appraisal and enforcement system involves the imposition of uniform standards and specialised staff whose base and loyalties, sooner or later, will become the EEC rather than their nation-state. In brief, the issues are raised of EEC policing and social control with its emotive prospects, rights of access, and powers of arrest, detention and legal proceedings. No member of the Council of Ministers will happily raise those issues with his/her government or party. The failure of the EEC to exercise adequate means to control fraud and abuse hence lies ultimately in the lack of transfer of adequate powers from member-states to the EEC and its institutions and acceptance of the loss of sovereignty this entails.

Having said this, however, it should be added that fraud and abuse are now on the agenda both of the EEC and of its member-states, where they were not a decade ago. If fraud has become an issue, it is worth enquiring how this happened and whether its

arrival betokens merely a continued inertia or whether there is evidence of any real willingness to change. It is with these matters that
the final section of this chapter is concerned.

FRAUD CONTROL: PROGRESS AND PROSPECTS

Reasonably informed British citizens might have anticipated fairly
decisive action on EEC fraud in 1989. Alerted by a *Panorama* programme on BBC1 a year earlier,[32] they were told in no uncertain terms
by *The Times* in February, 'Thatcher to attack 6 billion EEC fraud'[33]
and that the Prime Minister was to lead a British campaign on the
issue. The story was confirmed the following day, with the Prime
Minister telling MPs she would raise the issue at the forthcoming
meeting of heads of government. There was every reason to expect
that EEC fraud would be adopted as a British issue, given the government's long-term campaign against waste, inefficiency and abuse
in and against the British state and the Prime Minister's willingness
to point the finger at aspects of the EEC that called for reform. Such
an issue might also be argued to fit comfortably into the forthcoming
campaign for elections to the European Parliament: Tories will ensure that you get value for money in the EEC. Further, it was plain,
at least to a Conservative enquirer, that the root of the problem was
the Common Agricultural Policy (CAP) itself. Dismantle its un-
necessary and wasteful network of subsidies and establish a free
market in food, and opportunities for abuse necessarily disappear.
Such a radical approach was, however, likely to be counterproductive in the reactions stimulated among other member-states and
treated as yet another instance of Britain's anti-Community sentiment.
When the Prime Minister's former adviser and head of the Institute
of Directors, Sir John Hoskyns, sounded off a month later in characteristic vehement style denouncing fraud, corruption and mis-
management in the EEC, it provoked a prompt denunciation from
EEC President Jacques Delors, saying that fraud is a fake issue and
a distraction from more important matters, namely, the preparation
for the single market in 1992 and financial and monetary integration.
It was the latter which dominated the heads of government meeting
in June 1989, with Mrs Thatcher struggling to retain acceptable
conditions for progress towards monetary integration and in par-

ticular for Britain's joining the European Exchange Rate Mechanism, an issue so fraught that internal dissension over precisely how to manage it led to the resignation in the autumn of the long-standing Chancellor of the Exchequer, Nigel Lawson. By this time fraud seemed mysteriously to have been dropped from the government's agenda.[34]

It was perhaps not without significance that the House of Lords report on their extensive enquiries into the problem, undertaken by a select committee including such luminaries as a former Governor of Hong Kong, a former Governor of the Bank of England and a most distinguished accountant, to which reference has been made at several points above, should have concluded that the root cause of failure to tackle EEC fraud was lack of political will to do so. If Britain backed off from such an apparently prime Thatcherite target, what hope was there that it was ever likely to be tackled? What is it about the issue that makes members of the Council of Ministers so reluctant to confront it?

There is certainly evidence of a history of concern that EEC funds should be spent in a proper manner. As far back as 1970 the Council of Ministers issued regulations[35] requiring member-states to take all necessary measures to ensure EEC funds were properly spent, to pursue abusers and to recover losses. *In situ* checks on the adequacy of fraud control measures by the Commission were to be accepted by member-states. This was followed two years later by more stringent regulations[36] requiring member-states to inform the Commission within three months of the legal and administrative measures taken to implement the 1970 ruling, and the administrative agencies responsible for enforcement in each member-state. Member-states were also required to report quarterly on all frauds and abuses of EEC funds, the extent of losses and the measures taken to recover them. The obligation upon member-states to implement effective regimes to ensure that EEC funds were properly used was further emphasised in 1977.[37] Regulations required member-states to undertake a systematic check of commercial documents in at least half the undertakings (businesses) which received more than 100,000 units of account from the EAGGF. Despite the increasing stringency and detail of these regulations, the omens were not good. Member-states were being reminded of their obligations to see that EEC funds were being spent properly, but no real sanctions were in prospect for failure to do so – most obviously, denial of access to the funds and almost nothing by way of intrusion into member-states' management of the schemes by EEC staff was proposed to ensure that control systems were in place, were working properly, and were given adequate staffing, funding and training.

The most promising development was the establishment of the Court of Auditors in 1977 with responsibility for oversight of just these matters. It was and is, however, restricted in its rights of access. It can now make visits to member-states, but its staff are limited to 150, of whom only 65 are active professionally qualified inspectors. Its role is hence confined to annual reviews of expenditure, special enquiries into particular abuses (some of which have been referred to earlier in this chapter) and on-site checks on member-states' administration of EEC funds to verify that the systems in use are adequate for the tasks required of them. The auditors have neither the staff nor the authority to ensure that these systems are in fact working properly though they can identify obvious weaknesses in staffing, training, record-keeping and so on.

If fraud and abuse have become live political issues by the beginning of the 1990s it has been largely thanks to the persistent efforts of the Court of Auditors and of some members of the European Parliament. The Court produced a critical review of member-states' failure to implement the directives of the 1970s which was consolidated and intensified in the 1977 ruling, including an embarrassing table displaying the disparities in the level of inspections, frauds identified and monies recovered between member-states (cf. Table 6.2 above). To some extent, this disparity was the inevitable consequence of the continuing enlargement of the Community in the 1970s and 1980s from six to twelve members, but this was clearly not the entire explanation.[38]

This was followed by a special report in 1987 on the system of payment for refunds on agricultural exports – the scheme probably most abused – which analysed and criticised the various control systems in use in member-states and recommended modifications and the adoption of uniform and effective systems by all member-states. By this point the long-term strategy of the Court was plain: to use its own expertise to identify weaknesses in the current practises in member-states' verification procedures; to develop and publicise adequate systems; and by regular public reporting and comparison to goad and embarrass member-states gradually into improvement to an acceptable level. The disadvantage of this strategy is that it is evidently very slow. While some states, notably Germany, are keen to take a lead, and others, including Britain and more recently France, are susceptible to embarrassment, southern states which account for a large proportion of EAGGF expenditure either have become full members so recently as to require yet more time to come up to standard (Spain and Portugal), or lack the wealth and trained and experienced personnel (Greece), or are subject to such rapidly changing governments as to find it impossible to keep up with the legal and administrative changes required (Italy).

The Commission, arguably the most powerful EEC institution, has found itself between Scylla and Charybdis in this process. It is responsible for the implementation of policy, including the regulation and management of EEC funds, albeit most of the detail of the administration of the schemes is undertaken by member-states. It therefore often seems to have responsibility without real power. Goaded by reports from the Court of Auditors and regular complaints from the European Parliament, but subject to constraint by the refusal of the Council of Ministers to address the issue seriously, it has gradually shifted its position to one of greater public insistence that decisive action is now needed, and that such action should come from the Council and member-states. In a report in 1987 in response to a loud call from the Parliament for more effective anti-fraud measures it concluded:

> It should be clearly stated that the Commission must not be accused for failing in its duties [sic] because it does not deal directly with all the causes of fraud and is not always informed in detail of the situation by member-states. The main fight against fraud takes place in the field under the responsibility of national authorities.[39]

For its own part the Commission proposed to set up an anti-fraud co-ordination unit which would centralise information on fraud and fraud control and act as a focus for policy development. It is not and cannot be an EEC fraud squad. There is no such thing as EEC criminal law or any form of Euro-police with powers of enquiry and arrest under European legislation in any member-state. Failure by member-states to take action on EEC fraud cannot be remedied by this route.

Nor are other obvious remedies available. For example, without the agreement of the Council of Ministers, no initiative to staff the administration of EEC funds by Commission employees in member-states is possible. This again would increase EEC jurisdiction with proportionate loss of member-states' sovereignty. Even the largest power the Commission does have – that of disallowing expenditure which is improperly made by member-states – has been used cautiously by the Commission, though there are some signs that this weapon may be wielded more regularly now. Political will to introduce effective control of fraud against European funds inescapably involves ceding authority to European institutions to achieve it. This was anathema to the Thatcher government and it was the recognition of this point that resulted in the issue being dropped in 1989. Fraud, it emerged, was not something you could accuse others of tolerating; it was something that required powers of external scrutiny and control in all member-states. This was a point well appreciated by Lord Cockfield, a former Tory minister appointed as EEC Commissioner who 'went native' and converted to the cause of European integration. He asked pointedly, in the wake of Mrs Thatcher's declared anti-fraud campaign, why it was that the government had blocked his amendments to a 1986 EEC directive which would have enabled member-states to help each other trace illegal use of EEC funds.[40] The government could give no reply, but its action in 1986 stemmed almost certainly from concern at the inroads on British sovereignty implied by the amendment.

The sovereignty issue was one appreciated by the European Parliament, however. This produced a report under the chairmanship of Dutch Socialist Piet Dankert in early 1989,[41] timed to capitalise upon the more than usually trenchant report of the Court of Auditors on the EAGGF, which has been referred to several times earlier in this chapter. The Dankert Report's line was to insist on the scrutiny of all EEC legislation and administrative rules governing expenditure of funds, with a view to evaluating and minimising their potential for fraudulent abuse. It hence took its lead from the repeated complaints of various commentators that the complexity of schemes and their constantly changing regulations were an invitation to fraud, and that it meant that sufficient staffing to control it would be unduly expensive. Such a strategy, in emphasising prevention rather than intrusive investigation and embarrassing prosecution, was much more likely to command acceptance. It also left open the possibility that, if a scheme could be shown to be inherently susceptible to abuse, even after the most careful structuring, there might then be an argument for not going ahead with it at all. It was certainly a line of argument that appealed to Her Majesty's Government, whose tactics on an anti-fraud campaign had shifted by the time of the meeting of heads of government[42] to support for an enhanced budget for the

Commission's anti-fraud co-ordination unit, which was duly agreed, a review of rules governing EAGGF schemes to minimise fraud proneness, and a tougher line by the Commission on disallowing expenditure where member-states had been shown to be unduly lax in administering schemes. These are scarcely measures of the crusading and attention catching sort that had been heralded.

In conclusion, control of EEC fraud may be seen as a touchstone of willingness to progress towards European integration, with the piecemeal and cumulative loss of sovereignty of member-states which that entails. Watch this space, do no not hold your breath.

Notes

1. See, for example, N. Tutt, *Europe on the Fiddle* (London: Croom Helm, 1989), ch. 10. This polemic against the EEC from a militantly Thatcherite position is none the less accessibly written. Although some of its chapters are little more than tittle-tattle others are quite useful summaries of particular sectors.
2. Report of the Court of Auditors for 1987, *Official Journal of the European Communities*, C316, vol. 31 (12 December 1988) pp. 10.32–10.40
3. Ibid., pp. 10.41–10.60.
4. Ibid., pp. 5.20–5.43.
5. Tutt, op. cit., chs 7 and 8, figures from Tables 6.2 and 6.3.
6. Court of Auditors Report, 1987, op. cit. p. 4.92.
7. Ibid., p. 4.93.
8. Ibid., p 4.96
9. Ibid., p. 4.98.
10. Ibid., p. 4.105.
11. Ibid., p. 4.92.
12. *Official Journal of the EEC*, C297, vol. 30 (6 November 1987) p. 14.
13. 'Poisoned by Greed', *The Times*, 21 April 1986.
14. See Tutt, op. cit., pp. 127–32.
15. Court of Auditors Report, 1987, op. cit., p. 4.108.
16. Ibid., Table 4.1.
17. Ibid., pp. 4.4–4.19.
18. *Official Journal of the EEC*, C215, vol. 28 (26 August 1985) pp. 1–16.
19. Tutt, op. cit., p. 103.
20. Court of Auditors Report, 1987, op. cit., pp. 4.34 a–e, 4.36–4.38, 4.41 a–c, 4.42.
21. Ibid., p. 4.47.
22. Court of Auditors Report, 1987, op. cit., p. 3.26.
23. D. Magnusson, *Ekonomisk Brottslighet Vid Import Och Export – Brottsförebyggande Radet Rapport* (1981)2. See also House of Lords Select Committee on the European Community, *Fraud against the Community*, House of Lords Paper 27 (London: HMSO 1989) Q. 173.

This report, including the extensive expert evidence, is currently the best available source on the subject.
24. House of Lords report, op. cit., p. 88.
25. Ibid., Q. 285.
26. Ibid., p. 66, Tomlinson.
27. Ibid., p. 74 Waechter; p. 89 Tiedemann.
28. For a review and discussion of these matters see M. J. Clarke, *Business Crime* (Cambridge: Polity Press, 1990).
29. House of Lords report, op. cit., p. 41.
30. Cf. C. S. P. Harding, 'The European Communities and Control of Criminal Business Activities', *International and Comparative Law Quarterly*, 31 (1982) pp. 246–62.
31. Court of Auditors Report, 1987, op. cit., p. 4.68.
32. *The Two Billion Pound Rip Off*, BBC1, 8 February 1988.
33. *The Times*, 7 February 1989, p. 1.
34. Enquiries to the Cabinet Office in autumn 1989 produced a referral to 10 Downing Street and thence to the Ministry of Agriculture, Fisheries and Food which, after some persistence, undertook to discuss government policy on EEC fraud. A cautious source at MAFF then outlined the government's policy as indicated at the end of this chapter. Clearly the Prime Minister was not at this stage actively involved.
35. 729/70 EEC articles 8 and 9, *Official Journal*, L 94/16 (28 April 1970.
36. 283/72 EEC articles 2 and 3, *Official Journal*, L 36/1 (10 February 1972).
37. 77/435 EEC article 2, *Official Journal*, C172/17 (12 July 1977).
38. Special report on the implementation of directive 77/435 EEC, *Official Journal*, C336/1 (17 December 1984) Table 1.
39. Com (87) 572 (final), p. 7.
40. 'Young Baffled by EEC Questions', *The Times*, 5 February 1989.
41. European Parliament Session Documents 1988–9, A2-20/89/ Part A, *Report by the Committee on Budgetary Control on Preventing and Controlling Fraud Against the European Community Budget in a Post-1992 Europe*, rapporteur: Mr P. Dankert.
42. See note 34 above.

7

US Capital versus the Third World
Union Carbide and Bhopal

FRANK PEARCE and STEVEN TOMBS

INTRODUCTION

In this chapter we use the tragic disaster at Bhopal in December 1984 to question claims made by corporate capital to a new social responsibility. We demonstrate how Union Carbide Corporation (UCC), regarded by many as a safe and responsible company, both created the conditions whereby an accident was possible and would have unnecessarily disastrous consequences; how UCC sought to influence both public opinion and the legal process through a series of arguments and spurious claims concerning the accident, the nature of the Indian company, and the Bhopal plant and its employees; and how UCC was able to secure a favourable settlement, preventing that which was not at issue morally from being settled legally.

'SAFETY AT ANY COST': TOWARDS AN ENVIRONMENTALLY FRIENDLY CORPORATE CAPITALISM?

The 1990s look as though they will be the green decade. Major and the Conservative Party, Bush and the Republicans and many large corporations have all become brighter shades of green. Large supermarket chains in Britain, Canada and the US are selling 'environmentally friendly' products and large manufacturing companies have become leading conservationists. Tellingly, in recent advertising campaigns the US Chemical Manufacturers' Association (CMA) has appropriated an old radical slogan of the 1960s – that one is either part of the problem or part of the solution – to ask us to trust its 'technofix' of modern environmental problems.

On Earth Day 1990 in Washington, Browing Ferris Industries was 'very proud of the 25 wood duck nesting boxes and 25 bluebird boxes it has placed at the North Shelby landfill site in Tennessee' and DuPont preened itself for having 'dedicated a 7000-acre wildlife habitat park in North Carolina'. DuPont, along with Arco and Ciba Geigy and eleven other corporations is a member of the National Wildlife Foundation's Corporate Council. There are also many corporate members of the National Audubon Society and of the World Wildlife Fund/Conservation Foundation. The latter 'now lists as major donors Chevron and Exxon . . . Philip Morris, Mobil and Morgan Guaranty Trust . . . Waste Management Incorporated has been admitted to the Environmental Grantmakers Association and in the past three years has donated more than $900,000 to environmental causes'.[2]

Are these corporations, then, in the vanguard of a new, socially responsible capitalism? Even superficial scrutiny of their wider operations undermines such an interpretation. Waste Management Incorporated, 'known for its leaky landfills, its convictions for price-fixing, and its violations of environmental regulations', was penalised with fines of more than $30 million from 1982 to 1987.[3] Browning Ferris Industries was recently fined £900,000 'for 1,400 breaches of the regulations on hazardous waste disposal'.[4] DuPont was the major producer of CFCs and even in 1988 was opposing their regulation, branding as 'irresponsible' those scientists who warned of their danger to the environment.[5] Long after attention had been drawn to the dangers associated with the release of CFCs into the atmosphere two-thirds of all CFCs were used for the aerosols and hamburger cartons beloved of the consumer West. Yet now that it has become virtually impossible to deny the destructive effect of CFCs on the ozone layer, developing countries are expected to cut their use even for the essential purposes of refrigeration. Exxon's recent environmental accomplishments, when the *Exxon Valdez* ran aground off Alaska and dumped 250,000 barrels of oil in Prince William Sound resulting in an avoidable disaster, are only too well known.

Let us return to the US chemical industry. The CMA has 'developed a "Responsible Care Initiative" ' and has 'been a prime mover in implementing' legislation on 'Your Right To Know about what chemicals are being produced and used in your neighbourhood'.[6] The chemical industry is a particularly interesting site of enquiry

regarding social responsibility since not only is it here that environmental, safety and health problems are most clearly inextricably
linked, but it has also been this industry that has been at the centre
of debates around the potentially harmful consequences of corporate
activity. The CMA's initiative has some genuine positive consequences since it will contribute to the safer production, use and
disposal of chemicals. However, this initiative, like so many others
from the chemical industry, is tactical. Such initiatives have certain
defining characteristics. Being developed by the chemical industry,
they are 'pre-emptive' and are thus under the control of the industry:
they pre-empt rather than facilitate the genuine voicing of concerns
of various interested publics. Moreover, they make a virtue of
necessity: such initiatives obscure the fact that any 'responsible practices are likely to have been forced upon industry, by legislation and
the fear of legislation.'

Indeed, initiatives undertaken at the trade association level (for
example, the US CMA and the UK Chemical Industries' Association),
at the individual corporate level and even the international level[8]
have typically revolved around the development of fact-sheets for
public consumption, the attempts to use workers as 'ambassadors'
for the industry, the exploitation of 'communications opportunities'
and so on. Fundamentally, such initiatives begin from the premises
that publics need to be disavowed of their unjustifiably critical
attitude to the activities of chemical industries.

Thus the failure to promote dialogue between the industry and
various publics is a common characteristic of industry-inspired initiatives in both the UK and the US. Following the Bhopal disaster,
the US Chemical Manufacturers' Association introduced CAER,
'Community Awareness and Emergency Response'. A key element
of this is said to be dialogue with local communities, workers and
environmental groups. The limits to such dialogue were clearly
expressed by the Director of Environmental Communications,
Monsanto, in a presentation on the nature of CAER, in response
to a question asking which groups were to be engaged in such
dialogue:

You need to seek out commonality. It does not take very long to
see how rigid or flexible they might be. . . . You are not going
to get anywhere sitting down with the Greens, and we are not
going to get anywhere sitting down with Greenpeace.[9]

The UK's Chemical Industries Association's recent 'Responsible Care Programme' is based around a similar approach to informing publics of 'relevant' information, and improving the reputation of the industry.[10] Similar initiatives have emerged in continental Europe, both within and without the European trade association CEFIC.[11] However, the impetus for such initiatives has tended to come from two (closely related) types of sources, namely, 'political fallout' from disasters such as Bhopal and Sandoz, or the threat of impending legislation enacted by national or even supranational authorities.[12]

In terms of practical 'reforms', it needs emphasising that, for example, *if* there now exist emergency evacuation plans at some chemicals plants, these are relatively recent (and still rare) phenomena. And *if* pollution control devices are now installed, *if* some care is now taken to dispose of hazardous waste properly, prior to the 1970s these were simply released into the atmosphere, dumped into rivers and lakes or buried. When in the 1970s the disposal of solid and liquid waste became legally controlled the chemical companies successfully lobbied for an ineffective and indeed 'criminogenic regulatory structure'.[13] Instead of the producers of hazardous wastes being 'strictly liable' for their safe and effective disposal they were able to transfer the legal obligation by paying others to dispose of the waste. There emerged a highly competitive market which disposed of the waste cheaply and often illegally, but nearly always with a disastrous disregard for safety. Love Canal (25th of 115 Superfund-designated worst sites in the US) and the other 2500–10,000 sites that are imminently hazardous to public health[14] are a consequence of the pre-1970s lack of (and then subsequent inadequate) regulation. Similarly, prior to the 1970s Clean Air Act many chemicals were simply released into the air, but even then pollution control devices were, to put it mildly, inadequate. A 1980 EPA survey of Synthetic Organic Chemicals Manufacturing plants 'found that a significant number of equipment units . . . are expected to leak in "normal" operation".[15] Furthermore, in 20 years regulations were issued for only seven out of 300 chemicals that Congress determined were a health threat. For the first time, Title Three has forced the chemical companies to monitor and document their emissions for at least some chemicals. They now admit that 2.4 billion pounds of such chemicals are currently emitted every year in the US alone.[16] It is now also acknowledged that in the last 25 years the US has seen 29 major atmospheric releases of toxic chemicals, seventeen of them more dangerous than Bhopal.[17]

Interestingly, the Chairman of the Chemical Manufacturers' Association was also chairman of Union Carbide, which has itself recently published a whole series of pamphlets and press releases on environmental issues, including one entitled *Towards Environmental Excellence: A Progress Report* (1989), in which it lists its own achievements and gives itself more good marks. This report was published some five years after the Bhopal disaster; and Bhopal, like Flixborough and Seveso before it, has provided a key impetus in terms of pressure towards regulatory reform.[18] Yet claims to environmental and safety excellence on the part of Union Carbide Corporation are hardly the result of a corporate sea-change following that disaster. Indeed, there is no little irony in the fact that, in the early 1980s, prior to the accident, Union Carbide's slogan had been 'Production at a Cost: Safety at Any Cost', and that it prided itself on having one of the best safety records of the major American corporations. The worthlessness of the corporate slogan should have become apparent as news spread of the Bhopal disaster; it was brought home to the American public only months later when, in March 1985, an acetone/mesityl oxide mixture was accidentally released at the company's plant at Institute, West Virginia, and where five months later there was a leak of aldicarb oxime, a chemical of unknown toxicity.

We have argued elsewhere that Union Carbide is not an atypical, rogue company.[19] Indeed, its safety records *were* relatively good in the context of the US. What makes Union Carbide an extremely useful 'case-study' in corporate responsibility/irresponsibility is its reactions to the world's worst industrial disaster at Bhopal. Through our analysis of events surrounding that incident, we aim to call into question claims of a new social responsibility on behalf of corporate capital; indeed, what this paper most clearly demonstrates is that, through the (very old-fashioned) use and existence of power, the largest and most visible corporations continue to seek to avoid responsibility for the consequences of their activities – despite fine sounding corporate slogans.

EXPLAINING THE DISASTER AT BHOPAL

The 'Accident'

In Bhopal a chemical plant operated by Union Carbide of India Limited (UCIL), a subsidiary of Union Carbide Corporation (UCC), used the highly toxic chemicals carbon monoxide, chlorine, phosgene ('mustard gas'), monomethylamine and methylisocyanate (MIC) to produce the carbamate pesticides Carbaryl (Sevin) and Aldicarb (Temik). On the night of Sunday 2 December 1984 water somehow entered an MIC storage tank setting in process an exothermic reaction. This led to the build-up of excess pressure such that a cocktail of gases – including MIC, hydrogen cyanide, nitrous oxide and carbon monoxide – burst past the tank's rupture disk, through the relief-valve vent-header, past the vent-gas scrubber and into the atmosphere.[20] Over 200,000 local people were exposed to the toxic fumes, some 60,000 were seriously affected, more than 20,000 were permanently injured, and as many as 10,000 people may have died as a direct result of the tragedy. A simple listing of the numbers of deaths and injuries gives little idea of the overall impact of the tragedy. Women suffered particularly, and it is still unclear what the disaster's carcinogenic, mutagenic and terratogenic effects might be. One study has shown that of 2700 pregnancies in Bhopal in the year following the disaster, 452 ended in abortion or stillbirth, 132 died soon after birth and 30 were malformed.[21] Whole communities were devastated by the explosion – in the worst-hit areas, 90 per cent of families were affected through the death or severe incapacitation of at least one parent.[22]

Union Carbide's Response

Immediately after the gas leak the chief executive of UCIL had indicated that his company was willing to pay compensation which might run into millions of dollars. At the same time, UCC was asserting that since the disaster was totally unprecedented and unanticipated an 'evacuation or safety plan had never been developed'. They had the same safety standards in their American and overseas operations – 'in India or Brazil or someplace else . . . same equipment, same design, same everything'. They had not located the methylisocyanate (MIC) plant at Bhopal 'for reasons of economy or to avoid safety standards';[23] indeed, although it was managed exclusively by Indian nationals, this plant was the same as the one at Institute West Virginia, which was very safe.

In the year immediately following the disaster, UCC took almost every opportunity to develop a case as to the details of the accident and to deny its own responsibility for the series of events that had led to the gas leak. Most notably in its 1984 Annual Report, the 'Bhopal Methylisocyanate Incident Report' and its Memorandum of Law, as well as in a series of statements in a number of public forums, UCC made five basic contentions:

- UCC had an excellent safety record and the design of the plant's Standard Operating Procedures (SOPs), UCC's responsibility, was basically sound;
- the production of MIC in India, the siting of the plant and the quality of the materials used, were all the responsibility of UCIL and the Indian State;
- UCIL was an independent company responsible for its own affairs;
- India's cultural backwardness was responsible for the poor maintenance and management, poor planning procedures and the inadequate enforcement of safety regulations;
- there was a national proclivity to engage in sabotage, political or personal, and this demonstrated national immaturity.

In order to subject these contentions to careful scrutiny we shall provide a more detailed account of what is known to have happened that fateful night. But let us first deal with the implications of the last contention.

The Sabotage Theory

The 'sabotage theory' plays a key role in UCC's 'definitive version' of the sequence of events that led to the leak at the plant.[24] According to this 'theory', on the night of the accident a disgruntled employee who was not actually working at that moment removed a pressure gauge and then used a hose to put water into an MIC tank; his intention was to spoil a batch of chemicals rather than create a disaster. This version of events, circulated to the media and to UCC personnel, formed the basis of a paper presented by 'independent consultant' Dr Ashok Kalelkar at a London conference in May 1988. Kalelkar had in fact been a member of a team organised by UCC in March 1985 which even then had mooted the possibility of sabotage, although a lack of evidence meant that 'it was unable to develop this theory further at the time'.[25] Basing its eventual (1988) conclusions upon experimental data which have never been released, this team claimed that the accident was triggered by 1000–2000 pounds of water entering the tank. Kalelkar also claimed that an alternative explanation of the immediate circumstances of the accident did not withstand 'even minimal scientific scrutiny'. In this other view, water, possibly in a lesser quantity, gradually entered the tank over a period of time. It was inadvertently introduced when an in-adequately trained, inadequately supervised worker did not follow standard operating procedures when washing out a pipe. One rea-son that Kalelkar gave for the implausibility of this explanation was that, according to witnesses, three bleeder valves were open and would have drained away any water. What he failed to mention was that, according to other witnesses, two of these valves were partially blocked, the other completely. He also omitted mentioning another possible route of water into the tank, a temporary jumper line, despite the fact that UCC had reluctantly conceded its presence in August 1985.

This 'definitive version' of events was only the last in a series of such 'theories' involving alleged saboteurs. First, it had been claimed that the disaster itself was the result of the actions of careless or malicious employees who had placed a water line where a nitrogen line should have been used. The *New York Times*[26] pointed out that neither an accidental nor a deliberate incorrect coupling were possible since the relevant nitrogen and water lines were of a different colour and the nozzles were of different sizes. That same day Warren Anderson withdrew the contention on admitting at Congressional Hearings that he had no evidence of sabotage. Then, between 31 July 1985 and 3 January 1986, UCC claimed that a group of Sikh extremists called the Black June Movement were responsible.[27] But no such group was ever identified in any context other than allegedly putting up posters about Union Carbide; moreover, it was virtually impossible for anybody actually to plan a disaster of this kind. Not surprisingly, this was also quietly abandoned. In August 1986 a specific but unnamed employee was blamed but it was not until May 1988 that all references to nitrogen lines were dropped and a pressure meter was mentioned.

In a perceptive article Muchlinski has pinpointed the legal reasoning behind UCC's strategy of using the sabotage argument:

> Union Carbide and UCIL are hoping, first, to avoid vicarious liability on the ground that the employee would have been acting without authority and outside the course of his employment, and, secondly, to avoid liability under Rylands v. Fletcher, on the ground that an employee who comes onto his employers' premises without authority and causes the escape of a dangerous thing is a 'stranger' for whose acts the occupier is not responsible.[28]

Since Muchlinski's article an important ruling of the supreme court of India – *M. C. Mehta* v. *Union of India* – has radically changed the legal position. According to this judgment, where 'an entereprise . . . is engaged in a hazardous or inherently dangerous activity and harm results to anyone on account of an accident in the operation of such . . . activity the enterprise is strictly and absolutely liable to compensate all those affected by the accident'. And further, that 'it should be no answer . . . [for] the enterprise to say that it had taken all reasonable care and that the harm occurred without any negligence on its part'.[29] The law applies to all cases which are *decided* subsequent to the decision.

Kelley, Drye and Warren, UCC's attorneys, reacted by claiming that 'you can't go into a country and then totally change the law in order to convict a specific company. We have a right to due process.'[30] This is a red herring for two reasons. First, the maxim *nulla poena sine lege* was developed in the context of criminal not civil law. Secondly, it is perfectly acceptable in American law for the Supreme Court to overrule the law with retroactive effect.[31] These points aside, even if *Mehta* were not applicable, the case of *Rylands* v. *Fletcher* establishes the strong possibility that UCC would still be liable under tort law.[32]

Yet even without entering into such legal arguments, notwithstanding the significance of the *Mehta* ruling, and leaving aside the applicability of *Rylands* v. *Fletcher*, it remains clear that the very set of events that allegedly caused the disaster underline UCC's responsibility. For if the accident *was* caused by sabotage this shows how unsafe the plant was. Why as it possible to remove a pressure dial by hand when this was connected to such a toxic and volatile chemical? More generally, and these comments apply however water entered the tank, why were there water hoses in the area?

Since it is well known that water reacts violently with MIC, no water should have been allowed anywhere near the equipment, for washing out lines or any other purpose. If water is not there it cannot leak in, no matter how many valves leak or how many errors are made.[33]

Thus what is of import is not whether or not sabotage occurred, but the ease with which a disaster of almost unprecedented scale could be caused. The focus on sabotage drew attention away from UCC's responsibility for many other issues: the poor design of the Bhopal plant, its inappropriate siting, its inadequate safety systems, the lack of a proper emergency plan, and its generally run-down condition. Let us now turn to these questions.

THE CONTEXT AND CIRCUMSTANCES OF THE ACCIDENT

Let us focus, in more detail, on the circumstances of the accident. At Bhopal enormous amounts of MIC were stored in three 15,000-gallon tanks. The temperatures and pressures of these were routinely too high – they should have been kept at 0–5°C but were in fact between 15° and 20°C. Furthermore, these temperatures and pressures were not rigorously logged. Since plant instrumentation was inadequate to monitor normal plant processes, leaks were detected by smell (only possible at levels 20 times higher than its Threshold Limit Value). This was not the case at the plant in Institute, West Virginia, which in this context and in many others had superior technology. On the night of 2 December workers smelt MIC, could not locate its source but reported the leak to a supervisor who postponed investigating its source until after a tea break. Before that was over a tank was rumbling, concrete cracking, the tank's temperature was about 200°C, the pressure at over 180 psi – 140 psi in excess of the tank's rupture-disk limit. Gases burst past the rupture disk, shot through the relief-valve vent-header, then the vent-gas scrubber and into the atmosphere. The vent-gas scrubber was on standby, and although it was eventually turned on it probably never worked. The flare tower was inoperative, and an attempt to douse the gas with water was unsuccessful because the hoses had insufficient water pressure to reach the stack from which the gas was escaping. The operators could not dilute the MIC in tank 610 since it was already over-full and the emergency dump tank had a defective gauge which indicated that it was also 22 per cent full. Although the tanks should have been refrigerated, the refrigeration unit had been turned off – to save $50 per week. There is clearly no doubt that badly maintained equipment, lack of spare parts, inadequate SOPs and untrained staff all contributed to the accident. But equally important were *ad hoc* modifications to the plant designs, such as a jumper line that may well have been the means by which water entered the MIC tank.

There are also serious questions about the plant design itself. Plant instrumentation was inadequate to monitor normal plant processes. Furthermore, whilst large amounts of MIC were also stored at Institute it has larger dump tanks and an additional dedicated sump system with a capacity of 42,000 gallons.[34] It is possible that the Bhopal storage tanks had originally been used at Institute, since they were of a type unsuitable for Indian climatic conditions. The refrigeration plant at Bhopal, even when working, was not powerful enough to cool all of the MIC stored there, the vent-gas scrubber and flare tower were only designed to deal with single-phase (that is, gas, not liquid or *gas and* liquid) emissions. At Institute, moreover, there was an additional and more powerful emergency back-up system. *Bhopal* was *demonstrably inadequate and inferior to Institute.* Nevertheless, even with this inferior technology, far fewer people would have died: if the plant had not been sited near shanty towns; if there had been adequate risk assessment, modelling and monitoring of discharges and emergency planning and management; if the plant personnel, local medical services and the state and national government had known more about the nature and effects of the deadly gaseous emissions.[35]

Thus it appears, contrary to the claims of Anderson and others, that the Bhopal plant was inferior to the UCC plant at Institute, West Virginia. But this should not be taken as an indication that the latter was safe nor that the Bhopal plant was a maverick operation of an essentially law-abiding and socially responsible corporation. We noted above that in March 1985 an acetone/mesityl oxide mixture was accidentally released there and in August there was a leak of aldicarb oxime, a chemical of unknown toxicity. On the later occasion it became clear that alarm systems were shut off or not working, staff were inadequately trained, the SOPs were imprecise and management slack.[36] More generally, UCC has long been a prime example of 'toxic capital'. There was the Gauley Bridge disaster in West Virginia where

476 deaths from silicosis were recorded. It played a key role in the development and use of the carcinogen vinyl chloride. It has manufactured nuclear weapons in Oak Ridge, Tennessee. It owns dangerous graphite electrodes production facilities in Yabucoa, Puerto Rico.[37] Its plant in Alloy, West Virginia, puts 'out more pollution annually than the total emitted in New York City in a year' and, contrary to its claims to have reduced its production of hazardous waste, this has actually increased in recent years.[38] Clearly, Union Carbide's slogan of 'Safety at any Cost' portrays a corporate image that is hardly borne out by reality.

'UNION CARBIDE CORPORATION TNC'

Union Carbide Corporation and Union Carbide India Limited

Whether or not Union Carbide Corporation (UCC) was legally responsible for the accident has not been resolved by the decision in the Indian courts (see below, third part of this section); yet we can explore this issue sociologically. A useful starting point is Kelvin Jones's discussion of property relations in his *Law and Economy: The Legal Regulation of Corporate Capital*. He distinguishes three distinct and necessary functions of property in the sphere of economic production: *title* 'involves the sort of calculations an conditions which govern the more general provision of finance, the socialisation of debt, the exchange of guarantees and the constitutional position of shareholders'[39] *control* 'refers to the distribution of the relevant means of production to a particular use . . . to the more or less absolute power to dispose of the means of production within the relevant confines imposed by other relations of ownership';[40] while *possession* 'concerns the day to day relations of management'[41] and the 'strategies and calculations which comprise the use or actual operation of any particular process of production irrespective of who is the agent of possession'.[42]

In common with UCIL's other shareholders, UCC had 'title' to much of the revenue generated by UCIL. In fact, despite the rule that foreign companies should usually own 40 per cent of an Indian company's stock, UCC owned 50.9 per cent; and in 1982 UCIL remitted $1.43 million in dividends to UCC.[43] Such a majority shareholding allowed UCC to determine, to a large extent, the decisions made about investments and dividends and the assets of the company. According to UCC's charter, the objectives of the corporation would be realised through a management system which distinguished between 'Category I policies' which provide the worldwide directives of the company, and Category II policies which are operational procedures. Crucially,

> Both types of policy are issued to subsidiaries (*affiliates in which Union Carbide has more than 50 per cent ownership*) for adoption and implementation. A subsidiary cannot change the substance of any policy without review by the parent.[44]

UCC had a significant degree of 'control' over UCIL. UCIL's production and marketing strategies were dictated by the corporate strategies of UCC.[45] Moreover, the continued existence of the plant was its decision: it had commissioned a preliminary study of the cost of dismantling the methylisocyanate unit and other pesticide production facilities at Bhopal.[46] Despite such a threat to its existence, UCIL was not in a position to 'go to a competitor of Union Carbide and buy a pesticide plant' ready-made; and it would be prohibitively expensive to develop a 'pesticides plant from scratch'.[47]

UCC, to a large extent, 'possessed' the Bhopal plant. It had always dictated how and which chemicals were produced and stored. In the 1970s it had 'insisted that large amounts of MIC be stored in Bhopal over UCIL's objections. . . . [T]he UCIL position [was] that only token storage [of the chemical at Bhopal] was necessary.'[48] It monitored safety procedures and UCIL was forced to rely upon UCC for technological assistance and updates.[49] Indeed, at Bhopal UCC received significant revenues from its licensing, managerial, monitoring and marketing activities, a not-untypical arrangement when TNCs engage in joint ventures in less developed countries.[50] UCC had the right to intervene in day-to-day matters if safety was affected. A UCC safety team had monitored the plant in May 1982, and found 61 hazards, 30 of them considered major, eleven in the phosgene/MIC unit. Areas of concern were 'procedures training and enforcement together with attention to the equipment and mechanical deficiencies'.[51] Nevertheless, production was allowed to continue.

Detailed reports on safety and related matters were sent to UCC every three to six months.[52] This included decisions on plant expenditure – on investment and cutbacks, on staffing levels, on refrigeration and so on. All of these had certainly been cut back: for example, there were fewer operatives, and amongst these fewer first class BSc graduates; theoretical and practical training had been cut back or abolished; maintenance procedures were dangerously abbreviated.[53]

In short, then, even though it is clear that the actual social relations in the individual enterprises were 'lived' and fulfilled by specific Indian managerial personnel (and individual workers), UCC 'possessed' the enterprise.

In many ways, of course, this is only the case in so far as UCC exerted itself to ensure that UCIL would follow its SOPs. In fact it is not clear that it provided the resources adequately to monitor the SOPs at Bhopal, or whether it took into account the social and economic environments confronting UCIL. But UCIL's production of the pesticides Temik and Sevin took place under commodified conditions – that is, they were supposed to be produced and sold in such a way that subdivisions of the company showed a normal profitable return on investment. It is questionable whether it was possible for UCIL both to make pesticides safely *and* to sell these pesticides at a profit. In the event that they could not do so, either the company could have engaged in safe 'uneconomic' production, or it could have produced less safely but more economically. It is clear that UCC's SOPs were both inadequate and (to some extent) ignored, this with the collaboration of certain UCC's personnel. What is clear, however, is that the top management of UCC had represented itself to its shareholders as effectively controlling the different subsections of its organisation and had received the rewards and privileges commensurate with such control. Even if they were in fact not totally in control of the organisation's actions, top management at UCC seems to have been responsible for both the acts of commission and omission that created the Bhopal disaster.

More generally, Union Carbide has claimed that its own involvement in the Third World has been, and remains, benevolent. Its chairman, Warren Anderson, claimed that:

> without the technologies and the capital that multinationals help to introduce developing countries would have little hope of eradicating poverty and hunger.[54]

Whatever the intentions of individual actors within UCC, the events at Bhopal demonstrate only too clearly how this company, like all transnationals, operates in an imperialist manner.[55] Their economic power, combined with their monopoly of both scientific knowledge and sophisticated technology, allows them to 'export hazard'[56] to vulnerable, and often unsuspecting, Third World countries. Because of the lack of any countervailing power given acquiescent governments, inadequate regulatory agencies and unorganised workers and local communities – they can engage in cheap and dangerous production and be relatively indifferent to the social costs of their activities. Furthermore in order to achieve profits they will practise 'force and fraud' – they will tell lies and bribe and cheat.

On a number of specific points, as well as on the general issue of control and in the presentation of the sabotage theory, UCC seems to have engaged in some degree of calculated and conscious misrepresentation and manipulation. For example, while UCC claimed that it would rather have imported MIC to the Bhopal plant, this seems unlikely since it would have made it vulnerable to transportation problems. True, in 1983 UCIL, like many other affiliates of multinationals, was in the top twenty of profit-making Indian companies,[57] and the capital/labour relationship was highly favourable to UCC. Yet the pesticide and herbicide markets had been highly competitive for a number of years. Indeed, there was already a downturn in the market 'in 1977–78 when a consignment of MIC was delayed at sea . . . [Then in] 1984 . . . the plant was operating at less than one third of capacity'.[58] In the words of R. J. Natarajan, a director at Union Carbide Eastern, Bhopal was 'an oversized plant for an undersized market'[59] UCIL tried to maintain profitability, or minimise losses, in a number of different ways. It tried to restrict competition by increasing its licenced capacity, thereby pre-empting competitors from increasing their market share and in order thereby to try and 'maintain a monopolistic control over prices'.[60] They also cut back on operating costs to such an extent that the plant could not be run safely any more.[61] In the context of weak health and safety and pollution regulations it was not 'rational' for this capitalist corporation to spend money on these areas if this were matched by its competitors. This shows that UCC/UCIL was also *constrained* by the circumstances in which the Bhopal plant was operating. But much of this was the responsibility of the TNCs themselves: they had not pressured the Indian government to improve such regulations but rather they were happy to 'export hazard'. Then, some UCC executives used racist rationalisations to justify their carelessness and unusual level of risk-taking – life is not valued in Third World countries; Indians are technologically

unsophisticated, do not comprehend the purpose of safety procedures; and accidents are generally due to workers' incompetence.[62]
Thus it is not surprising that the lives of Indian people were so
recklessly put at risk nor that in other plants, but not at Bhopal, UCC
had been willing to engage in 'facilities writeoffs' of '$241 million' in
the face of unprofitable returns.[63]

Yet, while the existence of (somewhat) safer plants and production processes operated by UCC in the West (at Beziers, France, and
Institute, US) shows that the relatively poor state of the Bhopal plant
can only be understood in terms of a racist imperialism, this is only
partly true. One must also recognise that there are problems about
the relations between corporations and their workers, local communities and consumers, wherever they operate and whoever owns
and controls them. Such issues have often been addressed by the
more complex Marxist analyses of the operations of TNCs. These
approaches are useful in that they focus upon the class structure to
be found *within* particular countries, whilst relating such an analysis
to the *global system* in which individual states, corporations and
particular struggles are imbricated. In the case of India, itself now a
major industrial country, this means exploring the relations between
the different classes involved in different modes of production and
particularly in recognising that the capitalist class, which to a large
extent controls the state, shares many interests with foreign corporations, benefits from their and US government initiatives, such as
the 'Green Revolution', and shares a similar opposition to the interests
of the local working class. It is worth noting that in raising such
issues, the Union Research Group and many other commentators lay
some blame on those Indian interests who, through their commitment
to capitalist industrialisation at any cost, were responsible for the
attitude of the local and national state to UCC and other
transnationals.[64]

THE BHOPAL SETTLEMENT IN PERSPECTIVE

It seems clear to us that the contentions made by UCC concerning
the Bhopal disaster in its publicity and its legal arguments do not
stand up to scrutiny.

UCIL was not an independent company nor was it Indian backwardness that was responsible for the poor state of the Bhopal plant

and its unsafe manufacturing practices. The sabotage theory has been presented in a number of guises and remains unsubstantiated. The Bhopal plant's design and standard operating procedures were inadequate and they were the responsibility of UCC, not UCIL. Bhopal was an inferior plant to that at Institute, West Virginia; but that plant was not safe either. Indeed, contrary to the version of the history of its operations presented by the company, UCC has long been a prime example of 'toxic capital'.[65] Yet to a large extent it was UCC's ability to make these contentions seem plausible that allowed it to achieve such a small settlement. The initial sum demanded by the Indian government had been $3.3 billion. This was anything but excessive. It included no element of punitive damages, and can be placed into perspective via Everest's comparison with the $2.5 billion received by 60,000 claimants in the Johns-Manville asbestos suit or the $2.9 billion received by 195,000 victims of A. H. Robbins's Dalkon Shield. In fact, on 14 February 1989 UCC and the Indian government – the latter acting on behalf of the victims of the Bhopal tragedy – reached an out-of-court settlement of $470 million. It was agreed that this settlement would render UCC immune from all impending litigation, including criminal charges. The money is to compensate the families of the 3329 people officially recognised by the Indian government as having died as a result of the tragedy and the 20,000 seriously injured that it accepts as bona fide victims of the tragedy.

Does this mean that justice has been done and that the matter can be laid to rest? In two senses the answer is no. First, the current Indian government has reopened the question of the appropriateness of the settlement because, in its words, 'Indian life is not so cheap'. Secondly, the settlement itself can be better understood as a somewhat sordid compromise forced upon the weak by the strong rather than something determined according to equity and the facts of the case. Bhopal cannot be considered merely an unforeseen and unforeseeable event from which the chemical industry could learn some new lessons. UCC, with the aid of the American chemical industry, the American state and the American courts, has succeeded, albeit temporarily, in avoiding responsibility for the accident and in imposing an insulting and inequitable settlement.

Why did the government accept the settlement of $470 million? A large part of the reason was the successful effort by UCC to have the case tried in India rather than in the US. UCC argued that the witnesses to the disaster, the victims, the key players, the documentation and evidence were all in Bhopal, where the UCIL plant was 'managed, operated, and maintained exclusively by Indians residing in India, more than 8000 miles away'. The Company claimed that the real reason for the attempt to have the case tried in the US was the potential for a large settlement: 'as a moth to the light, so is a litigation drawn to the United States'.[66] On the question of litigation, UCC's particular (and real) concerns have to be related to the general interests of transnational capital whose Third-World operations might be threatened by any settlement with a punitive element.

Indeed, the Bhopal victims and the Indian government *had* wanted the trial in the US, articulating various reasons for this: that there was such a backlog of cases in India that the trial would take an inordinate amount of time; that tort law was underdeveloped and there was a lack of experienced legal experts; that there were inadequate discovery procedures in India and the laws were constructed around doctrines of negligence rather than strict liability; that this was largely due to the heritage of colonialism; that UCIL's assets in India were worth less than $100 million; and, finally and most important of all, that UCC controlled UCIL and the relevant documents and personnel were to be found in the US and not in India.

> Key management personnel of multinationals exercise a closely-held power which is neither restricted by national boundaries nor effectively controlled by international law. The complex corporate structure of the multinational, with networks of subsidiaries and subdivisions, makes it exceedingly difficult or even impossible to pinpoint responsibility for the damage caused by the enterprise to discrete corporate units or individuals.
>
> In reality there is but one entity, the monolithic multinational which is responsible for the design, development and dissemination of information and technology worldwide.[67]

Judge Keenan decided that the trial would be held in India but with three conditions: that UCC should itself consent to be tried in India; that it should accept the judgements of the courts there; that it should be willing to be subject to discovery under the model of the United States federal rules and civil procedures.[68]

UCC accepted the first two conditions but appealed against the third. It claimed that it was unfair for the Indian government to have unrestricted access to its records when its own access to the records of the Indian government was to be more limited. Keenan himself had implicitly indicated sympathy to such a plea when he wrote in a footnote that while 'the Court feels it would be fair to bind the plaintiffs to American discovery rules, too, it has no authority to do so'.[69] Not surprisingly, UCC won its appeal so that, instead of using American discovery procedures which had made possible the successful actions against asbestos producers such as Johns Manville,[70] the inadequate Indian, or rather Anglo-Indian, discovery procedures obtained.

An apparently even-handed settlement was nothing of the sort. Essentially, the American courts had accepted UCC's presentation of the case – that the crucial evidence and events were in India and simply ignored that of the Indian government. Baxi summarises Keenan's reasoning, on this point, as follows:

> India's claim was that Union Carbide was 'the creator of the design used in the Bhopal plant, and directed UCIL's relatively minor detailing program' . . . consequently only an American forum had the best access to the sources of proof. The court decides, in response, that 'most of the documentary evidence concerning design, safety, training, safety and start-ups is to be found in India'. In doing so, Judge Keenan relies on the affidavits of Messrs Brown, Woomer and Dutta, all Union Carbide employees.
> . . . [Then] the Court is 'struck by the fact' that the two agreements between UCIL and the Union Carbide ('Design Transfer Agreement' and 'Technical Service Agreements') were based on an arms-length corporate practice. . . .[71]

We have shown that to take such arms-length agreements at face value is ludicrous since it ignores the considerable evidence of the complex control exercised by UCC over its subsidiaries.

Similarly ludicrous is the fact that the American courts accepted that the interests of a sovereign (and democratic) state and a licensed (and autocratic) corporation were of an equivalent value. They did not believe that a government charged with the security of more than 650 million people had more specific and legitimate concerns with secrecy than was true of a corporation. Perhaps this was related to the fact that this corporation was a large America industrial (the 35th largest in 1984) with sales of $9.5 billion and assets of $11 billion.

Union Carbide did, however, make one particularly telling series of claims, namely that

> the Indian government may have granted a licence for the Bhopal plant without adequate checks on the plant; that the relevant controlling agencies responsible for the plant were grossly under-staffed, lacked powers and had little impact on conditions in the field. More particularly, the Bhopal department of labour office had only two inspectors, neither of whom had any knowledge of chemical hazards. . . .[72]

In other words, the Indian government bore a major responsibility for the Bhopal disaster. Now, there is strong evidence that Indian regulatory agencies were indeed inadequate;[73] but in arguing this position Union Carbide was being disingenuous. First, because it had itself cultivated relationships with personnel at all levels of the Indian state[74] and seems to have itself been party to the circum-vention of regulations.[75] Secondly, effective regulation in what was to all intents and purposes a 'deregulated' country would have partly curtailed UCC's ability to export hazard; and no corporation would (or could) altruistically or autonomously encourage the development of measures which restrict its own freedom to locate production.

In their desperate struggle for foreign investment and technology many less-developed countries have offered business environments with few controls on the movement of capital, hazardous production or pollution. Sometimes this has been the official policy of govern-ments, as in the case of 'free production zones';[76] on other occasions regulations exist but are simply not enforced. This was true not only of India but, to a lesser degree, was also true of the US and Britain in the 1980s.[77] In these countries there were cutbacks in the resources and powers of those regulatory agencies concerned with occupational health and safety and environmental dangers, whilst their enforce-ment responsibilities were extended.[78] Indeed, there is a crucial interrelationship between the possibility that capital will move to areas of weak regulation and this tendency of standards to drop in some advanced industrial countries. Yet, ironically, this is only a tendency. The political and economic fallout from Bhopal was such that in both the US and Europe as a whole there has been a tighten-ing of regulations.[79]

CONCLUSIONS

In this paper we have used the tragic disaster at Bhopal in December 1984 to question claims made by corporate capital to a new social responsibility. Despite public commitments to health, safety and environmental protection, we have argued that Union Carbide Corporation: created, or allowed to develop, the conditions whereby an accident was possible; had not taken the steps necessary to mitigate the effects of any accident; influenced public opinion and the legal process through a series of arguments and spurious claims; and secured a favourable settlement, one in which responsibility for the disaster was not, and will never be, determined legally.

However, we have emphasised throughout that UCC is not a rogue company amongst transnational corporations, just as Bhopal was not one maverick plant within an otherwise safety-conscious organisation. Indeed, *although the scale of the disaster at Bhopal was a unique one, its causes are all too common.* Workers and local communities regularly suffer death, injury and ill-health due to the actions or inactions of corporations. Understandably, they are perhaps the most sceptical audience for claims to a new corporate responsibility.

Notes

1. *Guardian*, 18 April 1990.
2. E. Pell, 'Movements Buying In', *Mother Jones*, vol. 15, April–May; vol. 3 (April – May 1990) p. 25.
3. Ibid.
4. *Guardian*, 19 April 1990.
5. *New York Times*, 26 March 1988.
6. *New York Times Magazine*, 15 April 1990.
7. S. Tombs, 'The Politics of Regulation', paper presented at the Workshops on Industrial Crisis Management, the European Consortium for Political Research, Bochum, 2–7 April 1990.
8. For example, the UNEP APELL programme; see United Nations Environment Programme 'APELL (Awareness and Preparedness for Emergencies at Local Level)', *Industry and Environment*, 11(2) (April/May/June 1988) pp. 3–7.
9. D. R. Bishop, 'The Community's Rights and Industry's Response', in M. A. Smith (ed.), *The Chemical Industry after Bhopal* (London: IBC Technical Services, 1985) p. 175. Similarly, in the course of a series of interviews and meetings between Steve Tombs and managers in various chemical companies operating in the UK, an explicit distinction

was made to one of us on several occasions between the average person's concern about the environment and the politically motivated agitation of groups such as Greenpeace and Friends of the Earth – though it must be added that the latter groups were afforded considerable legitimacy and respect by some individuals. This distinction between genuine and politically motivated environmental concern is reflected in the findings of Dawson and her colleagues (see S. Dawson, A. Clinton, M. Bamford and P. Willman, *Safety at Work: The Limits of Self-Regulation* (Cambridge: Cambridge University Press, 1988) p. 83).

10. *Chemistry and Industry*, 1 May 1989, pp. 279–80.
11. For details from an example of the latter, see A. Henry, 'Communication Concerning Technological Risk between Industry and its Surroundings at Pont-de-Claix', *Industry and Environment*, vol. 11 (April/May/June 1988) pp. 11–17.
12. See, for example, M. Hill, S. Aaranovitch and D. Baldock, 'Non-Decision Making in Pollution Control in Britain: Nitrate Pollution, the EEC Drinking Water Directive and Agriculture', *Policy and Politics*, 17(3) (1988) pp. 227–40; T. O'Riordan and A. Weale, 'Administrative Reorganisation and Policy Change: the Case of Her Majesty's Inspectorate of Pollution', *Public Administration*, vol. 67 (Autumn 1989) pp. 277–94; W. Stover, 'A Field Day for the Legislators: Bhopal, and its Effects on the Enactment of New Laws in the United States', in Smith, op. cit., pp. 69–126.
13. A. Szasz, 'Corporations, Organized Crime and the Disposal of Hazardous Waste: the Making of a Criminogenic Regulatory Structure', *Criminology*, 24 (1986) pp. 103–16.
14. S. Epstein (ed.), *The Disposal of Hazardous Waste* (San Francisco: Sierra Club, 1982) p. 448; Szasz, op. cit.
15. W. Morehouse and M. A. Subramaniam, *The Bhopal Tragedy* (New York: Council on International and Public Affairs, 1986) p. 164.
16. *Manchester Guardian Weekly*, 2 April 1989.
17. *New York Times*, 30 April 1989.
18. Bishop, op. cit.; J. K. Brooks, R. W. Haney, G. D. Kaiser, A. J. Leyva and T. C. McKelvey, 'A Survey of Recent Major Accident Legislation in the USA'; and D. A. Deieso, N. P. Mulvey and J. Kelly, 'Accidental Release Prevention: a Regulator's Perspective', both in Institution of Chemical Engineers, *Preventing Major Chemical and Related Process Accidents* (Rugby: Hemisphere Publishing, 1988) I.Chem.E. Symposium Series no. 110 and EFCE Publications Series no. 70).
19. F. Pearce, 'Socially Responsible Corporations Need Strong Independent Regulatory Agencies', *Political Quarterly*, 61(4) (1990) pp. 415–30; F. Pearce and S. Tombs, 'Ideology, Hegemony and Empiricism: Compliance Theories of Regulation', *British Journal of Criminology*, 30(4) (Winter 1990) pp. 423–43; F. Pearce and S. Tombs, 'Realism and Corporate Crime', in R. Matthews and J. Young (eds), *Realist Criminology* (London: Sage, 1991); F. Pearce and S. Tombs, *Crimes of Capital* (London: Sage, forthcoming).
20. We have drawn upon newspaper and magazine reports (Indian, British and American) and documents, interviews and discussions in

M. Abraham, *The Lessons of Bhopal: A Community Action Resource Manual on Hazardous Technologies* (Penang: International Organization of Consumers Unions, 1985); International Coalition for Justice in Bhopal, *We Must Not Forget: A Plea for Justice for the Bhopal Victims* (Penang: International Organization of Consumers Unions, 1987) and in many of the texts cited elsewhere in this article.

21. B. Dinham, B. Dixon and G. Saghal, *The Bhopal Papers* (London: Transnational Information Centre, 1986): APPEN, *The Bhopal Tragedy – One Year Later* (Penang: Sabahat Alam Malaysia (Friends of the Earth Malaysia), 1986); UCC Letter and Documents to International Coalition for Justice in Bhopal with excerpts from UCC Submission to the Indian Courts (1987); D. Weir, *The Bhopal Syndrome: Pesticide Manufacturing and the Third World* (Penang: International Organization of Consumers Unions, 1986).

22. L. Everest, *Behind the Poison Cloud: Union Carbide's Bhopal Massacre* (New York: Banner Press, 1986) pp. 84–5.

23. Ibid., pp. 47–8.

24. The controversy concerning the sabotage theory is discussed in Everest, op. cit.; T. Jones, *Corporate Killing: Bhopals Will Happen* (London: Free Association Books, 1988); D. Kurtzman, *A Killing Wind: Inside Union Carbide and the Bhopal Catastrophe* (New York: McGraw Hill, 1987); A. Kalelkar, 'Investigation of Large Magnitude Incidents – Bhopal as a Case Study', in Institution of Chemical Engineers, *Preventing Major Chemical and Related Process Accidents*, op. cit. There is a detailed refutation of the Kalelkar argument in Bhopal Action Group, 'Sabotaging the "Sabotage Theory": a Critique of the Paper by Ashok Kalelkar' (London: Transnational Information Centre, 1988).

25. Kalelkar, op. cit., p. 557; UCC, *Bhopal Methyl Isocyanate Incident Investigation Team Report* (Danbury, Conn.: Union Carbide Corporation, March 1985).

26. *New York Times*, 26 March 1985.

27. T. Jones, op. cit., p. 46.

28. P. T. Muchlinski, 'The Bhopal Case: Controlling Ultrahazardous Industrial Activities Undertaken by Foreign Investors', *Modern Law Review*, vol. 50(5) (September 1987) p. 575.

29. 1987 1 SCC 395 at p. 421.

30. *National Law Journal*, 29 February 1988, p. 42.

31. *Great N. R. Co. v. Sunburst Oil and Refining Co.*, 77.L. Ed. 360; *Tehan v. Us* 15.L. Ed. 2d. 543.

32. D. Bergman, 'The Sabotage Theory and the Legal Strategy of Union Carbide', *New Law Journal*, vol. 138 (17 June 1988) pp. 420-22.

33. T. Kletz, *Learning from Accidents in Industry* (London: Butterworths, 1988) p. 86.

34. Everest, op. cit., p. 38.

35. Weir, op. cit., p. 36.

36. T. Jones, op. cit., pp. 167–71.

37. A. Agarwal, J. Merrifield and R. Tandon, *No Place to Run: Local Realities and Global Issues of the Bhopal Disaster* (New Market, Tenn.: Highlander Center and Society for Participatory Research in Asia, 1985) pp. 14–23.

38.		*New York Times*, 10 September 1989.
39.		K. Jones, *Law and Economy: The Legal Regulation of Corporate Capital* (London: Academic Press, 1982) p. 78.
40.		Ibid., p. 77.
41.		Ibid.
42.		Ibid., p. 76.
43.		Everest, op. cit., p. 167.
44.		Muchlinski, op. cit., p. 571, emphasis added.
45.		Morehouse and Subramaniam, op. cit., p. 17.
46.		Dinham *et al.*, op. cit., p. 27.
47.		Muchlinski, op. cit., p. 582.
48.		Everest, op. cit., p. 31.
49.		Ibid., pp. 167–71.
50.		J. Kolko, *Restructuring the World Economy* (New York: Pantheon, 1988) p. 165.
51.		Everest, op. cit., p. 56.
52.		Ibid., p. 171.
53.		H. Sandberg, *Union Carbide Corporation: A Case Study* (Geneva: International Management Institute, 1985) p. 17.
54.		Cited in Everest, op. cit., p. 107.
55.		B. N. Banerjee, *Bhopal Gas Tragedy: Accident or Experiment* (Delhi: Paribus 1986); Dinham *et al.*, op. cit.; APPEN, op. cit.; Everest, op. cit.; Weir, op. cit.
56.		B. Castleman, 'The Export of Hazard to Developing Countries', *International Journal of Health Services*, 9(4) (1979) pp. 569–606; J. Ives (ed.), *The Export of Hazard* (London: Routledge and Kegan Paul, 1985).
57.		Everest, op. cit., p. 127; Sandberg, op. cit., p. 16.
58.		Sandberg, op. cit., p. 17.
59.		S. Hazarika, *Bhopal: The Lessons of a Tragedy* (Delhi: Penguin Books (India), 1987) p. 137.
60.		APPEN, op. cit.
61.		ARENA, *Bhopal: Industrial Genocide?* (Hong Kong: Arena Press, 1985); P. Shrivistava, *Bhopal: Anatomy of a Crisis* (Cambridge: Ballinger, 1987) pp. 48–51.
62.		Everest, op. cit.; see also Smith, op. cit., p. 16.
63.		Sandberg, op. cit., p. 11.
64.		Union Research Group, *The Bhopal MIC Disaster: The Beginnings of a Case for Workers' Control; A First Report* (Bombay: Employees Union Research Group (Union Carbide India Limited), 1985); Union Research Group, *The Role of Management Practices in the Bhopal Gas Leak Disaster; A Second Report* (Bombay: Employees Union Research Group (Union Carbide India Limited), 1985); Everest, op. cit.; ARENA, op. cit.
65.		Agarwal *et al.*, op. cit., pp. 14–23.
66.		T. Jones, op. cit.
67.		Affidavit of the Union of India, US District Court, South District of New York, 8 April 1985, cited in Hazarika, op. cit., p. 112.
68.		Hazarika, op. cit., p. 128.

69. Cited in U. Baxi, 'Inconvenient Forum and Convenient Catastrophe: the Bhopal Case', in U. Baxi and T. Paul (eds), *Mass Disasters and Multinational Liability* (Delhi: Indian Law Institute) p. 8.

70. P. Brodeur, *Outrageous Misconduct: The Asbestos Industry on Trial* (New York: Pantheon, 1985).

71. Baxi, op. cit., p. 23.

72. Muchlinski, op. cit., p. 575.

73. Everest, op. cit.; Hazarika, op. cit.; S. K. Chopra (consultant to Kelly, Drye and Warren), 'Bhopal Disaster and the Indian Legal and Administrative System: What is Wrong and What to Do', a paper presented at the International Bar Association, New York, September 1986.

74. ARENA, op. cit., p. 38.

75. Granada TV, *The Betrayal of Bhopal* (1986) (produced by Laurie Flynn).

76. R. Peet (ed.), *International Capitalism and Industrial Restructuring* (London: Unwin Hyman, 1987).

77. G. K. Wilson, *The Politics of Safety and Health* (Oxford: Clarendon Press, 1985).

78. Pearce and Tombs, 'Realism and Corporate Crime', op. cit., and *Crimes of Capital*, op. cit.

79. Pearce and Tombs, 'Realism and Corporate Crime', op. cit., and *Crimes of Capital*, op. cit.

8

The Politics of Corporate Crime Control

LAUREEN SNIDER

INTRODUCTION

Many of the most serious antisocial and predatory acts committed in modern industrial countries are corporate crimes. In dollar terms their cost far outweighs that of street crime – for example, all the street crime in the Unites States in a given year is estimated to cost around $4 billion, much less than 5 per cent of the take from corporate crime in an average year (excluding mammoth débâcles such as the Drexel case, discussed below). More significantly, in terms of lives lost corporate crime is a major killer. United States, the country with the highest rate of homicide in the developed world, reports 20,000 murders in an average year. By contrast, 14,000 deaths per annum are caused by industrial accidents, many of which stem from violations of safety codes; 30,000 deaths result from unsafe and usually illegal consumer products; and hundreds of thousands of cancer deaths are caused by legal and illegal environmental pollution. The high toll of deaths, injuries and occupationally induced illnesses, in addition to the heavy financial losses, make the emotional impact of corporate crime, the effects on the average victim, horrendous. And the loss of trust and confidence in business leaders and politicians that every new scandal generates further erodes democratic free-enterprise systems and feeds cynicism and apathy.

In Britain, 600 people are killed every year by accidents in the workplace and another 12,000 are injured. Estimates indicate that the majority of such accidents result from the law-breaking and negligence of employers, who fail to install protective equipment or allow dangerous conditions to stand uncorrected. Accident rates rose throughout the 1980s and now stand at 90–100,000 workers. However, evidence from a recent self-report study (the Second

212

Islington Crime Survey) indicates that the actual accident rate may be many times higher than official statistics indicate.[1]

Dollar losses are also horrendous. In the United States junk-bond king Mike Milken is under criminal indictment for 98 racketeering and securities fraud charges, involving insider-trading, failure to disclose information and assorted offences. The company he headed, Drexel Burnham, pleaded guilty to insider-trading and six felony counts and was assessed $650 million in fines. Because of the fraudulent activities of companies such as this, 312 savings and loan companies have defaulted, and 200–300 more are known to be in trouble. The cost of bailing out the companies and investors is conservatively estimated by the General Accounting Agency, the so-called 'watchdog' regulatory agency for the US Congress, at $325 billion dollars at minimum, $500 billion more realistically and $1.4 *trillion* according to yet another estimate. To put such amounts in perspective, $300 billion was the total US defence budget for 1989 and $100 billion is the gross national product of Saudi Arabia. This massive fraud, which is expected to cost every household in the United States a minimum of $5000, means that there will be less money to improve the environment, finance education, do research on AIDS or house the homeless. It also means higher taxes and interest rates for Americans. The cost to foreign governments, because of the hundreds of millions of dollars owed by Drexel to them, has yet to be assessed.[2]

In the light of this, why then is corporate crime so little understood and so inefficiently controlled? What, if anything, can be done about this? This chapter represents an attempt to answer these questions; an attempt premised on the belief that the relationship between the state and the corporate sector is the key to any analysis.

There is no shortage of material, as corporate crime and the role of the state in a capitalist economy has been extensively examined. Theorists from schools ranging from consensus to pluralist to interest group theory, and from instrumentalism to relative autonomy on the critical side have all examined this relationship. Unfortunately, pluralist approaches to corporate crime still predict far more effective state control than has ever been documented, while the critical approaches predict far less. The latter, even the relative autonomy approaches which identify the state as a site of struggle, retain elements of determinism by insisting that states *must* protect and secure capitalist relations of production. In other words, nothing can be done within the existing political and economic system. As O'Malley points out, such determinism is unwarranted. Just because every capitalist state (thus far) has more or less successfully used law to preserve capitalism, it does not follow that this was done because of some 'functional imperative' or that it will always be done in the future.[3]

This chapter represents an attempt to put theoretical insights to work and specify, for several major types of corporate crime, the origins and strength of resistance, and the probabilities of achieving meaningful control. It requires the assumption that it is possible to identify, and therefore predict, institutional and legal sites where effective action is achievable, as well as those where change will only be secured with great difficulty, if at all. The motivation in undertaking such an exercise is part praxis: if more effective control of corporate crime is only secured through unrelenting pressure on state authorities – which is apparently the case for all changes which go against the interests of capital, because the mechanism of enforcement is never self-generating in these situations – then it is important to develop a strategy, to know where and against whom pressure is most productively applied. The second motivation is theoretical, even though the danger in attempting prediction is that one will be forced into a determinist position or will retreat to an instrumentalist one which rules out counter-hegemonic forces and denies the impact that struggle and resistance can make. All the same, attempts at categorisation and generalisation must be made, to surmount the pluralist paralysis which has ironically been the result of two decades of sophisticated neo-Marxist analysis.[4]

The chapter begins by summarising what we know about the enforcement of corporate crime and the three models which have been advocated to control it. It then looks at the weaknesses of these models, identifies factors which appear to be key to securing meaningful state action, and applies these to the major variants of corporate crime.

SUMMARISING THE PROBLEMS OF REGULATION

First, some definitions are in order. This discussion will be restricted to corporate crimes, white-collar crimes which are committed with the encouragement and support of a formal organisation and intended, at least in part, to advance the goals of that organisation (as well as those of the individuals committing the offence).[5] It will relate to regulatory law, the 'intentional restriction of a subject's choice of activity by an entity not directly party to or involved in that activity.[6] That is, it involves control by the state through law over 'private (non-government) economic entitles'.[7]

The regulation of corporate crime has typically been accomplished (formally) through the use of civil, administrative and criminal procedures and sanctions, enforced by a special regulatory agency set up by the relevant level of government. Enforcement here is defined as the consistent application of formal rules, including sanctions, to secure compliance with the enabling legislation. While never totally achieved in practice, a full enforcement policy would be exemplified by the response of police forces to offences such as armed robbery. The outcome may be unsuccessful, in that the perpetrator may not be charged or convicted, but every suspected incident leads to an official investigation, and the legal assumption is made that everyone who commits such an act ought to be punished by law.

Studies of regulatory agencies have shown that present modes of control are woefully ineffective. Full enforcement is neither the goal nor the reality. Regulators, the government-appointed body of inspectors responsible for the discovery, investigation and prosecution of the bulk of corporate crime, attempt in the first instance to persuade and instruct offenders. They do not see themselves as essentially police, despite the fact that they usually have broader powers than police. Their official mandate, however, is more complex, in that they are often officially (and always unofficially) expected to balance the benefits of enforcement against the drawbacks. That is, they are directed to assess whether or not forcing corporations to obey the law will lead to negative results, such as loss of jobs in a community or loss of votes for a particular incumbent or party. They see their jobs as one of securing a certain level of compliance, and use an array of strategies to accomplish this end,[8] the primary one being non-use of the formal regulatory process. There are dozens of studies which document agency reluctance to utilise formal procedures against corporate offenders in Canada, Britain, Australia, the United States and elsewhere.[9]

Secondly, present modes of control focus on the corporate actors who do the least damage – the largest and most powerful organisations are the least sanctioned. This is not surprising, since major corporations tend to have the best relationship with regulatory agencies, to be held in the highest esteem by agency officials and to be best able to challenge and resist sanctioning efforts. Thus, the smallest and most peripheral concerns receive sanctions that are most severe both in quantity (number of visits, summonses and so on and quality (criminal versus civil law sanctions). This has been documented in such diverse areas as Canadian food and drug laws; false advertising and anti-combines laws;[10] tax violations;[11] and coal mining.[12] The advantages that large organisations have in managing regulatory agencies are of several types: political (large organisations are powerful, control more jobs and influence more politicians more efficiently); ideological (regulators tend to believe that only 'fly-by-night' business stoop to crime); and practical (cases involving large concerns are usually more complex, harder to document and prove, and more costly and time consuming for agency staff).

A third regulatory pattern is the perceived inadequacy of the sanctions meted out for corporate crime, especially those assessed by criminal courts. Both civil and criminal fines are so small that they amount to less than licensing fees, and for large organisations typically represent less than a fraction of the profits made in one hour of operation.[13] While imprisonment is called for in most of the written laws it is almost unheard of in practice, and is very lenient on the few occasions it is employed.

The empirical literature provides many illustrations. Offences against anti-trust and securities regulation in the United States have traditionally been among the most rigorously enforced corporate crimes; and one of the few where sentences of imprisonment have been used. McCormick, in a study of anti-trust cases launched under the Sherman Act between 1890 and 1969, found that 44 per cent of 1551 cases were prosecuted as criminal, but only 4.9 per cent of the defendants were sentenced to prison. In fact, in a telling commentary on the role of power and ideology in sentencing, the first eleven men sent to prison under this Act were labour leaders; the first business executive was not sent to prison until 1961, 71 years after the legislation was first passed.[14] Clinard and Yeager found that sixteen executives of the 582 corporations they studied received prison sentences; sentences which totalled 594 days in all. Excluding two atypical cases where the defendants received six-month terms, sentences averaged nine days each. Where monetary penalties were assessed, 80 per cent were under $5000, and the median fine for large firms was $1690.[15] Warnings were the most common 'sanction' recorded.

Lynxwiler *et al.* report $993.97 as the mean fine in their study of sanctions in 83 coal-mining firms between October 1978 and March 1980;[16] Carson's analysis of the British Inspectorate of Factories showed that only 1.5 per cent of the 3800 offences detected over the 4½-year period studied were prosecuted and the fines that resulted were minuscule;[17] a study of the Combines Investigation Act in Canada showed that $100 and $200 were the modal fines assessed under misleading advertising regulations in the mid-1970s.[18] Shapiro's intensive and excellent investigation of the Securities and Exchange Commission in United States found that only 11 of every 100 suspects investigated were selected for criminal penalties and only 46 per cent of those referred for prosecution were convicted. While an unusually high 55 per cent of these were given prison sentences, they were generally short. The 37 per cent who were fined were assessed a median of $2700 each despite the fact that their median profit per offence was $300,000.[19]

Achieving adequate control of corporate crime, then, is generally seen as a major problem for western democracies. This is despite the fact that new laws, agencies and sanctions are continually appearing, with each new example of regulatory failure leading to cries for more legislation. (Fels pointed out that the number of regulatory Acts passed by the Australian federal and state governments doubled between 1960–9 and 1970–9, and there is no reason to believe Australia is atypical.[20]) This in itself causes problems, as it yields a comparative enforcement advantage to formal bureaucratic groups, the quintessential example of which is the large corporation, which is perfectly suited to exploit and use legal complexity to its advantage.[21] Complex and extensive laws, then, may lead to greater inequality between rich and poor individuals, small and large organisations, and developed and undeveloped nations, because the entity with the greater resources can shape and use law better than its less-powerful counterpart.[22]

For those who see the damage done by corporate crime and wish to control it, this enforcement pattern is not a happy one. And the damage is severe. The National Product Safety Commission estimates that 20 million serious injuries and 30,000 deaths per year result from hazardous products sold in the American market place.[23] Accidents in the workplace are the third leading cause of death in Canada, after heart disease and cancer, and at least half of these are caused by unsafe and usually illegal working conditions.[24] In the United States 14,000 people per year are killed in industrial accidents;

data from Wisconsin have established that 45 per cent of all industrial accidents result from infractions against state safety codes.
Another 100,000 die annually from occupationally caused diseases,
with an additional 390,000 per year disabled; and the Occupational
Health and Safety Administration inspectors find law violations
(crimes, if this were criminal law) in 75 per cent of the firms they
investigate.[25] Despite this, one of the first actions of the Reagan
administration was to gut the Occupational Health and Safety Act,
repealing or fatally weakening its seven key standards, withdrawing
many of its films, pamphlets and slide shows, going so far as to burn
100,000 copies of a pamphlet telling workers about the dangers of
cotton dust and brown-lung disease because it was 'not neutral'.[26]
(This is a disease which kills 21,000 people per year in the cheap-
labour cotton industry of the southern states.) Thousands of painful
and protracted deaths have resulted from the illegal exposure of
workers and their families to asbestos, and from the 50-year cover-
up the asbestos industry embarked upon, denying the hiding research results which could have warned those being exposed to the
lethal fibres.[27] Hundreds of people were injured and killed because
the gas tanks on the Ford Pinto car, as part of a profit-maximising
strategy, were positioned where they were vulnerable in rear-end
collisions, causing cars to burst into flames on impact.[28] The Beech
Aircraft Corporation's use of a faulty fuel pump caused many plane
crashes and deaths.[29] Bhopal and Love Canal have become symbols
of corporate negligence and irresponsibility.[30] Despite all this, there
is little to suggest that enforcement is getting more effective and
efficient; indeed, the reverse has been the pattern of the 1980s with
deregulation becoming a rallying cry for the forces of the right.

PROPOSED MODELS AND REMEDIES

In the 50-odd years that corporate crime has been studied, a pro-
fusion of models and remedies have been suggested to improve its
control. All originate in an implicit or explicit analysis of the causes
of corporate crime. Theorists who see causes as primarily socio-
psychological, coming out of the personalities of corporate actors,
advocate reforms which will address these failings – schemes to
inculcate stronger ethical values into executives, to reward ethical

behaviour, to encourage whistle-blowers, and to promote the development of codes of ethics within trade associations.[31]

Organisational theorists, at the middle level of analysis, tend to advocate altering the decision-making and reward-generating structures of the organisation to allow boards of directors to take a more active role, to make top-level management responsible and accountable and to create and/or strengthen internal organisational units designed to ensure compliance.[32] Those who concentrate on enforcement deficiencies as prime causes develop theories of regulation, or schemes to increase the likelihood and severity of punishment.[33]

Beyond this are the macro-level theorists, who can be divided into the Marxist-orientated and the pluralists, both of whom support many of the remedies outlined above. However, because Marxist theory argues that corporate crime is related causally to the structure of capitalism, scholars in this tradition have been considerably more pessimistic about the possibility of finding feasible solutions within the capitalist economic structure than have the pluralists.[34]

Based on these divisions, several schools advocating very different remedies for corporate crime have developed. One group identifies enforcement deficiencies – specifically the reluctance of agents of the state to 'get tough' with corporate offenders – as the cause of proliferating corporate crime. They advocate increased use of imprisonment and much higher criminal fines as the remedy. The bulk of the arguments here are hortatory and normative rather than practical or policy-orientated – they tell us what should be done rather than how it can be accomplished. The key argument is that the stigma of criminality is the heaviest moral sanction that society provides, and its moral and educative impact must be utilised if corporate crime is to be taken seriously by either the offenders or society at large. Given the amount of corporate crime and the harm it causes,[35] the moral opprobrium symbolised by criminal law is the only appropriate sanction. The threat of criminal prosecution is one of the few that the corporate sector takes seriously,[36] whatever the problems of its practical application.

Proponents of criminalisation also point out the political advantages of criminal law. Legitimacy is an important factor in law enforcement: the state cannot afford to be seen to be utilising the 'soft' methods of persuasion and education with corporate offenders while imprisoning and harshly fining poor and traditional offenders –

despite the fact that states have managed to do just that up to this point.

Moreover, passing criminal laws has considerable political appeal. Laws against corporate crime have to be struggled for, and are usually secured only after a highly visible disaster has focused public attention. Given the role of moral outrage in getting state action, and the need for politicians after a crisis to appear to be 'doing something' to safeguard voters, it stands to reason that criminal laws are the sanctions politicians will most likely turn to in a crisis. They are visible and they symbolise moral indignation. And the fact that they can be ignored after the spotlight and pressure have shifted off corporate crime is a significant factor for many mainstream politicians. The ineffectiveness of such strategies in controlling corporate crime is explained by the fact that they have not been used to maximum effect. If criminal sanctions were to be deployed regularly, if corporations knew that their chances of escaping criminal conviction were slight, if fines commensurate with the size of the firm and the profitability of the crime were imposed, if gaol sentences were given, if these procedures were coupled with more enforcement personnel and more punitive laws, and backed up by civil and administrative remedies where appropriate, then criminalisation would be effective.[37]

Unfortunately, proponents of criminalisation share a defect common to would-be reformers: they analyse corporate crime in isolation from the wider society and thus are unable to tell us how more punitive laws and enforcement practices can be secured and made effective. And although they perceive, accurately, that the real obstacle to obtaining effective control is the power of the corporate sector,[38] they do not specify how this power can be overcome. Since the laws that now exist call for far more stringent and exacting sanctions than are ever assessed, this is a major weakness. Is getting even more unenforced criminal laws on the books really a solution?

This brings us to the second school, which targets the regulatory agency, and specifically its capture by the objects of regulation, as the source of enforcement problems. There are now a fair number of middle-range theories about the regulatory process and its employees. The ideal characteristics of the regulatory agency, the factors which create and nourish it (regulatory origin theories), its advantages and disadvantages and its various constituencies (from the general public to producers, competitors and government itself), have all been examined.[39] We can categorise regulatory agencies according to whether they employ the expert model, with few fixed legal rules and maximum discretionary flexibility in the hands of officials, or the legal model, where the emphasis is on obedience to rules and accountability to the legislative mandate of the agency.[40] What has not yet been done is to figure out how to render the agency and its employees immune to the power of those they regulate.

The issue of growth and 'capture', the process whereby the regulatory agency takes on the perspective of the industry it is supposed to regulate, is identified as a major factor in regulatory ineffectiveness. It is argued that regulatory agencies have historically displayed a long-term pattern of growth which, while irregular and cyclical, has outstripped growth in the target industry.[41] However, this growth is associated not with more efficient control of corporate crime but with greater rigidity of decision-making. A creative youth may presage a rigid and captured old age.[42] Sabatier argues that this process of rigidification and capture can be prevented or short-circuited if there are active public groups intervening in the policy arena, keeping the agency honest and uncomfortable (in non-pluralist terms, if there is resistance and political struggle), but he does not specify mechanisms by which this could be built into the regulatory system.[43] Critics such as Stigler and Peltzman argue that regulation is, in fact, designed and operated for the benefit of the regulated industry and not in the 'public interest' at all. Industries, they maintain, need the powers of the state to attain subsidies, control market entry by rivals, regularise the market and enhance public confidence in themselves and their products. The state, through the regulatory agency, needs the resources (votes, campaign donations, good will) which the industry can provide. The shape regulation takes, then, is determined by the interaction of these two symbiotic needs. Thus, this predominantly political-science literature leaves us with a pessimistic assessment of the potential of regulatory agencies to control corporate crime. Thus we should not be surprised to find that regulatory agencies are not efficient law enforcers.[44]

This does not mean that schemes to reform regulatory agencies have been absent. Scholars like Cranston suggest the following changes. First, states should introduce more controls against the 'revolving door' syndrome, to prevent regulators from moving from the regulated industry into the regulatory agency and back again. (After all, police never allow those they have regulated – ex-convicts – to become members of the force.) He also advocates an increase in the number of public representatives on regulatory and industry boards, though recognising the danger that they too will be co-opted by the regulatee. Both the regulatory agency and the regulated organisation should be compelled to hold bargaining sessions in public, and to publish the results of their investigations.[45] In addition, he wants pressure from public-interest groups on regulatory agencies increased, and advocates that governments regularly review agencies in order to eliminate those which are moribund. Sunset laws, allowing new agencies to be set up with provisions for their automatic demise after a certain period of time, are recommended for legislatures when new regulatory Acts are passed. Once again, however, there is much more emphasis on what should be done than on how it can be accomplished. Similarly, short shrift is given the political and ideological resistance which has created the existing paralysis.

Other organisational scholars have examined the target of enforcement, the regulated corporation or industry. Thus it has been suggested that business reference groups, such as chambers of commerce, introduce higher ethical standards; that corporations be reorganised to allow a more active role for the board of directors, altering boards to include representatives of the public; that all large organisations be required to secure charters from the federal government (to avoid corporate shopping for more-lenient provinces or states, though such measures do not prevent switching countries to avoid regulation); that sanctions, criminal and non-criminal, be made tougher and that they be expanded to include 'capital punishment' whereby the organisation loses its right to operate; that enforcement staffs and budgets be made larger and more effective; that penalties be proportional to assets or annual sales; that publicity and consumer pressure be used as a sanction; and that nationalisation of the recidivist corporation be utilised as a last resort.[46] Once again, while many of these ideas are worthwhile, how one would go about getting such measures passed and enforced has not, unfortunately, received much attention.

More recently, a school advocating the abandonment of confrontation and criminalisation in favour of co-operation has become popular. Based on the demonstrated deficiencies of past efforts to control corporate crime, theorists advocating co-operative models argue that the dependence of modern states on criminal law, and the adversarial relationship this necessitates, is a major cause of regulatory ineffectiveness.[47] Criminalisation strategies, according to theorists such as Braithwaite, are rigid techniques which alienate potentially co-operative individuals and corporations, cause them to be unresponsive to technological change and economic development and, being based in the nation-state, are totally unable to handle the transnational corporation.[48] He has suggested what he calls a pyramid approach, wherein the regulatory agency is mandated to move to criminal penalties only when all co-operative options have failed.[49] A variant of this has been developed by Scholz, who argues that co-operative strategies can be demonstrated, mathematically and logically, to be the most advantageous ones for both the regulators and the regulated.[50] However, co-operative models are also fatally flawed, because they refuse to recognise the importance of corporate power. The same structural forces, the same political and corporate resistance that vitiated efforts to use criminal law against corporations, will also destroy co-operative approaches. Indeed, the latter will be much easier targets because they legitimise the status quo by removing both the goal of full enforcement and the stigma of criminality; moreover, they weaken the potential for pressure groups to call the corporate sector to account.[51]

TOWARDS BETTER MODELS

Let us look, then, at what we need to know to create better models, beginning at the macro-level with the literature on the role played by the modern state in capitalist democratic systems. Although the initial formulations were too instrumentalist and have been extensively criticised, it has now been established that modern states do have an interest in facilitating accumulation by the private sector and promoting its extraction of surplus value. They do try, in other words, to build up capital and ensure that the private sector is profitable. As Gough, Offe and others have pointed out, the survival of the national political system and all its programmes (as well as the fate of the party in power) is dependent on this, both directly and indirectly.[52] Attracting capital and avoiding its flight are therefore central criteria by which policy initiatives are judged, whether these concerns are voiced up front or remain powerful background assumptions. They shape everyday government discourse most directly in matters of economic policy and corporate regulation, but indirectly, on the ideological level, affect virtually every government decision.

Under a capitalist system, this means making it possible for one class, the elite of upper-class men who own/control the means of production through giant corporations, to produce and amass capital. Thus states typically provide billions of dollars to the corporate sector in grants, income tax loopholes, corporate infrastructure, transportation, 'forgiveable loans' and so on in the belief that this is the only way to get them to invest, create jobs and ultimately produce the wealth which is crucial to the maintenance of the welfare state. States therefore are wary of offending capital, since they have little direct control over it. They are reluctant to try to prevent industries from moving out of a particular region (say the north of England), no matter how many millions of taxpayer dollars have been invested to lure them to that site. Similarly, the state is reluctant to pass – or enforce – stringent laws against pollution, worker health and safety; or monopolies. Such measures frighten off the much sought-after investment and engender the equally dreaded loss of confidence.

However, the political party in charge of this apparatus must also, in democratic societies, get elected. This may mean passing (and even occasionally enforcing) laws in the 'public' interest which promote the 'public' good, laws which go against the wishes of particular factions of the corporate elite. Generally such actions are taken when they are seen as necessary to protect long-range stability – that is, when danger threatens, or is perceived to threaten, systemic hegemony. Thus, for example, where there is a strong and organised working-class movement, the interests of manufacturers as a class in minimising production costs may have to be sacrificed to satisfy demands for safety equipment and laws which raise costs. The rhetoric of the democratic system is that lives are more important than profits: where this belief is revealed as false (when, for example, a major accident caused by faulty mine construction occurs) and where this contradiction has become public (when groups defending worker safety are strident, organised and persistent), the state will be forced, to maintain its legitimacy, to pass laws specifying minimum safety standards for manufacturers.[53]

This general thesis explains both state timidity to pass, and state reluctance to enforce, laws penalising corporations, since both potentially endanger accumulation. It also provides a model for understanding differences in regulatory laws and enforcement among the major democracies. The weakness of such analyses, however, is their tendency to reify the state, presenting it as a universal given with universally defined interests and strategies, thus minimising or overlooking the very real differences between nation-states and among the various levels within each one (federal or local). Allied to this is the danger of downplaying agency, struggle and resistance: organised pressure groups have played significant roles in achieving action in the face of corporate resistance. And positing economic power as the key determinant of state activity (or the lack of it) is the third problem. However, one can reject economic determinism and accept agency and still maintain that the goal of attracting capital and achieving 'confidence' in the investment community is and will remain one main factor in shaping state policy, despite local and national variations.

This means, contrary to much of the corporate-crime literature spelling out 'solutions', that states do not have a direct and unproblematic interest in eradicating most types of corporate crime. There is ample evidence that the modern state has frequently acted to vitiate laws against corporate crime. It has drawn up ineffective laws,[54] impeded enforcement[55] and savagely cut the budgets of regulatory agencies. Time and again a major crisis or law suit has been necessary to force political authorities to take action of any sort. Yeager presents an intriguing illustrations of state ambivalence when he tells how the US Justice Department quashed the news release publicising the Clinard and Yeager report documenting corporate criminality in the United States so that then-President Jimmy Carter's re-election chances would not be hurt. One must not annoy the corporate sector at election time![56]

Nor can one assume that states necessarily have the resource base to control the predatory activities of the private sector. There are instances where even the richest countries have been forced to back down because their resources were no match for corporate bankrolls, as with the failed attempt to lay charges against the oil companies after the 1973 oil crisis,[57] or to force chemical companies to clean up their toxic dumps and oil companies their disastrous spill.[58] The way in which Third World countries have been held hostage by multi-nationals is too well known to require reiteration, with chemical companies (Bhopal), infant formulae (Nestlés) and the dumping of unsafe drugs by pharmaceutical companies being the most publi-cised instances in the recent past. On the other hand, there have been some success stories over both the short and the long term, so one cannot argue that states always lack the motivation and the capability for enforcement. On occasion the state has strengthened the hand of regulators and conditions have improved.[59] In fact, one can see evidence of improvement – many rivers and some cities and towns are less polluted than they were 20 years ago; lead has been removed from gasoline in many countries; and automobiles are safer.

Putting this knowledge to work, then, what can we say about the potential of modern states to control corporate crime effectively? First, the state's willingness to crack down upon the corporate sector will vary with the strength of the forces promoting change; the visibility of the crime; its relationship to key structural factors such as the needs of capital; its relationship to dominant societal values; and the past and present relationship of that state and its bureaucracies to the major classes. Secondly, it is apparent that, for our purposes, corporate crime cannot be treated as an entity. Different factors will shape the chances of state action for different types of corporate misbehaviour. Thus, a classificatory scheme is necessary. Fels divided corporate crimes by victim and came up with a list of crimes against the public interest, against competitors, producers, employees, consumers and politicians/government.[60] Coleman identified five major types – fraud and deception, attempts to control the market, violent crimes, bribery and corruption, and those involving the violation of civil liberties.[61] Braithwaite and Geis worked with six types of offence: occupational health and safety; insider-trading and stockmarket manipulations; corporate frauds wherein creditors are the main victims; frauds where government bodies are victimised; anti-trust; and the omnibus category of crimes wherein consumers are the main victims. Because the literature is incomplete, we shall look in detail at occupational health and safety, anti-trust and monopoly, and insider-trading/stock-market frauds: three major variants which exemplify very different political economics of regulation.[62]

Occupational Health and Safety

Occupational health and safety laws are classified as 'social' or 'new', as opposed to economic or industry-specific regulations such as anti-trust laws.[63] The latter are usually considered more directly related to the viability of the economic system than the former, a factor of some significance for our purposes. Under occupational health and safety legislation, regulators are virtually always directed to balance the safety of workers against the need to keep down the costs of production. It is considered important not to jeopardise the regulated industry's competitiveness. Enforcement, then, must trade off one set of benefits and dangers against another.

A second factor affecting the chances of securing effective regulation is its potential impact on the viability of the target industry. This is important because it affects the strength of the industry's motivation to resist regulation. Health and safety laws directly affect the profits and ultimately the survival of virtually every business which hires workers. It is especially significant for primary and secondary industries, firms which extract resources or manufacture products; and is less significant to firms in the service or tertiary sector, because there are typically fewer hazardous substances or procedures (although the perils of ennui and the potential health hazards of daily contact with video-display terminals may change this). Because of this centrality, employers themselves have a strong interest in promoting weak health and safety laws; an interest which is only counterbalanced by industry's need to attract and sustain a productive supply of labour. States, on the other hand, are caught on the horns of a dilemma. They cannot appear to be enthusiastically helping the private sector accumulate without risking their own legitimacy, because the protection of life, limb and health is an absolute value under democratic capitalism. But they will not lightly choose to jeopardise the generation of surplus value upon which the economic system rests by being too fussy about providing safe working conditions for workers. As Walters states: 'Immediate expenditures would be high [to improve occupational health and safety] and returns could not be expected for decades'.[64] And the workers themselves have been known to demand even unsafe jobs over no jobs at all, if that is the choice polity and employers present to them.

Thus, one can predict that states will do as little as possible about enforcement. They will pass such laws only when public crises force them to do so, strengthen them reluctantly, weaken them whenever possible, and enforce them – except when the public spotlight is directed upon them (through elections, accidents, political opposition or pressure groups) – in a manner calculated not to impede profitability seriously.

When one examines case studies of regulation in this area, one finds the predictions borne out. Calavita, Gunningham, Walters,

Carson, Reasons and Tucker,[65] in studies done in Britain, Canada, the United States, Australia and Italy document the following patterns. Regulators are reluctant to get tough – though the definition of toughness varies from nation to nation. The state has typically been willing to back off enforcement whenever and wherever possible – although here again there are national variations, with right-wing regimes tending to admit and even brag about this, while left-leaning ones deny or downplay it. And public crises have been required to create pressure to secure passage and enforcement of occupational health and safety laws. Substantively, the variations between nation-states, which I am glossing over to emphasise the general point, do matter. They make real differences in the life-style and life-chances of the workers involved; differences which reflect struggles won and lost in the past, as well as cultural and historic differences. The prediction that strong resistance will be encountered, however, appears to be substantiated.

On the other side, there are also factors which promote regulatory action in the area of health and safety. Most important is the fact that violations in developed countries are relatively visible. Because they are both easy to understand and dramatic, sudden deaths due to employer and regulatory agency negligences make 'good copy'. Lingering deaths from continued exposure to carcinogenic substances, the most typical kind of victim, fit the criteria of newsworthiness less well and will therefore be less noticed. Unions, over the last decade, have increased both their vigilance and their knowledge of workplace hazards, even though their influence and membership have been seriously weakened by the economic retrenchment of the 1980s. For health and safety violations, it will be ideological struggle, a redefinition of the levels of risk deemed acceptable for workers in a particular nation-state at a particular time, in combination with industrial disasters, that will produce any toughening of standards which occurs.

Social action, then, should peak immediately following accidents, since the potential to strengthen regulatory agencies (with or without passing new laws) is highest then. A series of struggles for new rights in the workplace – and the discourse of 'rights' is an important one – by groups such as unions and left-wing political parties, has the potential to produce changes at the ideological level which will push up the lower limits of 'reasonable' business behaviour. As argued elsewhere, this process has resulted in long-term improvements for workers and is responsible for securing the generally less-hazardous working conditions of the twentieth century (com- pared with the nineteenth).[66] Getting more effective laws passed is a necessary part of this struggle, but as a goal in itself, without the power-base essential to making laws effective, it is useless. How- ever, criminal law should not be abandoned, because of the leverage and moral legitimacy it provides for regulatory watchdogs, opposition politicians and other pro-regulatory forces.

On the organisational level, many of the reforms already sug- gested are worth fighting for; such as the proposal that companies should be forced to draw up and register realistic self-regulation schemes and pay at least some of the costs of regulation.[67] More criminalisation might also increase the leverage of regulatory agencies; perhaps a statute prohibiting 'reckless employing' that would require employers to prove that they are taking every reasonable measure to prevent injury, rather than the reversed onus of proof now em- ployed.[68] While it may be impossible under the present socio- economic system to secure full and total enforcement of health and safety laws, or to punish adequately those responsible for the thousands of deaths and injuries which occur annually, this must paradoxically remain the official goal if even greater laxity is to be avoided.

Anti-trust and Monopoly Legislation

Anti-trust legislation illustrates a very different set of constraints. The principles of a free-market economy are that all sectors benefit by allowing the maximum amount of competition, the premises being that the most efficient businesses will win out, and the in- efficient will disappear. Neither prediction has turned out to be accurate. The theory in reality has produced an economy dominated by transnational corporations and giant oligopolies, with the result that real competition has virtually disappeared. Within the dominant or monopoly sector, one or a handful of giants control each industry, be it oil refining, insurance, car manufacturing or selling soap, and a number of small concerns fight for the spoils in the peripheral sector.

In Canada the number of dominant corporations declined from 170 in 1951 to 113 in 1972.[69] In the United States the largest 500 corporations control three-quarters of all manufacturing assets; 50 out of 67,000 companies in transportation and utilities control two- thirds of the airline, railway, communications, electricity and gas industries; three firms control most of the revenues in television and four control the movie industry; and two insurance companies alone have 25 per cent of the business.[70] Similar concentrations of power mark Western European and Australian economies as well.[71] Because of their market domination and size, monopoly-sector producers can realise higher profits at less cost, so they have a heavy structural bias against competition. Thus the largest and most powerful parts of the corporate sector do not want monopoly laws to be passed or enforced. However, such laws are in the interests of businesses in the peripheral sector, although there is less than total support even here, because of the ideological distaste for government regulation that such groups are likely to display. They also tend to be divided amongst themselves, which limits the amount of pressure they can exert.

The situation of the typical federal state *vis-à-vis* competition laws is quite unlike that in health and safety. States have a direct interest in promoting a certain amount of competition in the economic system. Although public pressure forcing the state to enact and enforce laws favouring competition is a weak and uncertain variable at best, states have an overall interest in maintaining an efficient economy in order to maximise the surplus value upon which their prosperity and fortunes ultimately depend. Moreover, they are major customers of private industry and need to obtain reliable, high quality goods and services for the public sector at minimum cost. Too much monopolisation carries the risk, for governments, of being held to ransom by suppliers. States also have an overall interest in preventing too much economic power being concentrated in too few hands, if there is perceived to be a danger that they will have trouble controlling this power. And in most countries enforcement is promoted because it can be initiated on the request of would-be competitors, thereby taking the initial onus off the state regulatory agency.

However, pro-regulatory forces are countered by strong opposition, because resisting forces, corporations in the monopoly sector, are huge and powerful.[72] Moreover, the relationship between competition and efficiency is a problematic one, in that a *laissez-faire* economy with many small economic units is functional internally up to a certain level. But it may well work against the interests of the nation-state and its corporations at the international level, making a profitable export market difficult. In addition, most countries have an extensive set of monopolistic operations that they themselves set up and control, in sectors such as uranium mining, airlines or telephone service. One might expect, then, that enforcement will be ambivalent and uncertain, varying with the dominant interests of the state at any particular time, and with the power of the central versus peripheral corporate sectors.

The literature offers support for this generalisation but shows, overall, that pro-regulatory forces in most countries are too weak to make regulation effective. Barnett argues that monopoly-sector firms are virtually ignored by regulators.[73] Coleman describes anti-trust laws in the United States as presenting an 'unbroken record of failure'.[74] In Australia the roughly comparable Trade Practices Act has been studied by Hopkins, who shows that business lobbyists from the monopoly sector shaped the very legislation which was to control them. He concluded, however, that the corporate sector was successful in shaping regulation and promoting the long-term interests of capital where no countervailing pressure from the electorate was exerted, but was less successful where such forces were present.[75] In Canada those studied the provisions against restraint of trade in the Combines Investigation Act have concluded that the interests of capital in retaining monopolistic power have consistently overcome the weak and disorganised pro-competition forces, in both law formulation and enforcement.[76]

The role of pressure groups in a complex and morally amorphous area such as anti-monopoly law is complicated, because it is very difficult to create public lobbies to promote competition. It is not clear that breaking up monopolies is always in the interests of consumers. And it is even less clear whether public pressure could secure the passage and enforcement of effective anti-trust laws, given that the strongest forces of capital oppose enforcement. The state, moreover, is ambivalent at best and 'captured' at worst.

Insider-trading and Stock-market Fraud

The third area to be examined provides the clearest illustration of successful regulation. Not surprisingly, controlling this type of corporate crime turns out to be in the interests of the corporate sector overall, as well as being compatible with state objectives. Such laws protect the sanctity of the investment market, which is central to the ability of corporations to raise money by issuing shares. Investors must therefore be able to have confidence in its operation. States, on the other hand, view a healthy stock market as a necessity for a profitable private sector. Moreover, as a player in the market, states have a direct interest in clean dealing. They will also experience public pressure from relatively high-income people when investors are cheated; state regulators may be accused of not doing their jobs, and they may have to bail out these investors – a very expensive proposition.

This does not mean that anti-regulatory forces are absent. Pressure against enforcement will still be significant, because powerful corporate actors and stock-brokers can potentially 'make a killing' from their knowledge and connections. However, the benefits are on the individual level, accruing to individual corporate entities. This weakens their leverage, since capital as a whole suffers if such imprecations become – or are perceived as becoming – too numerous.

Thus, we can expect enforcement to be relatively efficient, and that is indeed how it appears. The Securities and Exchange Commission in the United States is the most studied of such agencies, and scholars by and large agree that it is among the most effective regulatory agencies around.[77] Yeager has pointed out that even the Reagan administration, notorious for ignoring crimes against the environment, consumers and workers and for savaging regulatory agencies, was forced to take action to control insider-trading and stock-market fraud, because the offences being committed affected deleteriously not only the financial interests of powerful organisations but also those of government itself.[78]

We know considerably less about the other types of corporate crime. Levi, in his discussion of commercial fraud in Britain, argues that the state is unable to tighten regulation because of the overwhelming power of business. This is despite the facts that frequent fraud-induced bankruptcies threaten the very basis of capitalist relations, and that public opinion would apparently support more punitive measures. As he notes: 'The main policing burden falls upon the Department of Trade, who adopt a profile so low that limbo-dancers would find difficulty in getting beneath it.'[79] A moribund regulatory agency, then, can render enforcement much weaker than it would otherwise be.

Environmental protection has become a major issue recently. Although not identical with corporate crime, corporations are frequently responsible for major assaults on the environment, both through their manufacturing and discharge processes as well as their dependence on throwaway, high-consumption philosophies and life-styles. Control over corporate pollutors, thus far, appears to be very weak. Molotch and Coleman assert that environmental protection is poor to non-existent in the United States, due largely to the power of the business forces opposing it.[80] This is despite the fact that there are several organised lobbies promoting enforcement, a national regulatory agency (plus numerous state agencies), as well as considerable public sentiment opposing pollution. The paucity of action taken thus far on environment issues portrays most vividly the power of the corporate sector. In one celebrated instance, a federal court judge took the dramatic step of siding with a private environmental group to strike down a weak and ineffective statute on pesticides: a statute which was supported by the state legislature, the chemical corporations *and* the regulatory agency.[81] In this case, the group, the Environmental Defense Fund, took the regulatory agency to court to force it to do its job. Such legal victories, however, are usually hollow because the power to rewrite the offending legislation, and the responsibility for enforcing it, remain with the regulatory agency. Most development, and much of the surplus value which drives industrial capitalism, is premised upon the exploitation of human and natural resources, using them in the cheapest possible fashion to extract the maximum return. In light of this, 'sustainable development', however fashionable, assumes a great deal about the capacity of national states and international capital to put environmental issues in front of profitability. History does not allow us to view this scenario optimistically, despite the fact that the survival of our species is ultimately at stake.

CONCLUSION

This paper sketches out a political-economy perspective and illustrates its application to selected types of corporate crimes. Although preliminary, the empirical evidence available at the present time appears to support it. A fully developed model, one which considers all the factors identified in the literature, right down to the characteristics of inspectors in regulatory agencies, remains to be enunciated. However, in view of the horrendous number of lives lost and damaged by corporate crime, it is essential for all of us to look for solutions which might work, rather than advocate idealistic, 'pie in the sky' measures which the combined power of the corporate sector

234   *Global Crime Connections*

and its state allies will quickly wipe off the agenda: a scenario which
has been endlessly repeated in the past. Only by identifying the
factors which have defeated previous reform efforts, for each type of
corporate crime, can we hope to achieve any meaningful change.

Notes

1. Frank Pearce, 'The Contribution of "Left Realism" to the Empirical
    Study of Commercial Crime', paper presented to Realist Criminology
    Conference, Vancouver, B.C., May 1990, p. 10.
2. See *New York Times*, 10 June 1990; and *Observer*, 8 April 1990.
3. Pat O'Malley, 'Law Making in Canada: Capitalism and Legislation in
    a Democratic State', *Canadian Journal of Law and Society*, vol. 3 (1988)
    p. 69.
4. See, for example, Claus Offe, 'Some Contradictions of the Modern
    Welfare State', *Critical Social Policy*, vol. 2 (1988) pp. 7–16; Ralph
    Miliband, *The State in Capitalist Society* (London: Quartet Books, 1969);
    E. B. Pashukanis, *Law and Marxism* (London: Ink Links, 1978);
    J. Holloway and S. Picciotto, *State and Capital* (London: Edward Arnold,
    1978); and O'Malley, op. cit.
5. See J. W. Coleman, *The Criminal Elite: The Sociology of White Collar
    Crime* (New York: St Martin's Press, 1985) p. 8.
6. B. M. Mitnick, *The Political Economy of Regulation* (New York: Colum-
    bia University Press, 1980) p. 20.
7. R. Cranston, 'Regulation and Deregulation: General Issues', *University
    of New South Wales Law Journal*, vol. 5 (1982) pp. 1–29, see esp. 2.
8. See W. G. Carson, 'White Collar Crime and the Enforcement of
    Factory Legislation', *British Journal of Criminology*, vol. 10 (1970) pp.
    383–98; N. Shover, D. A. Clelland and J. Lynxwiler, *Developing a Regu-
    latory Bureaucracy: The Office of Surface Mining Reclamation and Enforce-
    ment* (Washington, DC: National Institute of Justice, 1983); K. Hawkins,
    *Environment and Enforcement: Regulation and the Social Definition of
    Pollution* (Oxford: Clarendon Press, 1984)); and John Braithwaite, 'White
    Collar Crime', *American Review of Sociology*, vol. 2 (1985) pp. 1–25.
9. See, for example, R. Kagan, *Regulatory Justice* (New York: Russell Sage,
    1978); R. Kagan and J. T. Scholz, 'The Criminology of the Corporation
    and Regulatory Enforcement Strategies', in K. Hawkins and J. Thomas
    (eds), *Enforcing Regulation* (Boston, Mass.: Kluwer-Nijhoff, 1984);
    D. King, 'The Regulatory Use of the Criminal Sanction in Controlling
    Corporate Crime', paper presented at the American Society of
    Criminology Meetings, San Diego, California, November 1985;
    M. Levi, 'Giving Creditors the Business: the Criminal Law in Inaction',
    International Journal of Sociology of Law, vol. 12 (1984) pp. 321–33, and
    *The Phantom Capitalists: The Organization and Control of Long Term
    Fraud* (London: Heinemann, 1981); M. Clinard and P. Yeager, *Corpor-*

ate Crime (New York: Free Press, 1980); J. Thomas, 'The Regulatory Role in the Containment of Corporate Illegality', in H. Edelhertz and T. Overcast (eds), *White-Collar Crime: An Agenda for Research* (Toronto: D. C. Heath Lexington Books, 1982); Laureen Snider, 'Corporate Crime in Canada: Preliminary Report', *Canadian Journal of Criminology*, vol. 20 (1987) pp. 142–68; Hawkins, op. cit.; C. Stone, 'Social Control of Corporate Behaviour', in D. Ermann and R. Lundman (eds), *Corporate and Government Deviance* (New York: Oxford University Press, 1978); N. Gunningham, 'Negotiated Non-Compliance: a Case Study of Regulatory Failure', *Law and Policy*, vol. 9(1) (1987) pp. 69–97, and *Safeguarding the Workers* (Sydney: Law Books, 1984), and E. Tucker, 'Making the Workplace "Safe" in Capitalism: the Enforcement of Factory Legislation in Nineteenth-Century Ontario', paper presented at the Canadian Law and Society Association Annual Meetings, Hamilton, 3–6 June 1987.

10.   See Snider, 'Corporate Crime in Canada', op. cit.

11.   See S. Long, 'The Internal Revenue Service: Examining the Exercise of Discretion in Tax Enforcement', paper presented at the Annual Meeting, Law and Society Association, Toronto, May 1979.

12.   See J. Lynxwiler, N. Shover and D. Clelland, 'Corporate Size and International Contexts: Determinants of Sanctioning Severity in a Regulatory Bureaucracy', paper presented at the Annual Meetings of the American Criminal Justice Society, San Antonio, Texas, 28–31 March 1983.

13.   See Frank Pearce, *Crimes of the Powerful: Marxism, Crime and Deviance* (London: Pluto Press, 1976); M. Green, *The Closed Enterprise System* (New York: Grossman, 1972); G. Geis, 'White Collar Crime: the Heavy Electrical Equipment Antitrust Cases of 1961', in M. B. Clinard and R. Quinney (eds), *Criminal Behaviour Systems: A Typology* (New York: Holt, Rinehart and Winston, 1967); W. G. Carson, 'Legal Control of Safety on British Offshore Oil Installations', in P. Wickham and T. Dailey (eds), *White Collar and Economic Crime* (Toronto: Lexington Books, 1982); D. M. Ermann and R. J. Lundman, 'Deviant Acts by Complex Organizations: Deviance and Social Control at the Organizational Level of Analysis', *Sociological Quarterly*, vol. 19 (1978) pp. 55–67; H. Edelhertz, *The Nature, Impact and Prosecution of White-Collar Crime* (Washington, DC: National Institute for Law Enforcement and Criminal Justice, Department of Justice, May 1970); and C. Goff and C. Reasons, *Corporate Crime in Canada* (Toronto: Prentice-Hall, 1978).

14.   See A. E. McCormick, 'Rule Enforcement and Moral Indignation: Some Observations of the Effects of Criminal Anti-trust Convictions upon Societal Reaction Processes', *Social Problems*, vol. 25(1) (1977) pp. 30–9.

15.   See Clinard and Yeager, op. cit., p. 291.

16.   See Lynxwiler *et al.*, op. cit.

17.   See W. G. Carson, 'The Institutionalisation of Ambiguity: Early British Factory Acts', in G. Geis and E. Scotland (eds), *White Collar Theory and Research* (Beverly Hills, Cal.: Sage, 1980a).

18.   See Snider, 'Corporate Crime in Canada', op. cit., pp. 154–5.

19. See Susan Shapiro, 'The Road not Taken: the Elusive Path to Criminal Prosecution for White Collar Offenders', *Law and Society Review*, vol. 19 (1985) pp. 189–90.
20. See A. Fels, 'The Political Economy of Regulation', *University of New South Wales Law Journal*, vol. 5 (1982) pp. 29–60, esp. p. 30.
21. See John Braithwaite, 'Inegalitarian Consequences of Egalitarian Reforms to Control Corporate Crime', *Temple Law Quarterly*, vol. 53 (1980) pp. 1127–46, esp. p. 1128.
22. See ibid.; and Marc Galanter, 'Why the Haves Come Out Ahead: Speculations on the Limits of Legal Change', *Law and Society Review*, vol. 9 (1974) pp. 95–160.
23. See Coleman, op. cit., p. 6.
24. See C. Reasons, W. Ross, and L. Patterson, *Assault on the Worker* (Toronto: Butterworths, 1981).
25. See Coleman, op. cit., pp. 6–7.
26. Kitty Calavita, 'The Demise of the Occupational Safety and Health Administration: a Case Study in Symbolic Action', *Social Problems*, vol. 30(4) (April 1983) pp. 437–48, esp. p. 442.
27. J. Swartz, 'Silent Killers at Work', *Crime and Social Justice*, vol. 3 (1975) pp. 15–20.
28. See V. Swigert and R. A. Farrell, 'Corporate Homicide: Definitional Processes in the Creation of Deviance', *Law and Society Review*, vol. 15(1) (1980) pp. 161–82.
29. G. Geis, 'Deterring Corporate Crime,' in F. Geis (ed.), *On White Collar Crime* (Toronto: Lexington Books, 1982) pp. 53–66.
30. See Frank Pearce and Steve Tombs, 'Regulating Corporate Crime: the Case of Health and Safety', paper presented to the American Society of Criminology Annual Meetings, Chicago, 1988.
31. See Clinard and Yeager, op. cit.
32. See John Braithwaite, 'Transnational Corporations and Corruption: Towards Some International Solutions', *International Journal of Sociology of Law*, vol. 7 (1979) pp. 125–42; and Stone, 'Social Control of Corporate Behaviour', op. cit.
33. See the work of G. Stigler, *The Citizen and the State: Essays on Regulation* (Chicago, Ill.: University of Chicago Press, 1975); A. Fels, op. cit.; and summaries in Mitnick, op. cit.
34. See Pearce, *Crimes of the Powerful*, op. cit.; H. Glasbeek, 'The Corporation as Criminal', *Our Times*, September 1984; and H. Barnett, 'The Production of Corporate Crime in Corporate Capitalism', in P. Wickham and T. Dailey (eds), *White Collar and Economic Crime* (Toronto: Lexington Books, 1982).
35. For summaries see Braithwaite, 'White Collar Crime', op. cit.; E. H. Sutherland, 'White Collar Crime in Organized Crime', in D. Ermann and R. Lundman, *Corporate and Governmental Deviance* (New York: Oxford University Press, 1978); D. R. Simon and D. S. Eitzen, *Elite Deviance*, 2nd edn (Toronto: Allyn and Bacon, 1986); and most of the articles in P. Wickham and T. Dailey (eds), *White Collar and Economic Crime* (Toronto: D. C. Heath, 1982).

36. See Hawkins, op. cit.; and Levi, 'Giving Creditors the Business', op. cit.
37. See C. Stone, 'The Place of Enterprise Liability in the Control of Corporate Conduct', *Yale Law Journal*, vol. 90 (1980) pp. 1–7; J. C. Watkins, 'White Collar Crimes: Legal Sanctions and Social Control', *Crime and Delinquency*, vol. 23 (1977) pp. 290–303; J. R. Elkins, 'Decisionmaking Model and the Control of Corporate Crime', *Hobarth Law Journal*, vol. 85 (1976) pp. 1091–129; R. Nader and M. J. Green (eds), *Corporate Power in America* (New York: Viking Press, 1973); J. C. Coffee, 'Corporate Criminal Responsibility', in S. H. Kadish (ed.), *Encyclopedia of Crime and Justice* (New York: Free Press, 1984) vol. 1 pp. 253–64; Glasbeek, 'Corporation as Criminal', op. cit.; and Braithwaite, 'Transnational Corporations and Corruption', op. cit.
38. For example, see E. Sutherland, 'White Collar Criminality', in G. Geis and R. F. Meier (eds), *White Collar Crime* (New York: Free Press, 1977) p. 45.
39. See Fels, op. cit., p. 32; and Mitnick, op. cit.
40. See Kagan, op. cit., p. 15.
41. See R. Meier and J. P. Plumlee, 'Regulatory Administration and Organizational Rigidity', *Western Political Quarterly*, vol. 31 (1978) pp. 80–95.
42. See J. E. Anderson, *Public Policy-Making* (New York: Praeger, 1975).
43. See P. Sabatier, 'Regulatory Policy-Making: Toward a Framework of Analysis', *Natural Resources Journal*, vol. 17 (1977) pp. 415–60; and 'Social Movements and Regulatory Agencies: Toward a More Adequate – and Less Pessimistic – Theory of "Clientele Capture"', *Policy Sciences*, vol. 6 (1975) pp. 301–41.
44. See J. Peltzman, 'Toward a More General Theory of Regulation', *Journal of Law and Economics*, vol. 19 (1976) pp. 211–40; and Stigler, op. cit.
45. See Cranston, op. cit., pp. 25–8.
46. See G. Geis, 'Deterring Corporate Crime', in Nader and Green, op. cit.; Stone, 'Social Control of Corporate Behaviour', op. cit.; Edelhertz, op. cit.; and John Braithwaite and G. Geis, 'On Theory and Action for Corporate Crime Control', *Crime and Delinquency*, vol. 28 (1982) pp. 292–314.
47. See B. Ackerman *et al.*, *The Uncertain Search for Environmental Quality* (New York: Free Press, 1974); E. Bardach and R. A. Kagan, *Going by the Book: The Problem of Regulatory Unreasonableness* (Philadelphia, Pa: Temple University Press, 1982); A. V. Kneese and C. L. Schultze, *Pollution, Prices, and Public Policy* (Washington, DC: Brookings Institution, 1975); and Kagan and Scholz, op. cit.
48. See John Braithwaite, 'Enforced Self-Regulation: a New Strategy for Corporate Crime Control', *Michigan Law Review*, vol. 80(7) (June 1982) pp. 1466–507; and Braithwaite, 'Inegalitarian Consequences', op. cit.
49. See John Braithwaite, 'Toward a Benign Big Gun Theory of Regulatory Power' (Canberra: Australian National University, unpublished manuscript, 1988), and 'White Collar Crime', op. cit.
50. J. Scholtz, 'Deterrence, Cooperation and the Ecology of Regulatory

Enforcement', *Law and Society Review*, vol. 18 (1984) pp. 179–224; and 'Voluntary Compliance and Regulatory Enforcement', *Law and Policy*, vol. 6 (1984) pp. 385–404.

51. L. Snider, 'Cooperative Models and Corporate Crime: Panacea or Cop-Out', *Crime and Delinquency*, vol. 36(3) (1990) pp. 373–91, esp. pp. 380–5.

52. See Offe, op. cit.; and Ian Gough, *The Political Economy of the Welfare State* (London: Macmillan, 1979).

53. See J. O'Connor, *The Fiscal Crisis of the State* (New York: St Martin's Press, 1973); Miliband, op. cit.; and Offe, op. cit.

54. See K. Calavita, 'Worker Safety, Law and Social Change: the Italian Case', *Law and Society*, vol. 20(20) (1986) pp. 189–229; W. G. Carson, 'The Other Price of Britain's Oil: Regulating Safety on Offshore Oil Installations in the British Sector of the North Sea', *Contemporary Crises*, vol. 4 (1980) pp. 239–66; and many previously cited case studies.

55. See Coleman, op. cit.; Levi, *Phantom Capitalists*, op. cit. and 'Giving Creditors the Business', op. cit.; and N. Gunningham, *Pollution: Social Interest and the Law* (Oxford: Oxford Centre for Socio-Legal Studies, 1974).

56. Peter Yeager, 'Managing Obstacles to Studying Corporate Offences: an Optimistic Assessment', paper presented to the Annual Meetings of the American Society of Criminology, Atlanta, Georgia, 30 October – 3 November 1986, pp. 3–4.

57. See A. Sampson, *The Seven Sisters: The Great Oil Companies and the World They Shaped* (New York: Viking, 1975).

58. See, for example, H. Molotch, 'Oil in Santa Barbara and Power in America', in W. J. Chambliss (ed.), *Sociological Readings in the Conflict Perspective* (Reading, Mass.: Addison-Wesley, 1973).

59. Some examples include B. J. Whiting, 'OSHA's Enforcement Policy', *Labour Law Journal*, vol. 31 (1980) pp. 29–45; I. Paulus, *The Search for Pure Food: A Sociology of Legislation in Britain* (London: Martin Robertson, 1974); M. S. Lewis-Beck and J. R. Alford, 'Can Government Regulate Safety?: the Coal Mine Example' *American Political Science Review*, vol. 74 (1980) pp. 745–81; A. Hopkins, 'The Anatomy of Corporate Crime', in P. Wilson and J. Braithwaite (eds), *Two Faces of Deviance* (St Lucia: University of Queensland Press, 1979); and Pearce and Toombs, 'Regulating Corporate Crime', op. cit., pp. 3–4.

60. See Fels, op. cit., p. 32.

61. Coleman, op. cit., pp. 74–7.

62. See Braithwaite and Geis, op. cit.

63. See Cranston, op. cit., p. 2; and Fels, op. cit., p. 31.

64. V. Walters, 'The Politics of Occupational Health and Safety: Interviews with Workers' Health and Safety Representatives and Company Doctors', *Canadian Review of Sociology and Anthropology*, vol. 22(1) (1985) pp. 58–79, esp. p. 59.

65. See again studies done by Calavita, 'Worker Safety', op. cit.; Gunningham, 'Negotiated Non-compliance', op. cit.; Walters, op. cit.; Carson, 'Legal Control of Safety ', op. cit.; Reasons *et al.*, op. cit.; and Tucker, op. cit.

66. See L. Snider, 'Towards a Political Economy of Reform, Regulation and Corporate Crime', *Law and Policy*, vol. 9(1) (1987) pp. 37–68.
67. See Braithwaite, 'Enforced Self-regulation', op. cit.
68. See Pearce and Tombs, 'Regulating Corporate Crime', op. cit.
69. See W. Clement, *The Canadian Corporate Elite* (Toronto: McClelland and Stewart, 1975).
70. See Simon and Eitzen, op. cit. p. 10.
71. See A. Hopkins, *Crime, Law and Business: The Sociological Sources of Australian Monopoly Law* (Canberra: Australian Institute of Criminology, 1978).
72. See Barnett, 'Production of Corporate Crime', op. cit.
73. See H. Barnett, 'Wealth, Crime and Capital Accumulation', *Contemporary Crises*, vol. 3 (1979) pp. 171–86, esp. pp. 171–2.
74. Coleman, op. cit., p. 174.
75. See Hopkins, 'Anatomy of Corporate Crime', op. cit., p. 79.
76. See Goff and Reasons, op. cit.; and W. Stanbury, *Business Interests and the Reform of Canadian Competition Policy, 1971–75* (Toronto: Carswell Methuen, 1977).
77. See Coleman, op. cit.; and Shapiro, op. cit.
78. See Yeager, op. cit., p. 4.
79. Levi, 'Giving Creditors the Business', op. cit., p. 323.
80. Molotch, op. cit.; and Coleman, op. cit.
81. A. Macintyre, 'A Court Quietly Rewrote the Federal Pesticide Statute: How Prevalent is Judicial Statutory Revision?', *Law and Policy*, vol. 7(2) (April 1985) pp. 250–79.

Bibliography

Abraham, M. (1985) *The Lessons of Bhopal: A Community Action Resource Manual on Hazardous Technologies* (Penang: International Organization of Consumers Unions).

Ackerman, B. *et al.* (1974) *The Uncertain Search for Environmental Quality* (New York: Free Press).

Agarwal, A., Merrifield, J. and Tandon, R. (1985) *No Place to Run: Local Realities and Global Issues of the Bhopal Disaster* (New Market, Tenn.: Highlander Center and Society for Participatory Research in Asia).

Allum, P. A. (1975) *Potere e societa a Napoli nel dopoguerra* (Turin); Italian version of *Politics and Society in Post-War Naples* (Cambridge: Cambridge University Press, 1973).

Alongi, G. (1890) *La Camorra* (Turin: Edizioni MCM).

Anderson, J. E. (1975) *Public Policy-Making* (New York: Praeger).

Anderson, W. J., Assistant Comptroller General (1986) Statement on 'General Government Programs', before the Subcommittee on Government Information, Justice, and Agriculture Committee on Government Operations, Unites States House of Representatives, *Hearings: Federal Drug Interdiction Efforts* (9 September) (Washington, DC: Government Printing Office).

Andreas, P. (1988) 'The U.S. Drug War in Peru', *Nation*, 13/20 August 1988.

Anslinger, H. J. and Oursler, W. (1962) *The Murderers* (London: Arthur Barker).

APPEN (1986) *The Bhopal Tragedy – One Year Later* (Penang: Sabahat Alam Malaysia (Friends of the Earth Malaysia)).

ARENA (1985) *Bhopal: Industrial Genocide?* (Hong Kong: Arena Press).

Arlacchi, P. (1983) *La mafia imprenditrice* (Bologna: Il Mulino).

Association of Chief Police Officers (ACPO) (1985) Final Report of a Working Party on Drugs Related Crime, chaired by R. F. Broome (ACPO unpublished report): extracts published as appendix in Dorn, Murji and South, 1991.

Bagley, B. M. (1988a) 'Columbia and the War on Drugs', *Foreign Affairs* 67(1) (Fall).

Bagley, B. M. (1988b) 'The New Hundred Years War: US National Security and the War on Drugs in Latin America', *Journal of Interamerican Studies and World Affairs*, vol. 30(1).

Bagley, B. M. (1988c) 'US Foreign Policy and the War on Drugs: Analysis of a Policy Failure', *Journal of Interamerican Studies and World Affairs*, vol. 30(2–3) (Summer/Fall) pp. 198–212.

Banerjee, B. N. (1986) *Bhopal Gas Tragedy – Accident or Experiment* (Delhi: Paribus).

Bardach, E. and Kagan, A. R. (1982) *Going by the Book: The Problem of Regulatory Unreasonableness* (Philadelphia, Penn.: Temple University Press).

Barnett, H. (1979) 'Wealth, Crime, and Capital Accumulation', *Contemporary Crises*, vol. 3, pp. 171–86.

Barnett, H. (1982) 'The Production of Corporate Crime in Corporate Capitalism', in P. Wickham and T. Dailey (eds), *White Collar and Economic Crime* (Toronto: Lexington Books).

Baxi, U. (1986) 'Inconvenient Forum and Convenient Catastrophe: the Bhopal Case', in U. Baxi and T. Paul (eds), *Mass Disasters and Multinational Liability* (New Delhi: Indian Law Institute).

BBC1 (1988) 'The Two Billion Pound Rip Off', 8 February.

Becchi Collioda, A. (1984) *Napoli Miliardaria. Economia e lavora dopo il terremoto* (Milan: Franco Angeli).

Belli, A. (1986) *Il labirinto e l'eresia: La politica urbanistica a Napoli tra emergenza e ingovernabilita* (Milan: Franco Angeli).

Bennett, W. J. (1986) *What Works: Schools without Drugs* (Washington, DC: US Department of Education).

Bergman, D. (1988) 'The Sabotage Theory and the Legal Strategy of Union Carbide', *New Law Journal*, vol. 138 (17 June) pp. 420–2.

Bhopal Action Group (1988) 'Sabotaging the Sabotage Theory: Critique of the Paper by Ashok Kalelkar' (London: Transnational Information Centre).

Bishop, D. R. (1985) 'The Community's Rights and Industry's Response' in M. A. Smith *et al.*, *The Chemical Industry after Bhopal* (London: IBC Tech nical Services).

Block, A. (1987) 'Ambiguities in US Caribbean Policy: the Bahamas, Narcotics, and American Foreign Policy', paper presented at the Southwestern Political Science Association meeting, Dallas, Texas (March).

Block, A. and Chambliss, W. (1981) *Organizing Crime* (New York: Elsevier).

Block, A. and McWilliams, J. (1989) 'On the Origins of American Counterintelligence: Building a Clandestine Network', *Journal of Policy History*, vol. 1(4).

Block, A. and McWilliams, J. (1990) 'All the Commissioner's Men: the Federal Bureau of Narcotics and the Dewey–Luciano Affair 1947–1954', *Intelligence and National Security*, vol. 5(1) (January) pp. 171–92.

Blum, W. (1986) *The CIA: A Forgotten History* (London: Zed Books).

Blumberg, A. S. (1967) *Criminal Justice* (Chicago, Ill.: Quadrangle Books).

Box, S. (1983) *Power, Crime and Mystification* (London: Tavistock Publica tions).

Braithwaite, J. (1979a) 'Transnational Corporations and Corruption: Towards some International Solutions', *International Journal of Sociology of Law*, vol. 7, pp. 125–42.

Braithwaite, J. (1979b) 'Corporate Crime: Regulating Corporate Behaviour through Criminal Sanctions', *Harvard Law Review*, vol. 9, pp. 1227–1375.

Braithwaite, J. (1980) 'Inegalitarian Consequences of Egalitarian Reforms to Control Corporate Crime', *Temple Law Quarterly*, vol. 53, pp. 1127–46.

Braithwaite, J. (1982) 'Enforced, Self-Regulation: a New Strategy for Corporate Crime Control', *Michigan Law Review*, vol. 80(7) pp. 1466–1507 (June).

Braithwaite, J. (1984) *Corporate Crime in the Pharmaceutical Industry* (London: Routledge and Kegan Paul).

Braithwaite, J. (1985) 'White Collar Crime", *Annual Review of Sociology*, vol. 2, pp. 1–25.

Braithwaite, J. (1988) 'Toward a Benign Big Gun Theory of Regulatory Power' (Canberra: Australian National University) unpublished manuscript.

Braithwaite, J. and Geis, G. (1982) 'On Theory and Action for Corporate Crime Control', *Crime and Delinquency*, vol. 28, pp. 292–314.

Brodeur, P. (1985) *Outrageous Misconduct: The Asbestos Industry on Trial* (New York: Pantheon).

Brooks, J. K., Haney, R. W., Kaiser, G. D., Leyva, A. J. and McKelvey, T.C. (1988) 'A Survey of Recent Major Accident Legislation in the USA' in *Preventing Major Chemical and Related Process Accidents*, I.Chem.E. Symposium Series no. 110 (Rugby: Institution of Chemical Engineers).

Browning, F. and Gerassi, J. (1980) *The American Way of Crime* (New York: G. P. Putnam's Sons).

Bruun, K. *et al.* (1975) *The Gentlemen's Club: International Control over Drugs and Alcohol* (London: University of Chicago Press).

Calavita, K. (1983) 'The Demise of the Occupational Safety and Health Administration: a Case Study in Symbolic Action', *Social Problems*, vol. 30(4) pp. 437–48.

Calavita, K. (1986) 'Worker Safety, Law and Social Change: the Italian Case', *Law and Society*, vol. 20(20) pp. 189–229.

California, State of (1950), Special Crime Study Commission on Organized Crime, *Third Progress Report*, Sacramento, Cal., 31 January.

Caputo, T., Kennedy, M., Reasons, C. and Brannigan, A. (eds) (1989) 'Overview – Political Economy, Law and Environmental Protection' in Caputo *et al.*, *Law and Society: A Critical Perspective* (Toronto: Harcourt Brace Jovanovich) pp. 164–72.

Caroll, L. (1990) 'Race, Ethnicity and the Social Order of the Prison', in D. Kelly, *Criminal Behaviour: Texts and Readings in Criminology* (New York: St Martin's Press) pp. 510–27.

Carson, W. G. (1970) 'White Collar Crime and the Enforcement of Factory Legislation', *British Journal of Criminology*, vol. 10, pp. 383–98.

Carson, W. G. (1980a) 'The Institutionalisation of Ambiguity: Early British Factory Acts' in G. Geis and E. Stotland (eds), *White Collar Theory and Research* (Beverly Hills, Cal.: Sage).

Carson, W. G. (1980b) 'The Other Price of Britain's Oil: Regulating Safety on Offshore Oil Installations in the British Sector of the North Sea', *Contemporary Crises*, vol. 4, pp. 239–66.

Carson, W. G. (1982) 'Legal Control of Safety on British Offshore Oil Installations', in P. Wickham and T. Dailey (eds), *White Collar and Economic Crime* (Toronto: Lexington Books).

Castleman, B. (1979) 'The Export of Hazard to Developing Countries', *International Journal of Health Services*, vol. 9(4), pp. 569–606.

Caute, D. (1978) *The Great Fear: The Anticommunity Purge under Truman and Eisenhower* (London: Secker and Warburg).

Cervantes, M. (1973) 'Rinconete e Cortadillo', in *Opere* (Milan: Rizzoli).

Chieppa, N. (1985) 'Dal contrabbando alla Camorra e dal colera al terremoto', *Osservatorio sulla Camorra*, vol. 4, pp. 18–31.

Chomsky, N. (1985) *Turning the Tide: US Intervention in Central America and the Struggle for Peace* (London: Pluto Press)

Chopra, S. K., Consultant to Kelly, Drye and Warren (1986) 'Bhopal Disaster and the Indian Legal and Administrative System: What is Wrong and What to Do', paper presented at the International Bar Association, New York (September).

Clarke, M. J. (1990) *Business Crime* (Cambridge: Polity Press).

Clement, W. (1975) *The Canadian Corporate Elite* (Toronto: McClelland and Stewart).

Clement, W. (1977) 'The Corporate Elite, the Capitalist Class, and the Canadian State', in L. Panitch (ed.), *The Canadian State* (Toronto: University of Toronto Press) pp. 225–48.

Clinard, M. B. (1979) *Illegal Corporate Behaviour* (Washington, DC: Government Printing Office).

Clinard, M. B. and Yeager, P. (1980) *Corporate Crime* (New York: Free Press).

Cobb, R. W. and Elder, C. D. (1972) *Participation in American Politics: The Dynamics of Agenda Building* (Boston, Mass.: Allyn and Bacon).

Cobb, R. W., Ross, J. and Ross, M. (1976) 'Agenda Building as a Comparative Political Process', *American Political Science Review*, vol. 70, pp. 126–38.

Coffee, J. C. (1984) 'Corporate Criminal Responsibility', in S. H. Kadish (ed.), *Encyclopedia of Crime and Justice* (New York: Free Press) vol. 1, pp. 253–64.

Cohen, A. (1977) 'The Concept of Criminal Organization', *British Journal of Criminology*, vol. 17(2), pp. 97–111.

Cohen, S. (ed.) (1971) *Images of Deviance* (Harmondsworth, Middx: Penguin).

Coleman, J. W. (1985) *The Criminal Elite: The Sociology of White Collar Crime* (New York: St Martin's Press).

Commissione Anti-Mafia, Documento XXIII, vol. 2 (Rome: 1976).

Comptroller General, Office of, General Accounting Office (1975), *Federal Drug Enforcement: Strong Guidance Needed* (Washington, DC: General Accounting Office).

Comptroller General, Office of, General Accounting Office (1983), *Federal Drug Interdiction Efforts Need Strong Central Oversight* (Washington, DC: General Accounting Office).

Cox, B., Shirley, J. and Short, M. (1977) *The Fall of Scotland Yard* (Harmondsworth, Middx: Penguin).

Cranston, R. (1982) 'Regulation and Deregulation: General Issues', *University of New South Wales Law Journal*, vol. 5, pp. 1–29.

Cutolo, R. (1980) *Poesie e pensieri*, (Naples: Carditi).

D'Agostino, G. (1988) 'Voto e Camorra', in F. Barbagallo, *Camorra e criminalita organizzata in Campania* (Naples: Liguori).

Dalla Chiesa, N. (1983) 'Mafia e potere oggi', *Democrazia e Diritto*, vol. 4, pp. 34–46.

Dawson, S., Clinton, A., Bamford, M. and Willman, P. (1988) *Safety at Work: The Limits of Self-Regulation* (Cambridge: Cambridge University Press).

De Blasio, A. (1897) *Usi e costumi dei camorristi* (Naples: Esti).

De Blasio, A. (1905) *La malavita a Napoli* (Naples: Esti).

De Forest, O. and Chanoff, D. (1990) *Slow Burn: The Rise and Bitter Fall of American Intelligence in Vietnam* (New York: Simon and Schuster).

Deieso, D. A., Mulvey, N. P., and Kelly, J. (1988) 'Accidental Release Prevention: a Regulator's Perspective', paper presented at Symposium entitled *Preventing Major Chemical and Related Process Accidents*, Queen Elizabeth II Centre, London, 10–12th May.

Dinham, B., Dixon, B. and Saghal, G. (1986) *The Bhopal Papers* (London: Transnational Information Centre).

Diver, C. (1980) 'Modesty and Immodesty in Policy-Oriented Empirical Research', *Administrative Law Review*, vol. 32.

Dorn, N., Murji K. and South, N. (1990) 'Mirroring the Market? Police Reorganisation and Effectiveness against Drug Trafficking', in R. Reiner and M. Cross (eds), *Beyond Law and Order* (London: Macmillan).

Dorn, N., Murji K. and South, N. (1991) *Traffickers: Policing the Drug Distribution Business* (London: Routledge).

Dorn, N. and South, N. (1990a) 'Profits and Penalties: New Trends in Legislation and Law Enforcement Concerning Illegal Drugs', in D. Whynes and P. Bean (eds).

Dorn N. and South, N. (1990b) 'Drug Markets and Law Enforcement', *British Journal of Criminology*, vol. 30(2), pp. 171–88 (Spring).

Downs, A. (1967) *Inside Bureaucracy* (Boston, Mass.: Little, Brown).

Draper T. (1990) 'Did Noriega Declare War?', *The New York Review of Books*, 29 March.

Drug Enforcement Report (1989) 'ONDCP (Office of National Drug Control Policy) Calls for National Drug Intelligence Centre, but Plan may be Delayed or Shelved', *Drug Enforcement Report*, vol. 5(22) 23 August.

Druglink (1989) 'Risk of Policy/Community Conflict'; 'The Stutman Connection'; and 'Government Backs Off Anti-Crack Drive', *Druglink*, 4, 5.

Edelhertz, H. (1970) *The Nature, Impact and Prosecution of White-Collar Crime* (Washington, DC: National Institute for Law Enforcement and Criminal Justice, Department of Justice) May.

Einstadter, W. J. (1969) 'The Social Organization of Armed Robbery', *Social Problems*, vol. 1, pp. 64–83.

Elkins, J. R. (1976) 'Decisionmaking Model and the Control of Corporate Crime', *Hobarth Law Journal*, vol. 85, pp. 1091–1129.

Enzensberger, H. M. (1979) 'Pupetta o la fine della nuova Camorra', in *Politica e gangsterismo* (Rome: Savelli).

Epstein, S. (ed.) (1982) *The Disposal of Hazardous Waste* (San Francisco, Cal.: Sierra Club).

Ermann, D. M. and Lundman, R. J. (1978) 'Deviant Acts by Complex Organizations: Deviance and Social Control at the Organizational Level of Analysis', *Sociological Quarterly*, vol. 19, pp. 55–67.

European Parliament Session Documents 1988–89, A2–20/89/ Part A, *Report by the Commission on Budgetary Control on Preventing and Controlling Fraud against the European Community Budget in a Post-1992 Europe.* Rapporteur Mr P. Dankert.

Everest, L. (1986) *Behind the Poison Cloud: Union Carbide's Bhopal Massacre* (New York: Banner Press).

Fazey, C. (1976) *The Aetiology of Non-Medical Drugs Use* (Paris: UNESCO).

Fellmeth, R. (1973) 'The Regulatory-Industrial Complex', in R. Nader (ed.), *The Common and Corporate Accountability* (New York: Harcourt Brace Jovanovich).

Fels, A. (1982) 'The Political Economy of Regulation', *University of New South Wales Law Journal*, vol. 5, pp. 29–60.

Ferracuti, F. (1988) *Forme de organizzazione criminali e terrorismo* (Milan: Giuffrè).

Fisse, B. and Braithwaite, J. (1983) *The Impact of Publicity on Corporate Offenders* (Albany, N.Y.: State University of New York Press).

Florida Development of Law Enforcement (1987) *Drug Abuse in Florida: Summary of the Problem and Statewide Initiatives* (February 17).

Fremantle, B. (1985) *The Fix: The Inside Story of the World Drugs Trade* (London: Michael Joseph).

Freudenheim, M. (1990) 'Booming Business: Drug Use Tests', *New York Times*, 3 January, p. D1.

Galanter, M. (1974) 'Why the Haves Come Out Ahead: Speculations on the Limits of Legal Change', *Law and Society Review*, vol. 9, pp. 95–160.

Gallo, E. and Ruggiero, V. (1989) *Il Carcere immateriale* (Milan: Sonda).

Gallo, E. and Ruggiero, V. (1985) 'Il crimine presunto e il delin quentelavoratore', *Primo Maggio*, vol. 23/24, pp. 34–52.

Garofalo, G. (1984) *La seconda guerra napoletana* (Naples: Javisano).

Geis, G. (1967) 'White Collar Crime: the Heavy Electrical Equipment Antitrust Cases of 1961', in M. B. Clinard and R. Quinney (eds), *Criminal Behaviour Systems: A Typology* (New York: Holt, Rinehart and Winston).

Geis, G. (1973) 'Deterring Corporate Crime', in R. Nader and M. J. Green (eds), *Corporate Power in America* (New York: Viking Press).

Geis, G. (ed.) (1982) *On White-Collar Crime* (Toronto: Lexington Books).

Geis, G. and Meier, R. F. (1977) *White-Collar Crime* (New York: Free Press).

Gilman, M. and Pearson, G. (1990) 'Lifestyles and Law Enforcement', in D. Whynes and P. Bean (eds).

Glasbeek, H. (1984) 'The Corporation as Criminal', *Our Times*, September.

Glasbeek, H. (1989) 'Why Corporate Deviance is not Treated as a Crime', in T. Caputo *et al.*, *Law and Society: A Critical Perspective* (Toronto: Harcourt Brace Jovanovich) pp. 126–45.

Goff, C. and Reasons, C. (1978) *Corporate Crime in Canada* (Toronto: Prentice-Hall).

Gough, I. (1979) *The Political Economy of the Welfare State* (London: Macmillan).

Granada TV (1986) 'The Betrayal of Bhopal', produced by Laurie Flynn.

Grayson, J. P. and Grayson, L. (1980) 'Canadian Literary and Other Elites', *Canadian Review of Sociology and Anthropology*, vol. 17(4), pp. 338–56.

Green, M. (1972) *The Closed Enterprise System* (New York: Grossman).

Gunningham, N. (1974) *Pollution: Social Interest and the Law* (Oxford: Oxford Centre for Socio-Legal Studies).

Gunningham, N. (1984) *Safeguarding the Workers* (Sydney: Law Book Co.).

Gunningham, N. (1987) 'Negotiated Non-Compliance: a Case Study of Regulatory Failure', *Law and Policy*, vol. 9, pp. 69–97.

Hall, A. (1988) 'Managing Contradictory Interests – Health and Safety in Mining', paper presented at the Annual Meetings of the Canadian Sociology and Anthropology Association, Windsor, June.

Harding, C. S. P. (1982) 'The European Communities and Control of Criminal Business Activities', *International and Comparative Law Quarterly*, vol. 31, pp. 246–62.

Hawkins, K. (1984) *Environment and Enforcement: Regulation and the Social Definition of Pollution* (Oxford: Clarendon Press).

Hazarika, Sanjoy (1987) *Bhopal: The Lessons of a Tragedy* (Delhi: Penguin Books (India)).

Helmer, J. (1975) *Drugs and Minority Oppression* (New York: Seabury Press).

Helmer, J. and T. Vietorisz (1974) *Drug Use, the Labour Market and Class Conflict* (Washington, DC: Drug Abuse Council).

Henman, A., Lewis, R. and Malyon, T. (1985) *Big Deal: The Politics of the Illicit Drugs Business* (London: Pluto).

Henry, A. (1988) 'Communication Concerning Technological Risk between Industry and its Surroundings at Pont-de-Claix', *Industry and Environment*, vol. 2. pp. 11–17 (April/May/June).

Hill, M., Aaranovitch, S. and Baldock, D. (1989) 'Non-Decision Making in Pollution Control in Britain: Nitrate Pollution, the EEC Drinking Water Directive and Agriculture', *Policy and Politics*, vol. 17(3), pp. 277–40.

Hinojoza, G. V. Garcia (1989) *An Analysis of the Relationship Between the Aggregate Value of Cocaine and the Bolivian Formal Economy*, Master's thesis, Pennsylvania State University (December).

Hobsbawn, E. J. (1986) 'Murderous Colombia', *New York Review of Books*, 20 November, pp. 27–35.

Holloway J. and Picciotto, S. (1978) *State and Capital* (London: Edward Arnold).

Home Affairs Committee (1989) *Drug Trafficking and Related Serious Crime*, vol. 1 (London: Her Majesty's Stationery Office.

Hopkins, A. (1978) *Crime, Law and Business: The Sociological Sources of Australian Monopoly Law* (Canberra: Australian Institute of Criminology).

Hopkins, A. (1979) 'The Anatomy of Corporate Crime', in P. Wilson and J. Braithwaite (eds), *Two Faces of Deviance* (St Lucia: University of Queensland Press).

Horgan, J. (1990) 'Test Negative: a Look at the "Evidence" Justifying Illicit Drug Tests', *Scientific American*, March, pp. 18–19.

House of Lords Select Committee on the European Community (1989) *Fraud against the Community*, House of Lords Paper 27 (London: Her Majesty's Stationery Office) Q. 173.

Hundloe, T. (1978) 'Heads They Win, Tails We Lose: Environment and the Law', in P. Wilson and J. Braithwaite (eds), *Two Faces of Deviance* (St Lucia: Queensland University Press).

Ianni, F. A. (1972) *A Family Business: Kinship and Social Control in Organized Crime* (New York: Russell Sage Foundation).

'Il Manifesto' (1983), 26 June.

'Il Manifesto' (1989) daily newspaper of Naples, 18 September.

Imbert, P. (1989) 'Do We Need a British FBI?', *Police Review*, 14 July.

Inciardi, J. (1986) *The War on Drugs: Heroin, Cocaine, Crime, and Public Policy* (Palo Alto, Cal.: Mayfield Publishing) pp. 208–9.

Institute for Race Relations (IRR) (1989) 'Operation Kingfisher – Police Raid Broadwater Farm', *IRR: Police–Media Research Project Bulletin*, vol. 55, p. 257.

Institute for Race Relations (IRR) (1990) '£100,000 Damages for Victim of Drug Plant by Notting Hill Police' in *IRR: Police–Media Research Project Bulletin*, vol. 57, p. 1.

International Coalition for Justice in Bhopal (ICJIB) (1987) *We Must Not Forget: A Plea for Justice for the Bhopal Victims* (Penang: International Organization of Consumers Unions).

Ives, J. (ed.) (1985) *The Export of Hazard* (London: Routledge and Kegan Paul).

Jamieson, M. (1985) *Persuasion or Punishment – The Enforcement of Health and Safety at Work Legislation by the British Factory Inspectorate*, unpublished M.Phil. thesis, Oxford University.

Johnson, B., Goldstein, P., Preble, E., Schmeidler, J., Lipton, D., Spunt, B. and Miller, T. (1985) *Taking Care of Business: The Economics of Crime by Heroin Abusers* (Lexington, Mass.: Lexington Books).

Johnson, E. (1963) 'Organized Crime: Challenge to the American Legal System', *J. Crim. Law Criminol. Polit. Sci.*, vol. 54, pp. 1–29.

Johnston, L. et al., (1989) *Drug Use, Drinking, and Smoking; National Survey Results from High School, College, and Young Adult Populations, 1975–1988* (Rockville, Md: US Dept of Health and Human Services).

Jones, K. (1982) *Law and Economy: The Legal Regulation of Corporate Capital* (London: Academic Press).

Jones, Tara (1988) *Corporate Killing: Bhopals Will Happen* (London: Free Association Books).

Kagan, R. (1978) *Regulatory Justice* (New York: Russell Sage).

Kagan, R. and Scholz, J. T. (1984) 'The Criminology of the Corporation and Regulatory Enforcement Strategies', in K. Hawkins and J. Thomas (eds), *Enforcing Regulation* (Boston, Mass.: Kluwer-Nijhoff).

Kalelkar, A. (1988) 'Investigation of Large Magnitude Incidents – Bhopal as a Case Study', in *Preventing Major Chemical and Related Process Accidents*, Institute of Chemical Engineers Symposium Series no. 110 (Rugby: EFCE Publications Series no. 70, Hemisphere Publishing Corporation).

Kefauver, E. (1952) *Crime in America* (London: Victor Gollancz).

Kennedy, P. (1988) *The Rise and Fall of the Great Powers* (London: Unwin Hyman).

Kinder, D. C. (1981) 'Bureaucratic Cold Warrior. Harry J. Anslinger and Illicit Narcotics Traffic', *Pacific Historical Review*, vol. 50, pp. 169–91 (May).

Kinder, D. C. and W. O. Walker III (1986) 'Stable Force in a Storm: Harry J. Anslinger and United States Narcotic Foreign Policy, 1930–62', *Journal of American History*, vol. 72, pp. 908–27 (March).

King, D. K. (1985) 'The Regulatory Use of the Criminal Sanction in Controlling Corporate Crime', paper presented at the American Society of Criminology Meetings, San Diego, California.

Kirby, T. (1989) 'Police Accused of Planting Drugs on Blacks', *Independent*, 17 June.

Kletz, T. (1988) *Learning from Accidents in Industry* (London: Butterworths).

Knapp Commission (1972) *The Knapp Report on Police Corruption* (New York: George Brazillier).

Kneese, A. V. and Schultze, C. L. (1975) *Pollution, Prices, and Public Policy* (Washington, DC: Brookings Institution).

Kobler, J. (1972) *Capone* (London: Coronet).

Kolko, J. (1988) *Restructuring the World Economy* (New York: Pantheon).

Kurtzman, D. (1987) *A Killing Wind: Inside Union Carbide and the Bhopal Catastrophe* (New York: McGraw-Hill).

Kwitney, J. (1988) *The Crimes of Patriots* (New York: Touchstone).
Lamberti, A. (1987) 'Dall'economia criminale all' economia legale: le linee di tendenza della Camorra imprenditrice', *Osservatorio sulla Camorra*, vol. 5, pp. 37–51.
Lamberti, A. (1988) 'Mercato politico e mercato criminale', *La Citta Nuova*, vol. 5, pp. 15–23.
Landesco, J. (1968), *Organized Crime in Chicago* (Chicago, Ill.: University of Chicago Press).
Le Goff, J. (1987) *La borsa e la vita: Dall'usuraio al banchiere* (Bari: Laterza).
Lernoux, P. (1984) 'The Miami Connection', *Nation*, 18 February.
Levi, M. (1981) *The Phantom Capitalists: The Organization and Control of Long Term Fraud* (London: Heinemann).
Levi, M. (1984) 'Giving Creditors the Business: the Criminal Law in Inaction', *International Journal of Sociology of Law*, vol. 12, pp. 321–33.
Levin, B. (1990a) 'What More Evidence Must They Have?', *The Times*, 25 January.
Levin, B. (1990b) 'Justice under a Blue Cloud', *The Times*, 12 January.
Lewis, R. (1985) 'Serious Business: the Global Heroin Economy', in A. Henman *et al.*, *Big Deal: The Politics of the Illicit Drugs Business* (London: Pluto Press) pp. 1–49.
Lewis, R., Hartnoll, R., Bryer, S., Daviaud, E. and Mitcheson, M. (1985) 'Scoring Smack: the Illicit Heroin Market in London, 1980–1983', *British Journal of Addiction*, vol. 80.
Lewis-Beck, M. S. and Alford, J. R. (1980) 'Can Government Regulate Safety? The Coal Mine Example', *American Political Science Review*, vol. 74, pp. 745–81.
Lindesmith, A. (1941) 'Organized Crime', *Annals of the American Academy of Political and Social Science*, vol. 217, pp. 32–54.
Linklater, M. *et al.* (1984) *The Fourth Reich: Klaus Barbie and the Neo-Fascist Connection* (London: Hodder and Stoughton).
Lippmann, W. (1967) 'The Underworld as Servant', in G. Tyler (ed.), *Organized Crime in America* (Ann Arbor, Mich.: University of Michigan Press) pp. 58–69.
Long, S. (1979) 'The Internal Revenue Service: Examining the Exercise of Discretion in Tax Enforcement', paper presented at the Annual Meeting, Law and Society Association, Toronto, May.
Lynxwiler, J., Shover, N. and Clelland, D. (1983) 'Corporate Size and International Contexts: Determinants of Sanctioning Severity in a Regulatory Bureaucracy', paper presented at the Annual Meetings of the American Criminal Justice Society, San Antonio, Texas, 28–31 March.
McCormick, A. E. (1977) 'Rule Enforcement and Moral Indignation: Some Observations of the Effects of Criminal Anti-trust Convictions upon Societal Reaction Processes', *Social Problems*, vol. 25, pp. 30–9.
McCoy, A. (1972) *The Politics of Heroin in Southeast Asia* (New York and London: Harper and Row).
Machetti, G. (1988) 'Le leggi eccezionali post-unitarie e la repressione della Camorra: un problema di ordine pubblico?', in F. Barbagallo, *Camorra e criminalita organizzata in Campania* (Naples: Liguori).

McIntosh, M. (1971) 'Changes in the Organization of Thieving', in S. Cohen (ed.), *Images of Deviance* (Harmondsworth, Middx: Penguin).

McIntosh, M. (1975) *The Organisation of Crime* (London: Macmillan).

Macintyre, A. (1985) 'A Court Quietly Rewrote the Federal Pesticide Statute: How Prevalent is Judicial Statutory Revision?', *Law and Policy*, vol. 7(2), pp. 250–79 (April).

Mack, J. (1975) *The Crime Industry* (Lexington, Mass.: Saxon House Lexington).

McQueen R. (1989) 'The New Companies and Securities Schemes: a Fundamental Departure?', *Australian Quarterly*, Summer, pp. 481–97.

McQueen R. (1990) *Why Company Law is Important to Left Realists*, paper presented to Left Realist Conference, Vancouver, BC, May.

McWilliams, J. (1989) *The Protectors: Commissioner Harry J. Anslinger and the Federal Bureau of Narcotics, 1930–62* (Newark, Del.: University of Delaware Press).

Magnusson, D. (1981) *Ekonomisk Brottslighet vid Import och Export*, Brottsforebyggande Radet Rapport, 2.

Mannheim, H. (1975) *Trattato di criminologia comparata* (Turin: Einaudi).

Marchak, P. (1975) *Ideological Perspectives on Canada* (Toronto: McGraw Hill Ryerson).

Marks, J. (1979) *The Search for the 'Manchurian Candidate': The CIA and Mind Control* (London: Allen Lane).

Marmo, M. (1988) 'La Camorra e lo Stato liberale', in F. Barbagallo, *Camorra e criminalita organizzata in Campania* (Naples: Liguori, 1988) pp. 28–52.

Meier, R. and Plumlee, J. P. (1978) 'Regulatory Administration and Organizational Rigidity', *Western Political Quarterly*, vol. 31, pp. 80–95.

Meier, R. and Short, J. F. (1982) 'The Consequences of White-Collar Crime', in H. Edelhertz and T. Overcast (eds), *White-Collar Crime: An Agenda for Research* (Toronto: D. C. Heath, Lexington Books).

Miliband, R. (1969) *The State in Capitalist Society* (London: Quartet Books).

Mirante, E. (1989) 'The Victim Zone: Recent Accounts of Burmese Military Human Rights Abuse in the Shan State', *Contemporary Crises*, vol. 13(3), September.

Mitnick, B. M. (1980) *The Political Economy of Regulation* (New York: Columbia University Press).

Molotch, H. (1973) 'Oil in Santa Barbara and Power in America', in W. J. Chambliss (ed.), *Sociological Readings in the Conflict Perspective* (Reading, Mass.: Addison-Wesley).

Moore, M. (1977) *Buy and Bust: The Effective Regulation of an Illicit Market in Heroin* (Lexington, Mass.: Lexington Books).

Moore, W. (1974) *The Kefauver Committee and the Politics of Crime* (Colombia: University of Missouri Press).

Morehouse, W. and Subramaniam, M. A. (1986) *The Bhopal Tragedy* (New York: Council on International and Public Affairs).

Mortimer, J. and Lait, J. (1950) *Chicago Confidential* (New York: Crown).

Mortimer, J. and Lait, J. (1951) *Washington Confidential* (New York: Crown).

Mortimer, J. and Lait, J. (1952) *USA Confidential* (New York: Crown).

Muchlinski, P. T. (1987) 'The Bhopal Case: Controlling Ultrahazardous Industrial Activities Undertaken by Foreign Investors', *Modern Law Review*, vol. 50(5), September.

Nadelmann, E. (1988) 'US Drug Policy: a Bad Export', *Foreign Policy*, no. 70 (Spring).

Nadelmann, E. (1989a) 'Drug Prohibition in the United States: Costs, Consequences and Alternatives', *Science*, vol. 245, 1 September.

Nadelmann, E. (1989b) 'Anyone Care What Works?', *Los Angeles Times*, 6 September.

Nader, R. and Green, M. J. (eds) (1973) *Corporate Power in America* (New York: Viking Press).

National Institute on Drug Abuse (NIDA) (1988) *Semiannual Report: Trend Data from the Drug Abuse Warning Network*, Series G, no. 21 (Rockville, Md: NIDA).

National Institute on Drug Abuse (NIDA) (1989) *National Household Survey on Drug Abuse: Population Estimates 1988* (Rockville, Md: NIDA).

National Institute of Justice (NIJ) Reports (1988) *Attorney General Announces NIJ Drug Use Forecasting System* (Washington, DC: US Department of Justice) March/April.

Naylor, R. T. (1987) *Hot Money and the Politics of Debt* (London: Unwin Hyman).

Naylor, R. (1989) *Denaro che scotta* (Milan: Mondadori).

Oakley, R. (1983) *Drugs, Society and Human Behavior*, 3rd edn (St Louis, Mo.: C. V. Mosby).

O'Connor, J. (1973) *The Fiscal Crisis of the State* (New York: St Martin's Press).

Offe, C. (1982) 'Some Contradictions of the Modern Welfare State', *Critical Social Policy*, vol. 2(2), pp. 7–16.

Official Journal of the European Communities (1970) 729/70 E.E.C. articles 8 and 9, L 94/16, 28 April.

Official Journal of the European Communities (1972) 283/72 E.E.C. articles 2 and 3, L 36/1 10, February.

Official Journal of the European Communities (1984a) 77/435 E.E.C. article 2, C172/17, 12 July.

Official Journal of the European Communities (1984b), Special report on the implementation of directive 77/435 E.E.C., C336/1, 17 December Table 1.

Official Journal of the European Communities (1985) C297, 6 November.

Official Journal of the European Communities (1988), Report of the Court of Auditors for 1987, C316, vol. 31, 10.32–10.40, 12 December.

Olson, S. (1985) 'Comparing Justice and Labour Department Lawyers; Ten Years of Occupational Safety and Health Litigation', *Law and Policy*, vol. 7(3), pp. 286–313 (July).

O'Malley, P. (1987) 'In Place of Criminology: a Marxist Reformulation', paper presented to the Annual Meeting of the Canadian Sociology and Anthropology Association, Hamilton, Ontario, 2–5 June.

O'Malley, P. (1988) 'Law-Making in Canada: Capitalism and Legislation in a Democratic State', *Canadian Journal of Law and Society*, vol. 3, pp. 53–70.

O'Riordan, T. and Weale, A. (1989) 'Administrative Re-organisation and Policy Change: the Case of Her Majesty's Inspectorate of Pollution', *Public Administration*, vol. 67, pp. 277–94 (Autumn).

O'Sullivan, J. (1989) ' "Framed" Club Owner is Cleared of Drug Charges', *Independent*, 17 June.

Palermo, C. (1983) 'Le forme nuove del crimine organizzato', *Democrazia e Diritto*, 4.

Pashukanis, E. B. (1978) *Law and Marxism* (London: Ink Links).

Paulus, I. (1974) 'The Search for Pure Food: a Sociology of Legislation in Britain' (London: Martin Robertson).

Pearce, F. (1976) *Crimes of the Powerful: Marxism, Crime and Deviance* (London: Pluto Press).

Pearce, F. (1990a) 'The Contribution of "Left-Realism" to the Empirical Study of Commercial Crime", paper presented at Realist Criminology Conference, Vancouver, May.

Pearce, F. (1990b) 'Socially Responsible Corporations need Strong Independent Regulatory Agencies', *Political Quarterly*, vol. 61(4), pp. 415–30.

Pearce, F. and Tombs, S. (1988) 'Regulating Corporate Crime: the Case of Health and Safety', paper presented to the American Society of Criminology Annual Meetings, Chicago.

Pearce, F. and Tombs, S. (1989) 'Bhopal: Union Carbide and the Hubris of the Capitalist Technocracy', *Social Justice*, vol. 16(2), pp. 116–45.

Pearce, F. and Tombs, S. (1990) 'Ideology, Hegemony and Empiricism: Compliance Theories of Regulation', *British Journal of Criminology*, vol. 30(4), pp. 423–43 (Winter).

Pearce, F. and Tombs, S. (1991a) 'Realism and Corporate Crime' in R. Matthews and J. Young, *Realist Criminology* (London: Sage).

Pearce, F. and Tombs, S. (forthcoming) *Crimes of Capital* (London: Sage).

Pearson, G. (1989) 'The Street Connection', *New Statesman and Society*, 15 September.

Peet, R. (ed.) (1987) *International Capitalism and Industrial Restructuring* (London: Unwin-Hyman).

Pell, E. (1990) 'Movements Buying In', *Mother Jones*, vol. 15(3), pp. 23–5 (April–May).

Peltzman, J. (1976) 'Toward a More General Theory of Regulation', *Journal of Law and Economics*, vol. 19, pp. 211–40.

Pizzagati, S. (1976) 'The Perverted Grand Juries', *Nation*, 19 June, pp. 743–6.

Pizzorno, A. and Arlacchi, P. (1985) *Camorra, contrabbando e mercato della droga in Campania* (Rome: Commissione Parlamentare sul Fenomeno della Mafia).

Police Review (1989a) '£100,000 Damages Against the Met.', *Police Review*, 8 December.

Police Review (1989b) 'PCA [Police Complaints Authority] Investigate Notting Hill Complaints', *Police Review*, 22 December.

Policy Studies Institute (1983) *Police and People in London*, vols 1–4 (London: Policy Studies Institute)

Porter, J. (1965) *The Vertical Mosaic* (Toronto: University of Toronto Press).

President's Commission on Law Enforcement and the Administration of Justice (1967) *The Challenge of Crime in a Free Society* (Washington, DC: Government Printing Office).

President's Commission on Organized Crime (Kaufman Commission) (1983–5) *Record of Hearings* (Washington, DC: Government Printing Office).

Presthus, R. (1973) *Elite Accommodation in Canadian Politics* (Cambridge: Cambridge University Press).

Reasons, R., Ross, W. and Patterson, L. (1981) *Assault on the Worker* (Toronto: Butterworths).

Reiman, J. (1982) *The Rich Get Richer and the Poor Get Prison* (Toronto: John Wiley).

Reinarman, C. and Levine H. G. (1989) 'The Crack Attack: Politics and Media in America's Latest Drug Scare', in J. Best (ed.), *Images and Issues: Current Perspectives on Social Problems* (New York: Aldine de Gruyer).

Report of the Commission of Inquiry Appointed to Inquire into the Illegal Use of The Bahamas for the Transshipment of Dangerous Drugs Destined for the United States of America (December 1984) (Washington, DC: Government Printing Office).

Reuter, P. (1983)) *Disorganised Crime: Illegal Markets and the Mafia* (Cambridge, Mass.: MIT Press).

Reuter, P. (1988) 'Quantity Illusions and Paradoxes of Drug Interdiction: Federal Intervention into Voice Policy', *Law and Contemporary Problems*, vol. 51(1), Winter.

Reuter, P. (1989) *Quantity Illusion and Paradoxes of Drug Interdiction* (Santa Monica, Cal.: Rand Corporation).

Reuter, P., Crawford, G. and Cave, J. (1988) *Sealing the Borders: The Effects of Increased Military Participation in Drug Interdiction* (Santa Monica, Cal.: Rand Corporation).

Reuter, P. and Haaga, J. (1989) *The Organisation of High-Level Drug Markets: An Exploratory Study*, A Rand Note (Santa Monica, Cal.: Rand Corporation).

Rigby, D. (1989) 'Inside the Crack Castles', *News of the World*, 30 July.

Rodgers, P. (1989) 'Small Banks Warned as War on Laundered Drug Money Hots Up', *Guardian*, 14 November.

Rossi, P. (1989) *Down and Out in America: The Origins of Homelessness* (Chicago, Ill.: University of Chicago Press).

Ruggiero, V. (1981) 'La Camorra oggi', *Controinformazione*, vol. 21, pp. 22–36.

Ruggiero, V. (1985) 'The Encounter between Big Business and Organized Crime', in *Capital and Class*, vol. 26, pp. 93–104.

Sabatier, P. (1975) 'Social Movements and Regulatory Agencies: Toward a More Adequate – and Less Pessimistic – Theory of "Clientele Capture"', *Policy Sciences*, vol. 6, pp. 301–41.

Sabatier, P. (1977) 'Regulatory Policy-Making: Toward a Framework of Analysis', *National Resources Journal*, vol. 17, pp. 415–60.

Sale, K. (1976) *Power Shift: The Rise of the Southern Rim and its Challenge to the Eastern Establishment* (New York: Vintage Books).

Sales, I. (1987) 'La Camorra massa: caratteristiche organizzative e radici sociali', *Osservatorio sulla Camorra*, vol. 55, pp. 123–420.

Sales, I. (1988) *La Camorra; Le Camorre* (Rome: Editori Riuniti).

Sampson, A. (1975) *The Seven Sisters: The Great Oil Companies and the World They Shaped* (New York: Viking)).

Sandberg, H. (1985) *Union Carbide Corporation: A Case Study* (Geneva: International Management Institute).

Scheflin, A. W. and Optom, E. N. (1978) *The Mind Manipulators* (London: Paddington Press).

Scholz, J. (1984a) 'Deterrence, Cooperation and the Ecology of Regulatory Enforcement', *Law and Society Review*, vol. 18, pp. 179–224.

Scholz, J. (1984b) 'Voluntary Compliance and Regulatory Enforcement', *Law and Policy*, vol. 6, pp. 385–404.

Schrecker, E. W. (1986) *No Ivory Tower: McCarthyism and the Universities* (New York: Oxford University Press).

Schrecker, T. (1989) 'The Political Context and Content of Environmental Law', in T. Caputo *et al.*, *Law and Society: A Critical Perspective* (Toronto: Harcourt Brace Jovanovich) pp. 173–204.

Seminar Program and Exhibits Directory (1980) 35th Annual Seminar and Exhibits, American Society for Industrial Security, 11–14 September.

Shapiro, S. (1985a) 'The Road Not Taken: the Elusive Path to Criminal Prosecution for White Collar Offenders', *Law and Society Review*, vol. 19(2).

Shapiro, S. (1985b) 'Nailing Sanctuary Givers', *Los Angeles Daily Journal*, 12 March, p. 4.

Shover, N., Clelland, D. A. and Lynxwiler, J. (1983) *Developing a Regulatory Bureaucracy: The Office of Surface Mining Reclamation and Enforcement* (Washington, DC: National Institute of Justice).

Shrivistava, P. (1987) *Bhopal: Anatomy of a Crisis* (Cambridge: Ballinger).

Simon, D. R. and Eitzen, D. S. (1986) *Elite Deviance*, 2nd edn (Toronto: Allyn and Bacon).

Simpson, C. (1988) *Blowback: America's Recruitment of Nazis and its Effect on the Cold War* (New York: Collier).

Sinclair, A. (1962) *Prohibition: The Era of Excess* (London: Faber and Faber).

Smith, D. (1975) *The Mafia Mystique* (New York: Basic Books).

Smith, M. A. (ed.) (1985) *The Chemical Industry after Bhopal: An International Symposium held in London* (London: IBC Technical Services).

Snider, L. (1987a) 'Towards a Political Economy of Reform, Regulation and Corporate Crime', *Law and Policy*, vol. 9, pp. 37–68.

Snider, L. (1987b) 'Corporate Crime in Canada: a Preliminary Report', *Canadian Journal of Criminology*, vol. 20, pp. 142–68.

Snider, L. (1990) 'Cooperative Models and Corporate Crime: Panacea or Cop-Out?, *Crime and Delinquency*, vol. 36, pp. 373–91.

Standbury, W. (1977) *Business Interests and the Reform of Canadian Competition Policy, 1971–75* (Toronto: Carswell Methuen).

Standing Conference on Drug Abuse (SCODA) (1989) 'Working with Stimulant Users', a conference report (London: SCODA).

Stigler, G. (1975) *The Citizen and the State: Essays on Regulation* (Chicago, Ill.: University of Chicago Press).

Stockholm International Peace Research Institute (SIPRI) (1985) *SIPRI Yearbook: World Armaments and Disarmament* (Stockholm: SIPRI).

Stone, C. (1980) 'The Place of Enterprise Liability in the Control of Corporate Conduct', *Yale Law Journal*, vol. 90, pp. 1–77.

Stone, C. D. (1978) 'Social Control of Corporate Behaviour', in D. Ermann and R. Lundman (eds), *Corporate and Governmental Deviance* (New York: Oxford University Press).

Stover, W. (1985) 'A Field Day for the Legislators: Bhopal, and its Effects on the Enactment of New Laws in the United States', in M. A. Smith *et al.*, *The Chemical Industry After Bhopal* (London: IBC Technical Services) pp. 69–126.

Stutman, R. (1989) 'Address to the Association of Chief Police Officers' Drugs Conference' (April); edited extracts reprinted in *Druglink*, 4, 5.

Sun (1989) 'Crack Crazy!: Evil Gangs Spread Drug Throughout Britain', *Sun*, 25 May.

Sutherland, E. H. (1977) 'White Collar Criminality', in G. Geis and R. F. Meier (eds), *White Collar Crime* (New York: Free Press).

Sutherland, E. H. (1978) 'White Collar Crime in Organized Crime', in D. Ermann and R. Lundman (eds) *Corporate and Governmental Deviance* (New York: Oxford University Press).

Swartz J. (1975) 'Silent Killers at Work', *Crime and Social Justice*, vol. 3, pp. 15–20.

Sweeney, J. (1989) 'Heirs to the Krays', *Observer Magazine*, 25 June.

Swigert, V. I. and Farrell, R. A. (1980) 'Corporate Homicide: Definitional Processes in the Creation of Deviance', *Law and Society Review*, vol. 15, pp. 161–82.

Szasz, A. (1986) 'Corporations, Organized Crime and the Disposal of Hazardous Waste: the Making of a Criminogenic Regulatory Structure', *Criminology*, vol. 24(1), pp. 103–16.

Thomas, J. (1982) 'The Regulatory Role in the Containment of Corporate Illegality', in H. Edelhertz and T. Overcast (eds), *White-Collar Crime: An Agenda for Research* (Toronto: D. C. Heath, Lexington Books.

Tombs, S. (1990a) 'The Politics of Regulation', paper presented at the Workshops on Industrial Crisis Management, the European Consortium for Political Research, Bochum, 2–7 April.

Tombs, S. (1990b) 'Beyond Technocratic Rationality? Managing Safety in the 1990s', Occasional Papers on Industrial Crises no. 2 (Leicester: Business School, Leicester Polytechnic).

Trebach, A. (1987) *The Great Drug War and Radical Proposals that Could Make America Safe Again* (London: Collier Macmillan).

Tucker, E. (1987) 'Making the Workplace 'Safe' in Capitalism: the Enforcement of Factory Legislation in Nineteenth-Century Ontario, paper presented at the Canadian Law and Society Association Annual Meetings, Hamilton, 3–6 June.

Tutt, N. (1989) *Europe on the Fiddle* (London: Croom Helm).

Union Carbide Corporation (UCC) (1985) *Bhopal Methyl Isocyanate Incident Investigation Team Report* (Danbury, Conn.: Union Carbide Corporation) March.

Union Carbide Corporation (UCC) (1987) Letter and Documents to International Coalition for Justice in Bhopal with excerpts from UCC Submission to the Indian Courts.

Union Research Group (1985a) *The Bhopal MIC Disaster, the Beginnings of a Case for Workers' Control: A First Report* (Bombay: Employees Union Research Group (Union Carbide India Limited)).

Union Research Group (1985b) *The Role of Management Practices in the Bhopal Gas Leak Disaster: A Second Report* (Bombay: Employees Union Research Group (Union Carbide India Limited)).

United Nations Environment Programme (1988) 'APELL (Awareness and Preparedness for Emergencies at Local Level)', *Industry and Environment*, vol. 2(2), pp. 3–7.

US Executive Office of the President (1989) *National Drug Control Strategy* (Washington, DC: Office of National Drug Control Policy).

US House of Representatives (1988) *Congressional Record*, vol. 134(2) March.

US Senate Hearings before the Permanent Subcommittee on Investigations of the Committee on Government Operations (1975), *Federal Drug Enforcement*, 94th Congress, 1st Session, 9, 10, 11 June.

US Senate Special Committee to Investigate Crime in Interstate Commerce (1951), 82nd Congress, *Third Progress Report* (Washington, DC: Government Printing Office).

US Senate Subcommittee on Terrorism (1989), Narcotics and International Operations of the Committee on Foreign Relations, *Drugs, Law Enforcement and Foreign Policy* (Washington, DC: Government Printing Office).

Vogel, D. (1983) 'The Power of Business in America: a Re-Appraisal', *British Journal of Political Science*, 13.

Vogel, D. (1986) *National Styles of Regulation: Environmental Policy in Great Britain and Unites States* (Ithaca, NY: Cornell University Press).

Vollmer, A. (1936) *The Police and Modern Society* (Berkeley, Cal.: University of California Press).

Walters, V. (1985) 'The Politics of Occupational Health and Safety: Interviews with Workers' Health and Safety Representatives and Company Doctors', *Canadian Review of Sociology and Anthropology*, vol. 22(1), pp. 58–79.

Watkins, J. C. (1977) 'White Collar Crimes: Legal Sanctions and Social Control', *Crime and Delinquency*, vol. 23, pp. 290–303.

Weir, D. (1986) *The Bhopal Syndrome: Pesticide Manufacturing and the Third World* (Penang: International Organization of Consumers Unions).

Whiting, B. J. (1980) 'OSHA's Enforcement Policy', *Labour Law Journal*, vol. 31, pp. 29–45.

Whynes, D. and Bean, P. (eds) (1990) *Policing and Prescribing: The British System of Drug Control* (London: Macmillan).

Wickham, P. and Dailey, T. (eds) (1982) *White Collar and Economic Crime* (Toronto: D. C. Heath).

Wilson, G. K (1985) *The Politics of Safety and Health* (Oxford. Clarendon Press).

Wilson, J. Q. (1985) *Thinking About Crime* (New York: Vintage Books).

Wilson, J. Q. (ed.) (1980)) *The Politics of Regulation* (New York: Basic Books).

Wisotsky, S. (1986) *Breaking the Impasse in the War on Drugs* (New York: Greenwood Press).

Woodiwiss, M. (1988) *Crime, Crusades and Corruption: Prohibitions in the United States, 1900–1987* (London: Frances Pinter).

Yeager, P. (1986) 'Managing Obstacles to Studying Corporate Offences: an Optimistic Assessment', paper presented to the 1986 Annual Meetings of the American Society of Criminology, Atlanta, Georgia, 30 October – 3 November.

Author Index

Subject Index

conspiracy theories on 6, 9
in United States 6, 17
Community Awareness and Emergency
Response *see* CAER (United States)
Comprehensive Crime Control Act,
1984 (United States) 51–2
conspiracy theories:
on communism 6, 9
on drug trafficking 3–4, 9–10, 20
ethnic 6–7
on the Mafia 3–4, 9–10, 12–14
Constantinou, Pericles 106, 107
construction industry *see* building trade
contaminated drugs 63
see also drug use
contraband 146, 149
agricultural 146
tobacco 149 50, 153
Contras, the (Nicaragua) 21–2
Cooper, Jack 101
Cooper, Joel 101
Cooper, Mel 101–3, 107, 108, 112, 114,
134–5
Cooper, Sam 101
Cooper Equities 101
Cooper Funding 101–3, 107, 113,
123–4
co-operative action:
against corporate crime 222–3
Corallo, Antonio 15, 103, 106
corporate crime 212–39
anti-trust laws 92–3, 100, 216–17,
229–31
causes of 218–19
control of 214–34
co-operative action against 222 3
cost of 212–13
criminalisation of 219–20, 223, 229
definition 214–15, 226
insider-trading 213, 231–2
models of 218–33
occupational health and safety
212–13, 217–18
regulatory agencies 215, 216, 220–2,
228–9
sanctions against 216, 217, 219, 225
securities regulation 216
stock-market fraud 213, 231–2
and trade unions 228
types of 226
corruption 25–6, 143
in FBN 12–13
political 8, 14, 102, 105, 106
in US Congress 102
Cosa Nostra *see* the Mafia

crack 73, 76–7
see also cocaine
crime:
and drug use 74, 82–3
see also organised crime
crime control 8, 13, 23–4
abuse of legislation on 14
constitutional amendments 13
regulatory agencies 215, 220–2,
228–9
see also organised crime
Criminal Justice Act, 1988 (United
Kingdom) 78, 89
criminal partnerships 157
criminalisation:
of corporate crime 219–20, 223, 229
of drug use 36
crop substitution 38–40
see also supply-reduction policies
customs officers:
Camorristi acing as 146
United States 45, 46–7, 48, 51
Cutolo, Raffaele 151, 152

Dankert, Piet 184
DAWN (United States) 63–4
DEA (United States) 45–6
death squads 21
DECO process 107–8, 109–12, 138
see also waste disposal industry
defoliation 40–1, 42
DeForest, Orrin 20
DelBroccolo, Vincent 99, 100
Delors, Jacques 180
demand-reduction policies 32, 37–8,
53–61, 66
drug education 57–8, 75
drug tests 23–4, 55–7
drug user rehabilitation 59–60
democratic systems 224–5
see also political systems
Department of Environmental
Resources *see* DEF (Pennsylvania)
Department of Trade and Industry
(United Kingdom) 232
DER (Pennsylvania) 91, 105, 115, 118
Devine, Donal A. 110
Dewey, Thomas E. 15
Dibiase, Peter 100
distillation:
of wine 165–6, 167
Donaldson, Bob 115–16
Donnelly Act (New York) 100
Drexel Burnham 213